GRACE AND AN OCCASIONAL MIRACLE

MY LIFE STORY

BEVERLY GEYER

D1400676

In memory of my beloved brother, Richard, who shared so much of this story with me

I dedicate this book to
my children, grandchildren, and all those who come after. I wish you a life of love, good health, a few struggles to bring wisdom and an occasional miracle.

Beverly Mae Geyer nee' Hier - 2013

To Patience —

You are indeed a miracle!

Bev. Beyer
2014

3

TABLE OF CONTENTS

INTRODUCTION

"These passions, simple but overwhelmingly strong, have governed my life, the longing for love, the search for knowledge and unbearable pity for the suffering of mankind."

Bertrand Russell
Excerpted from the prologue to The Autobiography of Bertrand Russell

Grace and Miracles

I was a very young girl the first time my heart was broken. It was the summer of 1944, and I was almost eight. I was taken to the Whaley Home, a place for children who cannot live with their parents. I don't remember any discussion ahead of time about where I would be taken and why, although something must have been said. I don't remember who took me, although it probably was my dad. What I do remember is lying in a small, single bed in the dark, sobbing. The pain in my chest was so intense I couldn't catch my breath. It felt like something was breaking. It was. I had not been away from my brother from the day they brought him home. None of my family was with me, but I wasn't alone. A woman sat on the floor by my bed, her face close to mine. She looked in my face and stroked my hair saying, "You'll be okay, it's okay, we'll take care of you, you'll be okay." She was kind, but I would not be okay for a long time.

Eventually I cried myself to sleep. I don't remember one other thing about that summer. Many, many years later I called the Whaley Home to see if I could learn anything about the woman who spent that first night with me. The woman who answered the phone told me a fire had destroyed most of their old files, a few had survived, and she would see if there was a record. She found a file with a single sheet of paper completed when I left the home. It noted the dates of my stay, June to August, 1944, and the reason I was leaving the home, *father wants her with him*. I was sixty years old when I heard those words and I cried as though I was that little girl again. I apologized profusely to the woman on the phone, and she told me that tears happen often when people call to learn about their stay.

I did not have bad parents. Sadly, there are many children who suffer unbelievable abuse. I was not abused. I was not neglected. My parents simply got caught up in their own drama and I was an innocent bystander. No one told them that a child's heart is fragile and can be badly damaged before they know why grownups do what they do. My heart has been broken many times. Heartbreak is part of life. You either get stuck in it or you grow. I grew. It took hard work, grace, and an occasional miracle before I became a strong woman, a survivor. Mine is a story of healing, a story of trial and error, of gaining wisdom, and doing better when I knew better.

INTO THIS FAMILY A BABY IS BORN

"A baby is God's opinion that the world should go on."
Carl Sandburg, U.S. biographer and poet (1878-1967)

1936: Hard times in the year of my birth

In 1929, the stock market crashed and the Great Depression began. Banks closed, people lost their jobs, and many went hungry. Recovery took a long time. Seven years later, in 1936, unemployment was still high, nearly 17 percent. President Franklin Delano Roosevelt was elected for a third term, the first and last time any president would serve more than two terms.

Flint, the city in which I was born, and the rest of southeast Michigan had become the home of the auto industry. The 1927 Ford Model T, mass-produced in Detroit, was more affordable. Two hundred fifty car companies without production line manufacturing disappeared, and by 1940 only seventeen car companies remained. Automotive parts industries were cropping up in Flint and young people, including my parents, began to hope for their future.

In 1936, the average new house cost $3,925, average annual wages were $1,723, and a gallon of gas cost nineteen cents. Television had been invented, but it would be another fifteen years before the average person had one at home. People listened to the radio, and unlike today, when the radio is primarily music and some news, there were comedy, variety, and drama programs as well. Our telephone had what was known as a *party line,* meaning it was shared by three or four families. Houses were mostly heated with coal. The average family did not go out to dinner, and fast-food restaurants were far in the future. Movies were popular for those who could afford to go, and The Great Ziegfeld, a musical, won an Academy Award. Monopoly was a brand-new game.

Most women worked at home and they worked hard. There were some conveniences: electric washing machines with wringers; electric irons, although they were much heavier and did not produce steam; vacuum cleaners, upright and almost too heavy to lift; running water; electric and gas stoves; and electric refrigerators. Milk in glass bottles was delivered daily to the doorstep of many homes. Kroger, Hamady, and the Atlantic and Pacific Tea Company, also known as the A. and P., were the major grocery stores in Flint. Older women did not wear pants, although younger women sometimes did. Wearing pants would become more common in the 1940s.

A few women, mostly single, worked outside the home as teachers, nurses, or store clerks and in offices. Women who could afford to usually quit work when they married. Women in poor families who did not have the luxury of staying home with their children often did domestic work for more affluent families--child care and cleaning. In some larger cities, poor women worked long hours for very little money in sweat shops making clothing.

My father's generation was the first in which many working-class young people completed high school. He and his youngest sister both did. My grandparents did not, and my mother did not. No one in my family went to college. This was typical in working-class families.

By 1936, the industrial revolution, which began in the 1800s, had reached its peak. President Roosevelt and Congress initiated programs focused on relief and recovery from the effects of the depression. The first *New Deal* legislation provided subsidies to banks, railroads, farmers, and other industries, and the second created the housing authority, farm security programs, social security, and the Work Progress Administration, the latter making the government the largest employer in the country. Everyone dreamed of owning an automobile. People were hopeful, and my parents were hopeful enough to create a new life.

An unsettling birth in an unsettled world

A favorite family story, told often by my dad, is that on Saturday, August 22, 1936, the day I was born, there was a raging thunderstorm in Flint, Michigan. At Women's Hospital the electric power failed, and my dad held a flashlight so Dr. Orill Reichardt, the same doctor who delivered him, could see to guide me into the world. Who knows the truth? Dad was a great creator of his own truth, the more drama, the more enjoyment. I suppose I could get the facts on the internet, but I kind of like the story. In any event, birthing a baby in the dark is surely a metaphor for the blind hope that all will be well

Mom's story of my birth was more personal to her. In July, 1936, the month before my birth, a heat wave set a record in Michigan. It was humid and Mom was miserable. I was her first child. She said the fact that I was a girl made the misery worthwhile. They named me Beverly Mae. My dad chose Beverly, the name of a former girlfriend. My mother was certainly more tolerant than I would have been. Mae is my maternal grandmother's name. Perhaps Mom accepted Beverly because dad could have named me after his mother, Lulu. Personally, I'm grateful not to be Lulu Mae.

My parents married in March and I was born five months later. At some point I figured out I wasn't planned, but the concept of planning for children wasn't viable in the 1930s. People had a lot on their minds, and bringing a child into the world was truly an act of faith. I was born smack in the middle of the biggest depression in our country's history.

Dad was almost twenty-two; Mom was nineteen. He was born into a traditional family, the oldest of three children and the only boy. When he graduated high school in 1932, he started work in the factory at A. C. Spark Plug. He was smart, responsible, and ambitious, and he quickly moved up to a line management job. By 1936, he could afford to marry and begin a family of his own.

Mom was the oldest in a troubled family and was thrust into responsibility for her siblings at a very young age. Just before my birth, two of her younger brothers, my uncles, Jay and Gene Reid, came to live with us. One was twelve and the other eight. They were my earliest babysitters. In 1938, my only sibling, Richard Lynn, we called him Dick, was born.

Later, when my parents individually discussed those early years, Dad talked about his pride in being able to provide for his family and his frustration that my mother was irresponsible. My mother talked about her hope for fun after a tough childhood, the strain of having responsibility for her siblings, and the difficulty of living with a man who had no time for fun and acted more like a father than a husband.

Five years after my birth, my family, the city in which I was born, and America itself were all unsettled; the future was uncertain. My parents' marriage was floundering, the auto industry where my father worked was changing rapidly, and America was on the verge of war.

My mother: The circumstances of your birth often determine who you become

Can we ever really know our parents in any other role except as our parents? The roles of mother and father carry such emotional weight. Most of us have some belief about what a mother is supposed to be, what a father is supposed to be. It's the rare parent who measures up to that ideal. Parents are, after all, human. They make mistakes. They follow their own desires, sometimes at the expense of their children. They have addictions. They are a product of their own upbringing. Some have the capacity to love unconditionally, some do not. We often judge our parents by whether they were able to meet our needs.

Confounding our ability to truly know them is that most parents withhold from their children at least some of who they are. Perhaps, they too believe in the ideal and fear they haven't measured up or, perhaps, they think they are protecting their children. Maybe their children don't really want to know. I've heard from my kids, "Too much information, Mom." But I do know some facts, and maybe I can, especially because I became a parent, discern some of who my parents were besides my parents.

My mom's name was Nola Mary Reid. She was born on March 7, 1917, in Flint, Michigan. Her father was John Wesley Reid, and her mother was S. Mae Reid. I think the S. stands for Sallie. Mom was born on her mother's nineteenth birthday; her father was twenty-one. She was the oldest of six children. Her siblings, in order of their birth, were Faye, born in 1922; Earl, 1923; Jay, 1924; Gene, 1928; and Joyce, 1933.

Grandma Reid had difficulty in childbirth. There were several miscarriages between Mom's birth and the birth of her sister Faye, more between brothers Jay and Gene, and more between Gene and Joyce. When Grandma was pregnant for her fourth child, Jay, grandma's sister, Edith Audsley, took both Faye and Earl to live with her and her husband. Faye was old enough to know who her parents were. Earl was raised as Aunt Edith's child and given their last name. He never knew who his biological parents were, and he believed his siblings were his cousins.

The first defining event in my mom's childhood was her father's alcoholism. He lived to drink. Everything revolved around his drinking. The rent didn't get paid, food didn't get bought, and he didn't show up when it mattered. Mom woke in the night to arguments between her parents about his drinking and the lack of money to take care of his family. The arguments often escalated, ending with Grandpa Reid physically abusing his wife.

When he was sober Grandpa worked for Inter-City Trucking Company driving supplies between Flint and Detroit, but much of what he made went for alcohol. Family members who were better off helped when they could. Jay, the oldest son living with the family, recalls many times when he had to go with his dad to the store to buy food in the hope that having a child along would ensure he got to the store. Instead, Grandpa would leave Jay in the car while he went to the bar for *just one drink*. Like most alcoholics, the drinking came before work, before family.

17

The second defining event in Mom's childhood was her mother's death in childbirth on September 15, 1933, at age thirty-five. She had been told that if she continued to have children she would die, but she continued because she had no choice. My mom said my grandfather when drunk was a force to be reckoned with. While he was physically a small man, my grandmother was even smaller. She never weighed more than one hundred pounds. Her death certificate says the cause of death was *sixth pregnancy, had numerous miscarriages with severe pelvic cellulitis.*

Mom was sixteen years old when her mother died. As the oldest girl, and with a mother who was often ill, she already had considerable responsibility for her siblings and the work it took to keep the house going. Her siblings still at home were nine, five, and a newborn. Grandpa was not capable of raising the children. The new baby, Joyce, was adopted by friends of the family, Ruby and Doug Setterington. Earl and Faye continued to live with Grandma's sister, Edith, in Canada. Mother's brothers, Jay and Gene, were sent to foster homes and later to the Whaley Home. My mom's route out was to marry her current boyfriend, Johnny Potter. She told me she married him not only to get away from home, but because he was a good dancer and she loved to dance. She also told me that she took her best friend, Toots, with them on their honeymoon because it would be more fun. Her life had not much fun, and, at sixteen, I don't think she would be expected to be mature. The marriage lasted six weeks.

Mom was pretty by any standards. She was small, four feet, eleven inches, and never weighed more than one hundred ten pounds, even when she was pregnant. She had thick, wavy, auburn hair, which she wore long most of her life. She was fun and flirtatious and men liked her and wanted to take care of her, or they thought they did.

By the time she married my dad, Mom was drinking as her father had. She was young, so it's hard to tell at that point if she was an alcoholic or if drinking too much was just part of having a good time. My dad was a frequent drinker, too, but he also was responsible about work. He had definite ideas about the role of wife and mother and the role of husband and father. His parents had a long-time traditional marriage. His dad was in charge and earned the living, and his mom stayed home, did the housework, and raised the children. My mom struggled to live up to the model my dad was used to. She never managed to do so, and arguments about Mom's drinking were increasingly frequent.

An early memory, maybe when I was between four and five, was typical. Dad came home from work to find Mom gone and Dick and I in bed asleep in the bedroom we shared. Uncles Jay and Gene, Mom's brothers, were living with us and Jay was in charge. When she came home, I woke up to loud voices in the kitchen. I pulled the covers up around me and lay awake, a little frightened because Mom was crying. In a short while, Dad was kneeling by my bed. He said, "I'm taking you with me to Grandma and Grandpa Hier's house." Mom came into the room, still crying, and pulled on my father's arm. "Leave the kids here, don't take my babies," she cried over and over. Dad said, "I'm only taking Beverly. I'm sure she's mine and I'm not sure Dick is." I had no idea what he meant. I loved my dad, but I didn't want to leave my mom.

Dad stood me up on the bed. I was in my pajamas and he took off his jacket and wrapped it around me. I remember it was big, reaching nearly to my ankles. My arms were in the sleeves and I lifted my arms trying to uncover my hands. He wrapped the jacket tighter and it felt scratchy around my neck and face. He picked me up and carried me to the car. I was crying. "I don't want to leave Momma," I told him. He put me in the front seat and said, "We have to go," and drove me to my grandparents. When we got there and he carried me in the house, Grandma and Grandpa came into the living room in their night clothes and asked what was wrong. Dad was

crying and told my grandparents, "I don't know what I'm going to do with her." I knew that *her* was my mother.

At some point, not long after, my dad moved out and got an apartment, leaving us with Mom and my uncles, Jay and Gene (above), I remember walking with her one day after he moved and she pointed to a building and said, "That's where your dad lives." I don't think they lived apart long. When I was about six, Dad, Mom, my brother, and I moved away from the city to a small town, Fenton, and lived in a cottage on Fenton Lake. Again, I remember Dad coming home and finding Mom not there and my brother and I left with a neighbor. He shouted and asked where she was. I don't know what the neighbor said, but I knew my dad was mad. He took us home and sat up waiting for her. I couldn't sleep because I worried that something had happened to Mom. "Where is Momma?" I asked. "I don't know," he said. I tried to stay awake but I couldn't. When I woke the next day, Mom was there and Dad was gone, and that was normal, he must have been at work. Within the year, in 1943, they were divorced and my brother and I moved in with our Hier grandparents. I was seven, my brother was five.

I remember those years between birth and age six with my mother, aside from the fighting between my parents, as happy years. My mom loved to sing and today I can recall the words to many of the songs that were popular in the late 1930s and early 1940s. She was fun and people liked her. I thought she was beautiful. She always had girlfriends. Mostly I felt safe because my Uncle Jay was there when Mom wasn't, and he took care of us when mother's addiction took over.

I saw very little of Mom after the divorce. For a long while I was sad; I missed her, and I didn't understand why she was gone. Sometimes she came to visit and sometimes she promised to come and didn't show up. It bothered me but it bothered Dick even more. I don't think I expected much. Dick stood looking out the window for a long time, waiting for her, and no one could convince him to leave. He was sure she would come. When we were with her there was often a man around, different men, and it made me angry. She seemed to pay more attention to the men than she did to me. She laughed when she was told she looked too young to have kids our age, which was often, and said, "I was a child bride but these are my kids."

In 1945, Mom married Clarence North. He was older, a handsome man who also drank a lot. I remember meeting

him only once. The marriage lasted about a year. Dad moved Dick and me to Detroit that same year. I don't remember seeing my mother very often while we lived in Detroit.

In 1947, Mom moved to Pentwater, Michigan, where her brother Jay was living. She met and married Fred Stenberg (left), whom everyone called Fritz. Fritz was a commercial fisherman and owned a fishing tug, the *Maggie Lynn*, with his brother, Bud, and his uncle, Frank Larson. They also had a market where they sold smoked fish in the summer. This was Fritz's first marriage and my mother's fourth.

When Mom and Fritz were first married they lived with his mother and step-father in the house where Fritz had lived most of his life, on the main street across from Pentwater Lake. Bud and his wife and children lived in a little house just behind their mother's house. In 1948, at ages ten and twelve, my brother, Dick, and I spent half a school year living with my mom and Fritz. Fritz had difficulty dealing with Mom diverting her attention away from him and sharing it with us. He tolerated me, but he continually criticized Dick.

On and off, my mother worked in a small factory, Pentwater Wire Company. She did this more to keep busy than because they needed the money. They bought several lots on Pentwater Lake, and Fritz built a home on one; their address would be 95 Lake Street. He sold the other lots at $200 each to help pay for the house. Today those lots would cost more than $50,000. When he finished the home around 1949 or 1950, they moved in. It had a large living room and kitchen, a utility room, bathroom, a master bedroom, and a small bedroom with room for only a twin-size bed. Every year Fritz planted a vegetable and flower garden behind the house. Mom was expected to can all the vegetables and she did, although not without complaint. The canning was definitely Fritz's idea. I remember her saying once, "If you bring one more tomato into this house, I'm going to throw it at you."

During summer vacation from school I rode the Greyhound bus from Detroit to Pentwater to visit Mom, a full day's trip. In 1952, when I was sixteen, I asked to live with her. She asked Fritz; he said yes, but Dick isn't invited. Mom and Fritz were having some struggles. Both drank a lot, although much more attention was focused on Mom's drinking than on Fritz's. In those days, and maybe still, it was more acceptable for men to drink and to go to the bar alone.

But even with the drinking, Mom tried hard to be a present mother and I was happy to be living with her. She attended the school plays I was in. She went to events our class held to raise money for our senior trip. We had family gatherings with her sister Faye and brothers, Jay and Gene. Grandpa Reid came to visit, usually when he was coming off of a drunk, hadn't paid his rent, and needed a place to crash. Mom always took him in. All of her siblings were disgusted by his behavior, but Mom never turned him down if he needed something.

I graduated from high school and left my mother's home in 1954, moved to Muskegon, and went to business school. I visited regularly. In 1958, when I was twenty-one and married with one child, Mom and Fritz adopted a little girl, Frances, (left) who was five years old. Fritz did not have children and didn't bond with my brother and me. He wanted a child of his own. Mother had been sober for at least a year and was regularly attending the Episcopal Church. The priest helped with the adoption. Mother stayed sober for a while after Frances came to live with them, but soon started drinking again.

One morning in 1965, when she was forty-eight years old, Mom woke with a terrible headache. She walked toward the bathroom and fell. Fritz put her in the car and rushed her to the hospital in Hart, Michigan, about ten miles away. She had an aneurism; that hospital did not have a neurosurgeon, so she was immediately transported by ambulance to Muskegon. They operated to close off the bleeding in her brain, but considerable damage had been done. She was unconscious for six weeks, and when she regained consciousness, she had lost much of her memory and was paralyzed on her left side. She thought she was still married to my dad and that I was a young child. Frances was twelve and had lived with Mom for seven years, but Mom didn't remember her at all.

The stroke changed her in many ways. She loved my children who were eight, five, and three at the time. After the stroke, she didn't remember them, and even though she was told they were her grandchildren, the attachment was gone. She went home in a wheelchair with a brace on her left leg and her left arm contracted up close to her body. A physical therapist came to the house to try to improve mobility in both. She screamed and cried through the treatment; it was painful, and she begged Fritz to stop the therapist from coming. Sadly, he did and she never regained the use of her leg or arm.

In the next few years Mom mostly sat on the couch in the living room and smoked. She didn't drink because she didn't have access, but Fritz increased his drinking. Fritz did not handle my mother's illness well. He was very traditional and Mom had always done the caretaking. He did the things that needed to be done, bathed her and dressed her and fixed meals, although it was difficult for him, and he told everyone who would listen, *"she left me with a terrible mess."* Each time I visited he walked with me to the car as I left and told me that he couldn't take anymore and he wished he and my mother were both dead. I had never been close to Fritz. He was always jealous of Mom's relationship with me. I tried not to judge because I'm sure it wasn't easy, but his complaints annoyed me and my compassion was reserved for my mother. Each time he told me how miserable her illness was making his life, I wanted to ask him how wonderful he thought her life was.

For a while, in order to relieve Fritz, Mom came to stay with me and my children in Muskegon. I hired, and Fritz paid for, a daytime caregiver. My children laugh at some of the memories they have from that time. The stroke had turned Mom into a person who frequently swore. Her favorite was, *damn it all to hell anyway!* She was a smoker and burned holes in her nightgowns. She coughed a lot from the smoking and the cough wracked her frail body. One time, feeling considerable compassion for how difficult the coughing was, I told Mom I was so sorry she was having such a hard time with the coughing. Her response was, *"Don't worry, honey. It's not the cough that will carry me off, it's the coffin they will carry me off in that you need to worry about."* Her sense of humor was not affected by the stroke.

She loved her home in Pentwater and wanted to move back, so she did. On October 29, 1977, Fritz was working in the yard and came in to fix lunch. After lunch, Mom lit a cigarette. She had learned to do this by putting the cigarette in her mouth and managing her lighter with her right hand. Fritz went back outside, came in a few hours later, and discovered the living room couch had caught fire. Mom was dead and her body was badly burned. The couch had smoldered for some time. She was sixty-one years old. Her death was investigated, and the first report said there was no smoke in her lungs. Her original death certificate said she died in a house fire. It was later changed and the cause was listed as *burns and smoke inhalation, house fire, patient had been smoking*. As I read those words, I had a sick, uncomfortable feeling: Was there smoke in her lungs or not? She and Fritz had been married thirty years when she died. At the funeral he told me to pick up her cedar chest, a gift from my dad when Mom and he were married, and its contents, some photos, and cards and letters to and from my brother and me. I did and that was the last time I saw Fritz.

Here are some of the things I remember about my mom. She liked green apples with salt. She had a music box with a dancing ballerina that she played often. She liked baked bean sandwiches. She had a red halter dress with white polka dots and she had a green winter coat with a fur collar. She loved to sing and dance and she had a terrific sense of humor. She drank coffee all day long. She loved her original family and was the one who made sure everyone kept in touch. She drank vodka and carried it around in a medicine bottle in her purse. She told me often that I was strong and could do anything I wanted.

In those two years I lived with her, I never doubted that she loved me and she certainly loved my children. She was so thrilled when I had a little girl and called her, "Little Princess." Although I was sometimes frustrated with her drinking, I loved her and I seemed to always understand that her drinking was a sickness. As I gained maturity, I stopped thinking of Mom as just my mother. I learned more about her early years, the dysfunction in her family, the loss of her mother, her dependency on men and marriage as a way to survive and support herself, and her frustration at that dependency. She often told me *"If one more man pats me on the head and tells me how cute I am, I think I'll shoot him."* She meant it to be funny, but it contained a lot of truth. I felt her frustration.

Mom did her best. She was born into a family with a genetic disease, alcoholism. I don't know what part of who we are is genetic and what part is learned behavior, but I do believe that both count in forming our character. Yes, we can take a different path from what was laid out for us genetically, but it takes some miracles. She had too few miracles. She did not have a happy life, and she had a tragic death. Even so, she never lost the capacity to love, laugh, and forgive. She wanted more for me than what she had. She had no personal resources to make that happen except to try very hard to make sure I knew that I was smart and strong and didn't need to repeat her mistakes. I miss her. I wish I could call her and tell her how my children turned out, what a wonderful granddaughter I have, and that she was right, I am smart and strong.

*My father: A difficult
relationship ends in peace*

Dad's graduation picture
shows a handsome man with a
full head of wavy dark brown
hair. He was five feet, seven
inches tall and barrel-chested
like his dad. He had one blue
eye and one brown eye with a
little bit of blue in it, an odd thing. He played football in high
school. His nickname was Speed because he liked to drive
fast. That's what my mother always called him. Three years
after graduation, in a picture of my father when he and my
mother got married, he had lost most of his beautiful hair and
was bald from front to back with a fringe around the edges.

Lynn J. B. Hier was born to Julius Benjamin and Lulu
Fern Hier on October 18, 1914, in Owosso, Michigan. The J. B.
was to honor his father, Julius Benjamin, and his grandfather,
Julius Brumson. It was not unusual in the Hier family to use
initials instead of names. He had two younger sisters, Floris
Jean, they called her Jean, and Phyllis, and one older half-
brother, Gerald, from his father's first marriage. His father
was thirty and his mother twenty-one when he was born.

Dad was fifteen when the U.S. stock market crashed
beginning the Great Depression, which lasted nearly to the
end of the 1930s. In 1932, when he graduated from Flint
Northern High School, the economy was still difficult and few
jobs were available. The employment picture in Michigan was
a little brighter than much of the rest of the nation because of
the auto industry, and my father was able to find work at A.C.
Spark Plug, an auto-related industry.

In December, 1941, five years after my parents
married, and when Dad had just turned twenty-seven, the
Japanese attacked the United States at Pearl Harbor, Hawaii.
The war expanded and soon we were fighting in both

27

Germany and Japan. The country was in peril and so was my parents' marriage. Two years later, in 1943, they divorced. Dad was awarded custody of my brother and me. As the war continued, the draft age had been raised and he was eligible to serve, but as a single parent with custody he was exempt. My mom told me this was the reason she did not fight for custody. I don't know if this is true. I know it was rare at that time for a father to have custody of his children when the mother was living, and I know Mom could never have stood up to Dad.

World War II ended in armistice with Germany and Japan in 1945. Before my father's thirty-second birthday, his country had engaged in a World War and experienced the Great Depression. He had married in hope and divorced in despair. The complexity of that beginning profoundly affected my father. The world in general and his personal world were chaotic for many of those first thirty-two years.

Memories are a tricky thing. Even though my dad had custody of my brother and me, I don't remember that he was around that much. I was almost seven at the time of the divorce, and my brother and I lived with my grandparents for the next two years. I remember my dad visited, but he did not live there. I also remember good times with him. He took us for Sunday drives. We told him where to turn and tried to get him lost. We were amazed that after directing him to turn again and again, he still got us back to where we started. Often we had dinner at a restaurant on these outings. This was a big treat. Dad would sometimes sing in the car although he really only knew the words to one song. I've searched for these lyrics online to learn the name of the song and can't find them so maybe he made them up just as he made up many things. It made us laugh when he sang.

> *"Told you once, ain't gon' to tell you no more, if the bed breaks down, you're gon' to sleep on the floor, now. How come you do me like you do, do, do? You ain't gon' to do me no more."*

In 1945, when I turned eight, Dad got a job working as a supervisor in the factory at Fruehof Trailer. He married his girlfriend, Verla Procunior, and the four of us moved to Detroit. She was good to us. She had homemade treats ready after school and she put together a dress-up box for me with some of her beautiful clothes. Sadly, the marriage lasted less than a year. There was a noisy fight, yelling and crying, and Dad slapped her and accused her of seeing someone else. When she left, I sat in Dad's lap and cried and asked why she left. He told me she had no children of her own and didn't want the responsibility of two children. I remember thinking her leaving was our fault, but it was confusing because she had been so nice to us. I wondered why we couldn't keep mothers.

For the next four years, my brother and I did not live with Dad, and we were moved frequently. Dad left Fruehof Trailer for a better job at U.S. Tire and Rubber Company. In 1949, I was fourteen and for the next two years we stayed in one place; Dad lived with us. The three of us did the housework and the cooking. I moved alone back to Pentwater in 1952 to live with my mother. My dad was angry and hurt that I did this. He sent a small amount of money weekly and told me that if I needed anything else I could get it from my mother. I knew he meant it.

After I moved to Pentwater, my dad met and married Pauline Beard, a tall, very pretty, redhead who worked for him in the factory at U.S. Tire and Rubber. Pauline had a great sense of humor and when I was around her we laughed often. She had two sons who lived with their father. Dad said that he liked it that other men looked when they walked into a room and she was on his arm.

My dad has been described by my friends as charming and I understand why. He was friendly and funny and told wonderful stories. Many of them were not true. In telling his stories, my dad created the world as he wished it was, and he did such a good job of it that he believed the stories he told.

29

The stories were always about something he did at work that was extraordinary, how much money he made, how much he spent on something, a beautiful woman who was attracted to him. He told us that when he lived in California he dated movie stars, named names, and said they were crazy about him. These stories embarrassed my brother and me because we were sure they weren't true. My brother told me that he sometimes caught himself exaggerating and had to stop and retract because he so disliked Dad's embellishment and imagined stories.

Dad was quick to criticize and slow to praise. He never directly praised my brother or me. He said it would *give us the big head.* He did praise my brother to me and me to my brother. This only led us to think that he liked the other one better. I imagine praise from his parents was scarce as he was growing up. It wasn't like today when many kids are praised for nearly everything they do. It was also difficult to depend on his promises. Too often he would make a promise and not follow through. His criticism of me mostly focused on my appearance, and as I went through puberty, it was especially painful when I wore something I thought looked nice on me and he said I looked fat.

Dad and Pauline moved from Detroit to Flint where Dad became president of Katzman Concrete Manufacturing Company. He also owned and leased two semi-trucks. He and Pauline began to have marriage problems. They decided that leaving Flint would help the marriage, and he bought a cement plant in the southwestern United States. I was married and had children by this time, and dealing with my own struggles left me with little time to know what was going on in my dad's life. I do know that Pauline had two children in Michigan and was not happy living away from them. Dad and Pauline divorced, Pauline moved back to Detroit where her children lived, and Dad moved to Ventura, California, alone. I don't know what happened to the cement plant. He studied, got his real estate license, and set up his own real estate business. That area of California which had been mostly farm land was growing quickly and he did well. Later, he bought a bar, not a wise move for a man who drank too much. Later he sold it, saying his employees were stealing him blind.

After Pauline, Dad never remarried. He visited in Michigan from time to time but the visits to my house were a stop-by. He stayed with my brother, who had more in common with him. They both drank and liked spending time in bars.

From the time I came of age at eighteen, I asked my dad for help only three times. The first time was to ask for financial support to attend college after high school. He said no. The second was during my first marriage when my husband was physically abusive and I wanted to leave. He said that I had made my bed and now I had to lie in it. The third was when I was a single mother with three children ages one to six, working full-time, not making much money and getting little support from my children's father. My car died and I asked for one hundred dollars to buy a used car. He said no. I never asked again. I think his values around helping your grown children were directly related to his own upbringing. As a young man who started working in the middle of a depression, he was expected to contribute to his parents. There was never any question that when you turned eighteen you were to support yourself.

Dad did lend my brother money to buy a cement business. My brother said Dad went to the local bars, drank too much, and told everyone that my brother would have amounted to nothing had he not stepped in to help. That left me grateful that Dad said no to me. Later though, in 1978, out of the blue and without my asking, he came to visit me in Muskegon, went to the Oldsmobile dealership, and bought me an Oldsmobile Cutlass Calais, my first-ever new car. He said that since I had been elected to the City Commission, an important position, I couldn't be seen driving in those old junky cars I was used to. Appearances were important to him and that was his way of saying he was proud of me. At least, that's what my brother told me.

As a young person, I never fully understood my dad. My brother felt the same way. He was a difficult man to understand, often harsh and critical, and as I've said, he made up stories when the truth would have worked as well. He never said the words I love you; there were no affectionate hugs or pats on the back. He may have kissed us when we were babies, but not after that. He always made sure we had the basics, shelter, food, and health care, but he could not have been described as generous. He spoke respectfully of his mother, but made negative and demeaning comments about women in general. He was racist and used racist language to describe people from a variety of ethnic and religious backgrounds. His third wife, Pauline, once told me he hired a private detective to investigate me after I moved to live with my mother, and that he asked her when I came to visit to try to find out whether I was sexually active. I don't know why she told me, but I did believe her. It didn't at all sound like something that was out of character for him.

He was there when we needed him, depending on your definition of need. In 1947, I spent most of a summer in the hospital with what the doctors thought might be polio. There was an epidemic that year. It turned out to be a mild case. Dad visited every day. We had fun times too, especially when we were little and he came to visit. We were so glad to see him and he seemed glad to see us. I know he was proud of us, although it was not in his nature to say so. From a child's point of view, there were long periods of time when we lived with strangers and seldom saw him. I now believe that his alcohol problem explains a lot about the inconsistency.

In 1999, my dad's neighbor in California called and said Dad was not doing well and should not be living alone. I flew out and brought him to Michigan. He wanted to stay with my brother. Dad's health deteriorated, and one weekend when I came to visit he said that he thought it best if he came to live with me because I would be able to make the hard decisions ahead. He was eighty-five years old. He had lost his vision to macular degeneration and he couldn't hear. He had congestive heart failure, was tethered to an oxygen tank, and was in the early stages of dementia. My husband, Jose, and I lived in Muskegon and I was still working, so we hired a nurse's aide to come in each day to stay with Dad. Home health nurses came twice weekly.

By this time his height had shrunk to about five feet, three inches, and he was very frail. He still, however, retained his sense of humor. He mostly slept during the day and wandered at night. One night he set off the alarm system. We jumped out of bed and my husband said, *"You can't go outside, Mr. Hier. It's dark outside."* My dad responded, *"What the hell, I can't see anyway so what difference does it make if it's dark outside."* Another time we were walking on the sidewalk in front of our house and a neighbor stopped to talk. Dad kept walking. I had my back to him, the neighbor's eyes widened, and she gasped. I turned around and Dad was a half block away pulling his pants down. I ran to him, grabbed his pants on both sides, and yanked them up. I said sternly, *"Dad, you can't take your pants off in public."* He responded, *"I guess you don't know much about men's clothing, do you."* After that I got suspenders for his pants and put a sweater over the suspenders so he couldn't get them off so fast. It was funny, but it was sad too.

The dementia got worse and so did his congestive heart. His kidneys were not functioning well. We took him to the emergency room several times. He couldn't sleep lying down and he couldn't sleep at night. The doctors said he needed twenty-four- hour care. I found a nursing home nearby, and visited him every day after work. My daughter, Julie, was there two or three times weekly. He continued to decline. It was humbling to see my father, the man who had been such a powerful figure in my life, so vulnerable, dependent, and helpless. I brought pictures of him when he was in his prime to the nursing home, and wrote a short history of his life and posted them on a bulletin board by his bed for the nursing home helpers to read. I wanted them to understand he was more than a body they washed and fed and moved about as needed. He was a real person and he was loved.

On October 31, 2000, the nursing home staff called in the morning and said they thought Dad would die that day. I called my brother and he came to say good-bye. Dad knew he was there and kept saying his name. My daughter and her husband came after work. In the evening, Dad roused from his morphine-induced sleep and wanted to sit up. The orderly moved him to a chair. After fifteen minutes or so he wanted to lie down again. The orderly came, started to lift him, and realized that Dad was struggling. He called the nurse who came running. Julie and I were on one side of Dad and the nurse on the other. Dad was agitated and the nurse was speaking softly to him. She told him it was okay to let go, that he was going to a wonderful place where he would see all the people who had loved him, his father, his mother, and his sisters. Dad began to relax. I could feel his heart still beating, but slowly. He opened his eyes, looked off into the distance as though he saw something we couldn't, and in an awed and peaceful way, he said slowly, "Oh, oh, oh," and his heart stopped. Julie and I felt sure he saw those who would help him cross over to his final home. We kissed him and said our final goodbye. The funeral home director came for the body. Dad was cremated, and a few days later his ashes were buried in a gravesite next to his mother and father at Sunset Hills Cemetery in Flint.

In caring for our father at the end of his life my brother and I were able to forgive him. As Dad became more vulnerable, we learned compassion and understanding. He did the best he could. He never said the words, "I love you." He was not affectionate. He showed his love in the only way he knew how, by making sure we had the material things we needed. We never went without. Now, he was at peace, and my brother and I had forgiven him for those things that were hurtful in our childhood. We were at peace, too.

My paternal grandparents: Julius B. and Lulu F. Hier

My father often said that his parents loved each other so much there was little left for the kids. When I was almost seven, my brother and I moved in with my grandparents. We joined my first cousin, Patty, who had lived with them from birth in 1935. We left when I was nine. After we moved out, they turned their second floor into an apartment. In 1947, we moved back and lived in the apartment. I was eleven at the time. As young as I was, I doubt I had any concept about how much two people might love each other, but I do remember what life with them was like for me.

Grandpa was born on April 27, 1884. He was about five feet, eight inches tall, barrel-chested, and had thick, strong arms. His face was round, he was bald on top with a fringe of graying hair, and he wore glasses. In earlier pictures, his hair was dark and wavy and he had a nice smile. He had a third-grade education. Grandpa worked at Flint Cut Stone and Monument Company engraving granite tombstones. When he got home he did the man chores, cutting the grass, clipping the hedge in front of the house, keeping things repaired, taking care of the coal furnace. He sat at the head of the table during dinner and did very little talking. His box of Serutan, *"Nature's spelled backwards,"* the ad said, sat by his plate. He must have had digestive issues because he added it to water and drank it at every meal. He was stern with the three grandchildren who lived with him, my cousin Patty, my brother Dick, and me. We were taught table manners. *"Don't reach in front of someone to get something, ask, don't put your elbows on the table, when you eat soup move the spoon away from you to scoop the soup,"* he would say in a stern voice and without a smile. If our table manners slipped, we were corrected with a tap on the knuckles or elbow with the heavy end of his table knife. Children were not to speak at the table unless spoken to, another of his maxims. We weren't often spoken to unless it was to ask if we wanted something on the table or to pass something. Grandpa never spanked us. That was Grandma's job.

After dinner Grandpa took an apple from the refrigerator, turned on the radio, sat in his rocker, and listened to the radio while he peeled the apple. We watched, fascinated that he could peel the whole thing in one long curl, and sure that one day the peel would come off in two pieces. Later, he went to his bedroom and brought out a little brown paper sack filled with his favorite candy: round, chalky-chewy pink peppermints. He shook the bag a little because his hands were too big to reach in, spilled candy into his other hand, put down the bag, and handed each of us kids a peppermint. I tried to suck it so it would last, but always ended up chewing it. If we were outdoors when he came home from work, he stopped at the approach to the driveway and we stepped up on the running board, held on and he drove us to the garage behind the house. It seemed like a long drive but as an adult I recognize that it was your average driveway. The only affection I saw between my grandparents was a kiss good-bye if one or the other was going someplace. Grandpa was not warm and approachable, he didn't laugh much, but he was not mean and we were not afraid of him.

Grandma was born on October 6, 1893. Her maiden name was Hershey. She was about four feet, ten inches tall, short-waisted, chubby but not really heavy. She had curly gray hair and wore glasses. We never saw her in pants. She wore cotton print housedresses at home and silk or rayon, dark-colored dresses when she went out. Her shoes were black with laces and a chunky two-inch heel. Before she and Grandpa married, she was a servant working in private homes. After marriage she was a homemaker--not much difference between the two as far as I could tell.

The house was always tidy and she organized an annual spring cleaning involving Patty, Dick, and me, a time when everything was taken apart and put back together. The rugs were hung outdoors on the clothesline and it was our job to beat them with the wire rug beater. All of the wallpaper was cleaned with a pink doughy substance that looked like Silly Putty; she climbed the ladder and we did the lower part. Mattresses were turned and all the lampshades came off the lamps for cleaning.

Every Monday Grandma washed clothes, cutting up cakes of Fels-Naptha soap in the washer. She fed the clothes into the wringer, sending them to the rinse tubs where she had added bluing and sloshed them around to remove the soap. They went back through the wringer for a second rinse, she sloshed them around again, and finally they were hung on a clothesline to dry. The lines were outdoors in summer and in the basement in winter. Sometimes she let us feed clothes into the wringer. We always worried about catching and crushing our fingers. Tuesdays were ironing days. It took nearly all day because everything was sprinkled with water, rolled up, and then ironed piece by piece. She listened to the radio while she ironed. Wednesday was cleaning day, Thursday was baking day, and Friday was shopping day.

Grandma in the kitchen was something to behold. It was her domain, she was in charge. We kids were welcomed, often given small tasks, and always told what good helpers we were. She was a wonderful cook and her cooking is something my brother and I both looked back on fondly. Everything was delicious. My personal favorite was her meat pies. She bought a cheap cut of meat, placed it on a wooden cutting board, and cut into bite-size chunks. She dipped the meat pieces in flour, sprinkled them with salt and pepper, melted Crisco in her cast iron skillet, and put the meat in to brown. While the meat was browning, she cut up potatoes, carrots and celery. The meat and vegetables were tossed into a large casserole dish with water, salt, and pepper, and maybe some other spices too. Then she moved to her flour cupboard, and in another bowl mixed the ingredients for the crust. She sprinkled flour on the wooden shelf that pulled out from the cupboard, plopped the mixture onto the flour, and used her hands to shape it, not thin like pie crust but thicker, almost like flat bread. She placed the crust over the meat and vegetables and stuck the dish in the oven. It came out with the meat and vegetables bubbling in gravy and the crust browned.

Another fun time in her kitchen was when she asked us to help make donuts. Our job was to shake the donuts in a bag with granulated or powdered sugar after Grandma fried them. When the donuts were cut, we rolled the donut holes between our palms into balls so she could fry them for us to eat as she cooked. Everything was made from scratch and nothing was wasted. When she cooked chicken even the feet were used to make broth for soup.

Grandma gave us other kitchen chores. We colored the oleo for her. It was white and came with a little orange packet of coloring that we stirred in to make the oleo yellow. She washed the dishes and we dried. Her kitchen sink was lower than standard because Grandma was short and it had been installed to fit her height.

It was Grandma who did all the work of caring for us, and she was the disciplinarian. We were pretty good kids, and usually the only time we were spanked is if we swore, and that especially included using the Lord's name in vain. Once, when talking in my sleep, I said Jesus Christ in a tone that meant I wasn't praying. She pulled me out of bed. I was barely awake and frightened. I knew Grandma was angry at me, but I didn't know why. She began to spank me on my bottom saying, "If you say Jesus Christ in your sleep, you're saying it when you're awake." It felt unfair because I didn't swear on purpose, although she was probably right. My father and my mother both said *Jesus Christ* to express frustration so I picked the words up early, but when I was awake I knew better than to take the Lord's name in vain in front of Grandma.

Grandma drilled us in our multiplication tables and checked our schoolwork. She washed Patty's hair and mine, usually in rainwater she saved in a washtub that sat in the back yard. She said it made our hair softer. She parted our hair and wound it around rag strips, and tied the ends. The next day we went to school with little sausage-like curls.

She played the piano by ear and we sang the songs of her day, "Daisy, Daisy," "The Old Mill Stream," "Ka-Ka-Ka Katy," and "Casey Would Waltz With a Strawberry Blonde." She also played hymns. "In the Garden" and "Old Rugged Cross" were two she especially loved. I still know the words to all of those songs. Grandma loved soap operas on the radio and we listened at noon when we came home from school for lunch. *Helen Trent* and *Our Gal Sunday* are the ones I remember.

At meal time Grandma never ate when we did. She sat next to Grandpa and jumped up frequently to get whatever was needed. We kids had to carry our plates to the kitchen when the meal was done. Grandma cleared Grandpa's place and then she sat down and ate while we all went to the living room. She had a best friend, Maude, and they went shopping together.

The only clue I have that Grandma wasn't always happy was that sometimes while standing at the sink doing dishes she would cry silently, tears running down her face. I don't remember if we ever asked her why. When we were living in the apartment, Patty was in her early teens and giving them a lot of trouble. She was boy-crazy, the popular phrase for focusing most of her energy on boys. Patty was impulsive and did not have a lot of common sense, so the combination was a big worry. Also, now that I am a grandmother, I realize one does not plan to raise her grandchildren. Grandma raised her kids and there were struggles, especially with her daughters, and now she was raising three grandchildren. My brother was very attached to her and as an adult he reminisced about our time with her, calling her a saint. He was the baby, and the only boy, and I believe she did have a special feeling about him. Patty had always lived with her, so she was special too. From birth I had been the oldest child; at their house I was the middle child. I thought she liked me well enough, but I never felt that she had special feelings about me.

Grandma and Grandpa seemed like perfect grandparents, salt of the earth people, sensible and hard-working, but as adults, their children had problems. Dad was the oldest and he was hardworking, successful in his work. Not so in his personal life. He married and divorced three times. He was jealous and often drank too much. Aunt Jean was married four times. Patty was her only child and she left her with my grandparents immediately after she was born. Jean rarely came to visit. I remember her as self-centered, full of drama, immature, vain and without a lot of common sense. Aunt Phyllis, my favorite, was more stable and married only once, to a man who was a heavy drinker. She had a great sense of humor and was always fun to be around. She had three children and often said that playing with the kids was a lot more important than cleaning house. She was a compulsive overeater, and before she died of heart disease she was so heavy that she could not get up from a sitting position without help.

Grandma died of cancer on October 6, 1950. She was fifty-seven. Patty was fifteen and had been sent to California to live with her mother two years earlier. I was fourteen, Dick was twelve, and we lived with my dad in Detroit. Grandma must have been sick for some time. The cancer spread throughout her body and her death certificate says *cirrhosis of the liver, hepatic insufficiency.* I'm not sure what that diagnosis means. I was told she had cancer and it spread to her liver. I remember visiting when she was sick and her skin was yellow. I've thought as an adult that the tears at the sink when we lived with her in 1944 and 1945 may have been because she was already sick and in pain, but maybe not.

Grandpa remarried not more than six months after grandma died. His wife, Olive, did not like my dad. I don't know why. The only time I called on my own, when I was in Flint visiting my cousin Patty, she said they were about to sit down for supper and there wasn't enough for a guest. I never called again. I saw Grandpa once more in early 1958, when I took my oldest son, Brad, who was seven or eight months old, to Flint to visit my dad. Grandpa died of heart disease that same year on September 24, at age seventy-four. He also had diabetes.

So, I don't know if my grandparents loved each other and had too little left over for their children as my father said. Whatever affection that was expressed was undoubtedly expressed in private. While they were good to their grandchildren, they were not hugging and kissing grandparents. They showed their love by taking us in when we needed to be taken in and taking care of us after their children were raised. It can't have been easy.

My maternal grandparents: John Wesley and S. Mae Reid

This is not a happy story. Grandpa Reid was a small man, maybe five feet, six inches tall, with a huge appetite for alcohol. He was not a responsible husband, father, grandfather, or friend. I never heard anyone talk about him without talking about his alcohol addiction.

Grandpa Reid was born on December 23, 1895, in Ontario, Canada, the youngest in a family with five children. Grandma Reid was born on March 7, 1898, also in Ontario. They married in Canada in February, 1916, and shortly after moved to Flint, Michigan. He was twenty-one and she was almost eighteen. Their first child, my mother, was born on her mother's birthday a little over a year later. Grandpa was a truck driver.

Most of what I know about my Reid grandparents is from stories told to me by my mother and her brother, my uncle Jay. Mom's memory of her childhood was focused on her mother's struggles in a household where her husband worked sporadically, and when he did work spent the money first on alcohol. There was no public assistance at that time, so the family was often dependent on the goodwill of other family members, particularly Grandpa Reid's sisters.

Uncle Jay's memory of his childhood was focused on the responsibility thrust on him, at a very young age, to police his father in the hope that he could be persuaded to not spend all of his money at the bar. He was sent along when Grandpa went out to buy food on payday. Uncle Jay's presence made little difference. He talks about sitting in the car outside of a bar waiting for his dad, sometimes for hours.

43

Grandma Reid died on September 15, 1933, at age thirty-five. She was buried in Gracelawn Cemetery in Flint. Her death certificate lists the cause of death as *ruptured uterus during labor at term.* She died in childbirth. The child, Joyce, lived. My mother talked frankly about Grandpa coming home drunk, aggressive, and abusive and Grandma doing whatever was necessary to avoid violence. Grandpa's drinking literally and emotionally tore his family apart.

Aunt Pearl, Grandpa's oldest sister, tried to help. She and her husband, Sam Griffin, lived in Detroit and owned a large Victorian house, remodeled into several apartments, on Court Street in Flint. When I was small, before I started school, she gave Grandpa an apartment and put him in charge of maintaining the house. He sometimes spent money on alcohol that was intended to pay the electric bill, the lights were cut off, and the tenants complained. Eventually my mother and father took over management of the Court Street house, and Grandpa slept in a small apartment in the basement.

Grandpa married again to a woman whose name was Helen. I was a young child but I remember occasionally visiting with them. They lived in an apartment above a bar. I guess it saved Grandpa from driving home drunk. The marriage didn't last; Helen left him within a couple of years.

Great-aunt Pearl and Great-uncle Sam moved to Pentwater in the 1940s. They lived there until they died. Both Mom and my uncle Jay later moved there, and Grandpa Reid moved to nearby Muskegon, a larger city, where he got a job in the maintenance department at Sealed Power, an automobile parts manufacturer. He visited Pentwater often. When he went on drinking binges, he came to Mom's to sober up before returning to Muskegon to work. She always took him in and so did Sealed Power, something I never understood.

I came to know my grandfather better, as well as you can know someone who is almost always drunk, when I lived with my mother in Pentwater. He rarely talked to me beyond hello or to tell me that I was just about the ugliest granddaughter he had. That was his idea of being funny. It didn't affect me much. Even at sixteen I was wise enough to know you can't pay much attention to a drunk.

After high school graduation in 1954, I moved to Muskegon. Grandpa lived in a boarding house on Henry Street. Sometimes my friend, Shirley, also from Pentwater, and I would ride from Muskegon to Pentwater with him. He stopped at three bars for a shot on the way. I tried to distract him before the third, hoping for a shorter trip. Sometimes it worked, not often.

By late 1955, Grandpa was very sick. He had bleeding ulcers and his hands shook badly, both a result of a lifetime of alcohol. Every night before bed he poured a shot of whiskey and set it on his nightstand. When he woke up, in withdrawal and shaking, he picked the glass up with his teeth and downed it. That would steady him so he could continue to drink. He wasn't eating and he was rapidly losing weight. I called a doctor who came to the house, examined him, and told him if he didn't quit drinking he would be dead within six weeks. I gave him money to buy groceries and the groceries didn't get bought. I stopped giving him money and bought groceries, but I'm not sure he ate. He couldn't leave his room to buy alcohol, but another boarder, also an alcoholic, went to the liquor store for him and shared the bounty. Within six weeks, on January 6, 1955, at age sixty-one, grandpa died. His death certificate read, *chronic alcoholism*. This bothered my mother a lot and she wanted it changed. She was trying to rescue him to the end and beyond.

Grandpa is buried in the Pentwater cemetery and Mom had her mother's body moved so they rest eternally side by side. This would be touching if I could see a love story in there somewhere. Love for another is difficult when alcohol is your first love. My grandfather inherited his disease from his father. Three of his six children inherited the disease from him: my mother, my Uncle Gene, and my Aunt Faye. Uncle Earl never was told about his original family and my mother and her siblings lost track of him so we don't know if he inherited the addiction. Aunt Joyce, the youngest, kept in touch with her original family. She does not drink. Uncle Gene lives in Traverse City with his wife, Alma, and no longer drinks. Uncle Jay, the non-drinker who spent all those hours in his childhood waiting outside bars for his father, never touched alcohol. He died in 2010 at age eighty-six. My mother, Nola, drank until she had a cerebral hemorrhage in 1965 at age forty-eight and couldn't get alcohol on her own.

For any future generations who may read this, pay attention. Mom's is not the last generation to deal with alcohol issues. To my knowledge, no one in the family has let alcohol completely take over his or her life as my grandpa Reid did, although my brother came close. It is my hope no one ever will.

*My brother: A joy and sometimes
the bane of my existence*

My brother, Richard Lynn
Hier, my only sibling, was born
on June 6, 1938. We called him
Dick until he was grown. He had
natural curly red hair and a face
full of freckles. Our mother
entered him in a cute baby
contest, and he won a prize. I
had straight, brown hair and was
never entered in a cute baby contest. Until he entered the
picture I was the center of attention. I was only twenty-two
months old when Dick was born, so my first real memories of
him were when I was four and he was two. At that point I
both adored him and wished they would send him back.

We had moved from the apartment house on Court
Street, where my parents lived when I was born, to Myrtle
Street in Flint, Michigan, just before my brother was born.
Shortly after his birth, my mother's aunt and uncle asked her
and my dad to move back to Court Street and manage their
property, an old single-family Victorian which had been
converted. Court Street was a main street not far from
downtown; all of the houses were large, some were still single
family, but most were not.

Our apartment on the first floor had a big living room,
a kitchen that was also our dining area, a bathroom, and two
bedrooms. On rainy days we played in the unattached garage
in back, and on sunny days we played on the wrap-around
front porch. My brother and I shared a bedroom.

The house was heated with coal, and one of my
parents' duties was regularly shoveling coal into the furnace.
The coal bin was in the basement right next to the apartment
where my Grandpa Reid had previously lived. Another daily
job was getting rid of the ashes from the burnt coal. Heat

reached our apartment through iron registers in each room. Once, when Dick was about two, he was playing with a pop bottle, swinging it from side to side, when he hit one of the registers and the bottle broke. He dropped the broken bottle on his foot, cutting his toe, and he had to be taken to the doctor for stitches. I cried because he was hurt and because they wouldn't let me go with him to the doctor.

When Dick was very little I dressed him and tried to lug him around. I begged Mom to let me help push him in his buggy before I could even reach the handle. Mom held me in front of her and I thought I was helping her push. She said that whenever anyone came to visit, the first thing I did was to grab their hand and take them to meet my baby brother.

Uncle Jay, my mother's brother, who also lived with us, says his favorite memory of my brother as a little boy was his imitation of a famous radio comedian, Red Skelton. Skelton played many different characters, including a little boy who frequently got in trouble. Dick made us all laugh when he contemplated doing something he was told not to do, did it anyway, and when he got caught, grinned and said just what Red Skelton's little boy character said: *"If I dood it I get a lickin, oh-oh, I dood it!"* Of course, my parents were tickled at his cleverness and he was rarely punished. I wasn't so clever and when I did something wrong, I did get spanked. I didn't think that was fair and often suggested that he should be spanked too.

We had a little Pomeranian dog whose name was Ming Toy. One day when I was about four, my little brother, the dog, and I were on the front porch. There was an accordion-like gate across the steps. Mom had stepped into the house and left me in charge of my brother for a minute. I tried to open the gate, I don't remember why, and the dog dashed out onto busy Court Street and was hit by a taxi cab. I sobbed loudly and screamed, "Momma, Momma." My mother ran out and asked me if something happened to my brother. She realized Ming Toy had been hit and talked to the taxi driver.

Ming Toy didn't make it. Later, Mom sat down to talk with me. She said, "Bev, opening the gate was not a good idea. I was really scared and thought something happened to your brother." I replied, "I wouldn't have cried that hard if something had happened to my brother." I'm sure I would have cried, but maybe not so hard.

I remember always feeling that my brother had to be taken care of. I didn't resent it. It was just the way it was. When we were tucked in at night my father would tell us, "Sleep tight and don't let the bedbugs bite. Good-night Buckaroo, good-night Sister Sue, and Sister Sue, take care of your little brother." When my parents fought and Dick got scared, I got out of bed and went to him to tell him it was all right.

But I wasn't always nice. I also regularly smacked him if he got into my things, wouldn't let him play with my friends and me, and later, when we lived in a two-story house, threatened to throw him out the window if he didn't do what I wanted. That stopped when he got bigger than me. My brother was a charming little boy. Family loved him and with the family he was happy and outgoing. He was shy with others. When my parents divorced and we moved in with my grandparents, my cousin Patty and I frequently played tricks on him. He went to Grandma crying and we called him a baby, which only made him cry more. But, neither one of us would let anyone else pick on him. When boys at school tried to beat him up we made sure they didn't.

Dick did not have friends. As a child, he played with whoever I played with. He stuck by my side. It was annoying sometimes, but mostly I didn't mind. He suffered more than I remember suffering when our parents were divorced and Mom rarely came to see us. Dick never gave up on her.

Mom remarried when I was thirteen and Dick eleven. We were living with Dad in Detroit. She asked us to stay with her for a while, and in January at mid-term in school we did. Mom's husband, Fritz, tolerated me but he did not like Dick.

He called him sneaky. It was not a happy time. I made friends but again Dick was a loner. At the end of the summer we moved back with Dad.

Dick was seventeen when Dad married his third wife, Pauline. I was on my own living in Muskegon at the time. Dick didn't like Pauline, so he quit school and joined the navy. He had done some experimentation with drinking as a teenager, but his serious drinking began then. No one had ever talked to us about alcohol addiction, its prevalence in our family, and the increased propensity we might have for alcohol addiction. When you're young, getting drunk is just  something you do, and at that time, particularly something young men did.

When his enlistment time was up, Dick, now called Richard, came home and went to work for our father in the cement business. He married his girlfriend, Joanie, and had a daughter, Karen, who would be his only child. His drinking continued and the marriage ended when Karen was very young. Women were attracted to Richard. They wanted to fix things for him, much like I did when he was a little boy. He married a woman named Hazel who had two small children. The drinking continued, and they divorced. While going through records on Ancestry.com, I uncovered two more marriage licenses listed for him. I didn't see him often then. I was busy with my own life and he rarely came to visit.

Richard bought a cement manufacturing company in Clio. I'm not sure when that was, but not long after that he met a wonderful woman, Marilyn Finley, hard-working, steady as a rock, and not surprisingly, a rescuer of people. She was to stand by him through the next very difficult years.

In 1988, Richard turned fifty. He was drinking heavily and not paying much attention to work. His primary employee ran the business, and Richard hung out in bars. He liked to spend money and attracted a number of much younger women. It was a time when many young people were experimenting with cocaine, and Richard experimented. He was an addict, and, of course, he got hooked. Much later in his life Richard told me he was flattered by the attention he got when he had cocaine available for these young women he met in bars. Cocaine was expensive. He sold his business, and before long he could not support his habit and he started to deal.

Within two years, Richard was caught selling drugs, and sent to prison where he spent almost two years. Incarceration began at Jackson State Prison and ended at Carson City State Prison about seventy-five miles from Flint. This didn't stop the addiction; in fact, Richard told me that drugs were easier to get in prison. Marilyn visited regularly and when Richard was released he again lived with her.

We all thought prison would be the shock Richard needed to quit practicing his addictions. He did stop drinking. Alcohol no longer interested him. But he had not given up cocaine. Again, he had to deal to pay for his drugs. He was back in the very business that put him in prison. I did see Richard two or three times a year after he was released from prison. Each time I left deeply saddened. Richard could not hold a conversation beyond ten minutes or so. We chatted and then he would excuse himself to go up to his bedroom. I later learned he snorted cocaine and then smoked marijuana to level the effect of cocaine. After an hour or so, he came back downstairs and we could talk a little longer.

Occasionally I visited Richard for lunch while Marilyn was at work. It was then that I learned he was still dealing. He never did it when Marilyn was around. People drove up to the house and got out of their car, Richard went into the garage with them, and then they got back into their car and drove away. Marilyn, hard as it is to believe, never knew he was dealing. She thought he was drinking and occasionally used marijuana. It was a miracle the police never found out.

When Richard was around sixty-five, he was still using and dealing cocaine. He accidentally dropped a packet of powder in the downstairs bathroom and didn't see it. Marilyn's grandchildren were visiting and her grandson was roughhousing with a friend in the kitchen. Their play spilled over into the bathroom, which was right off the kitchen. Marilyn went in to break up the scuffle and saw the packet. Fortunately, the kids did not. She picked it up and confronted Richard. She told him he had to leave and move into his own place within six weeks. He could stay through Christmas. I visited around that time and he told me she had asked him to leave and he was scared. He loved Marilyn, and he needed her. She made him feel safe. She was the woman who was there for him as his mother never was.

He made a promise to her that he would not use and he would not sell. A miracle occurred, and somehow, in some way, he totally quit using. No cocaine, no marijuana, and no alcohol. When I came to visit I had my brother back, the brother I could be close to, the brother I had when we were teenagers together, before his addictions took over. We visited and we reminisced. We laughed together and shared our sadness over the difficulty of our childhood.

Richard had been dealing with alcohol-related diabetes for some time and it had progressed. He had neuropathy in his feet, and in 2009, at age seventy-one, Richard went into the hospital to have part of his foot amputated. When I visited we talked a bit, and then he looked at me wistfully and said, "I suppose the reason I'm having these health problems has a lot to do with the way I lived my life." He got very still and quiet. Then he looked at me, and with a grin said, "It seemed like such fun at the time." We laughed together. I kissed him goodbye and told him I would visit when he got home. Those were the last words he said to me.

After the operation the doctors put a dye into his system to determine whether the veins in his legs had the capacity to provide enough blood to his feet. The dye weakened his already damaged kidneys. Marilyn called me and his daughter, Karen, and told us we needed to come. The doctor put Richard on life support. He was unconscious when I came and Karen arrived. We hugged him, cried over him, cried with each other, and then the doctor came in and took him off life support. He was gone.

Until the very end Richard was part of my joy. He was the only person who shared the same parents, the same history, knew the same family stories. There were many times when as his big sister I was his protector, and many times when the things he did were serious enough that he could not be protected. As I write, I often find myself wanting to call and ask him something about our childhood that I can't remember. I loved him. When he died I lost a part of myself. I will miss him always.

Dick's Family

Karen age four   Karen today

Marilyn Finley

GROWING UP – MY SCHOOL YEARS

*"Ring the bells that still can ring, forget your perfect offering.
There is a crack in everything and that's how the light gets in."*
Leonard Cohen, "The Anthem"

A depression ending, a war beginning, and more

On December 7, 1941, when Japan attacked Pearl Harbor and the United States joined World War II, I was five years old and in kindergarten. My beloved uncles, Jay and Gene, my babysitters, lied about their ages and joined the navy.

As time went on, there were things I began to know about the war. Almost every Saturday, my cousin Patty, my brother Dick, and I walked several blocks to the Nortown Theater where we paid fourteen cents to see a movie. There was always a newsreel before the movie that began with big cannon-like guns swiveling until they pointed directly at the audience. Eerie music played and a man's deep voice announced, *"The eyes and ears of the world are upon you."* We knew something important was about to be said. The newsreel lasted about ten minutes and the biggest stories were about the war, soldiers in battle, airplanes roaring through the skies, booming guns, and the rat-a-tat-tat of machine guns. Sometimes we saw pictures of women working in factories that supplied our soldiers with tanks, Jeeps, guns, and other equipment they needed. We watched wives and children bravely smiling as their men left for war. Actors urged us to buy war bonds and conserve gas.

In the newsreels and in regular movies, Hitler with his big, black mustache, was shown giving a speech, shouting in a language I didn't understand, while people saluted him with their right arm extended. *"Heil Hitler,"* they shouted while he saluted back with his right arm extended. We watched people who looked different from us, people the newsreel called Japs, and we knew that both the Japs and Hitler were our enemies. In play, we put our index finger under our nose, imitating Hitler's mustache, put out our other arm, and yelled in a loud voice, *"Heil Hitler."* Sometimes we would chant, *"Hotsy, Totsy, no more Nazis."* I guess we thought it was funny.

56

I knew our country was fighting Germany and Japan, but I had no idea the extent to which the war affected people's lives. I had no idea that innocent Japanese Americans were being forced from their homes and interned in fenced camps out of fear that they were collaborators. I didn't know that Hitler was systematically ordering the imprisonment and killing of Jews. I remember sitting in the living room next to Cousin Patty, leaning on the Philco floor model radio, feeling the vibration and listening to the voice of President Roosevelt talk about the bravery of our soldiers and thanking the people for their sacrifices. Our grandparents were silent during the broadcast and would quickly shush us if we talked. I remember neighborhood drills when the neighborhood air raid warden checked to see that house windows were covered so no light could be seen should an enemy bomber fly over.

On April 12, 1945, just before the war ended, when I was almost nine, President Franklin Delano Roosevelt died. He was sixty-three years old. He had led us out of the Great Depression and gotten us through the war. His voice on the radio had been a comfort to my grandparents and to people all over the country. I know my grandparents were sad. It was almost as though they had lost a family member.

I remember the excitement on May 8, 1945, VE Day, V for victory, E for Europe, when the radio announcer declared the war in Europe had ended. The neighbors were out on their porches and in their yards talking to each other. The Germans had surrendered. Then, on August 6 that same year, with orders from our new president, Harry Truman, an atomic bomb was dropped on Hiroshima, Japan, killing 140,000 men, women, and children. On August 15, the Japanese surrendered. It was VJ Day, J for Japan. We saw pictures in the *Flint Journal* of people celebrating in the streets downtown. I knew that people were happy and excited that the war was over, but I didn't understand the depth of relief they must have felt.

It would be years later when we had television that I would see images of Japanese children running in the streets of Hiroshima, their clothes burned off from the bomb. It would be even longer before I understood how dropping the nuclear bomb changed the course of history. There was fear around the possibility of using the devastating power of a nuclear weapon for evil. In our country, tension existed between those who were relieved that the war was over and those who were shocked and saddened by the loss of so many innocent Japanese lives. What if it had been Japan that had the nuclear bomb? There were also scientists who knew that nuclear power could be a force for good as well as evil. In 1946, President Truman responded by creating the Atomic Energy Commission, and scientists began to look at peaceful ways to use nuclear energy.

Soldiers came home ready to re-establish their lives, including marriage and babies. Some seventy-six million babies were born between 1946 and 1964, a baby-boom it was called. By the force of their numbers, boomers are a demographic bulge of people who have remodeled our country as they passed through each decade. After the war, there was a huge marketing push encouraging women to come back home, to leave the jobs they held during the war, to create jobs for veterans in factories as they returned. Most did, some did not, but the independence women gained during those war years would never go away. The seeds for the second wave of the women's movement were planted then.

It would be wonderful to say there were no more wars after World War II; however, the aftermath was the impetus for the Korean War. Japan had occupied Korea for generations, and the surrender agreement that ended the war divided Korea, allowing the Soviet Union to occupy the north and the United States the south. The Soviet Union increasingly exerted control over central and Eastern Europe, spreading the doctrine of communism in every country it controlled. In the United States communism was viewed as evil and President Truman pledged assistance to any nation threatened by communism. The Cold War had begun.

The United States prepared to withdraw from South Korea which, in 1948, had held its first election and established its own government. In 1950, the ruler of North Korea, Kim Il Sung, went to the Soviet Union and asked for and was granted permission to invade South Korea. President Truman ordered air and sea forces to give support. In June 1950, North Korea captured Seoul, South Korea, and the United States sent ground troops into battle. In October, China entered the war fighting on the side of North Korea. By 1951, the war was at a stalemate with neither side making much headway. America was tired of war. Dwight Eisenhower was elected in 1952 with a promise to negotiate an honorable truce and withdrawal of American troops. Armistice was declared in July 1953, but North and South Korea remain divided today.

Other important events when I was growing up in the 1940s, in addition to President Roosevelt's death in 1945, included Democrat Harry Truman narrowly winning the presidency in 1948. Everyone thought Thomas Dewey, the Republican, would win, and in fact, early morning newspapers headlines declared that he did. That same decade, a former military vehicle, the Jeep, was introduced as a personal vehicle, ballpoint pens replaced ink pens, women wore bikini bathing suits at the beach, Polaroid cameras were invented, and Slinky toys were popular.

When I was in high school in the 1950s, a constitutional amendment passed limiting presidential terms to two. DNA was discovered, a polio vaccine was created, and the television remote control and Velcro were invented. The 1950s saw the beginning of the black civil rights movement when Rosa Parks refused to give up her seat on a bus to a white passenger as was required in many southern states. The peace symbol was created, Elvis Presley became a phenomenon when he gyrated his hips on the Ed Sullivan Show, and hula hoops and Lego were popular. In 1952, the Today show debuted, and in 1954, the year I graduated high school, the Dow Jones average hit an all-time high of almost 383 points. (As of this writing it has hit another all-time high of over 16,000.) Also in 1954, the *Tonight* show aired for the first time, *On the Waterfront* won Best Picture; Marlon Brando, its star, won Best Actor; and *I Love Lucy* starring Lucille Ball and her husband, Desi Arnaz, was a favorite television show.

Living with Grandma and Grandpa: A stable home where we could just be kids.

In 1943, when our parents divorced, my brother and I moved to Grandpa and Grandma Hier's house at 914 E. Philadelphia Street in Flint, Michigan. It was the summer I turned seven and my brother turned five. That fall I entered second grade and Dick started kindergarten. Our first cousin (above), Patricia Jean Steib, Patty, was nine. She was daring and funny, a most wonderful companion, and she could make my grandmother laugh and forget that she had been naughty. For example, one day Grandma asked Patty to run the broom around the dining room floor. That meant give it a light sweeping. Patty procrastinated. After several minutes went by Grandma, in a firm voice, said, "Patty, I told you to get in here and run the broom around the dining room floor." Patty got up, clutched the broom handle with both hands, and proceeded to run around the table with it, hollering, "It's getting away from me, Grandma." Grandma laughed and no discipline ensued.

My grandparents' house was two stories, sided with brown shingles. It had a basement, an attached shed, and a detached garage in the back. A kitchen, bathroom, dining room, bedroom, living room, and formal parlor were on the first floor. The second floor had four bedrooms and an entrance to the attic. The basement held the furnace, a coal bin, laundry area, lots of shelves for home canned goods, and an open area where we played when the weather was not good enough to go outside.

There was a swing on the front porch, and in the summer Grandma filled white wicker plant stands with geraniums. Hedges bordered the front, and in the side yard Grandma had a vegetable and flower garden. My favorites were peonies and hollyhocks.

61

The kitchen had a gas stove, flour cupboard, kitchen sink lowered to fit Grandma's height, and cupboards for dishes, pots and pans, and groceries. Grandma was a great cook. Everything was made from scratch.

The bathroom was off the kitchen and it held a tub, sink, toilet, and a cabinet for bathroom supplies and towels. There was no shower in those days. We sponged off every day and took a bath and had our hair washed weekly. We brushed our teeth with Teel, a liquid tooth cleaner instead of paste, shampooed our hair with Prell, and bathed with Palmolive soap, all were Grandma's favorite brands.

The teachers at our school regularly lined us up and used a pencil to part our hair in several places, looking for lice. Even if we didn't have them, a note was sent home if someone in the class did. Grandma took no chances. She took us in the bathroom, rubbed kerosene in our hair, and combed it through, killing any lice eggs that might be hiding there. It smelled awful, worse than grandpa's ashtray and that was pretty bad. Then she vigorously shampooed. It was a matter of pride to Grandma that no one ever found lice on Patty, Dick, or me.

The dining room held the refrigerator, which was too large for the kitchen; a round oak pedestal table with six chairs; and a matching buffet. A small radio on the buffet was always on when we came home from school for lunch, and we listened with Grandma to the soap operas she loved. In one corner of the dining room was a small desk-like table where the heavy black telephone sat. It had a drawer for the telephone book. Our phone number was 33767; there was no letter prefix, which came later, and no area code, which came much later. We had a party line and each family's phone had a different ring. I think ours was three longs and a short. We could, if we didn't get caught by Grandma, listen in on a neighbor's conversations.

Five doors off the dining room led to the back shed, my grandparents' bedroom, the basement, the living room, and the kitchen. Most of our activity took place in the dining room. We did our homework around the table. Grandma drilled Patty on her multiplication tables. She curled Patty's and my hair at the dining room table. While our hair was wet, she took several rag scraps that she had cut in 1 x 3 inch pieces, wrapped them around strands of our hair, and tied them. The next day we went to school with little sausage-like curls. Of course, we ate at the table. We asked to be excused from the table when we were through eating; when company came, we stood up until told to sit down; and we never called grownups by their first name. Manners were important to my grandparents.

My grandparents' bedroom had a double bed, a dresser, and a cardboard-like closet. There were no built-in closets in any of the bedrooms. Patty and I kept a secret. Their bedroom was off limits for kids but we sneaked in to search for Christmas gifts we knew Grandma kept in their closet, and we found a bottle of whiskey under the presents. We kept the secret because we knew we would be punished if they found out we were snooping. There was one exception to the *"Don't go in our bedroom"* rule. Patty, Dick, and I slept in an upstairs bedroom, but any time one of us was sick we were kept in our grandparents' bedroom during the day. Once, I was sick, Dr. Reichardt was called, came to the house to examine me, diagnosed me with German measles, posted a quarantine sign by the door on the front porch, and said I had to be isolated. I was put to bed in my grandparents' bed with all of the shades drawn and no lights in the room. It was believed that you could lose your eyesight if you were exposed to bright light when you had the measles. I was isolated for several days. I liked being served meals in bed, but when I started feeling better, I was bored. The other kids couldn't visit.

Grandpa's big rocking chair sat in a corner of the living room along with an overstuffed fabric couch and a matching chair. The floor model Philco radio took up one corner. It was probably three to four feet tall, with a rounded top, two large knobs for volume and tuning, and a numbered backlit screen so you could tell which station you were tuned to. A burlap-like fabric covered the speakers in the front lower half. The front door led directly into the living room. An area rug, almost the size of the room, covered the wood floor where Patty, Dick, and I would often lie and color. It was exciting when we graduated from the twenty-four to the sixty-four Crayola crayon boxes. The goal was to get very good at coloring within the lines. Patty always did better than Dick and me. I never minded, anything she did was okay with me.

After supper, Patty and I sat in the living room with our backs against the radio, probably because we didn't want to miss a word of the programs we listened to. We were thrilled and scared when the sound of a squeaky door opening welcomed us into *The Inner Sanctum*. We laughed out loud at Jack Benny, his wife, Mary, and their servant, Rochester. We were mesmerized by *The Shadow* and waited for the opening, *"Who knows what evil lurks in the hearts of men? The Shadow knows."* And we loved the Lone Ranger and his faithful companion, Tonto. We were ready for a good story when the announcer said, *"From out of the west come the thundering hoof beats of the great horse Silver, hi ho Silver, away!"*

The parlor was off the living room. It was furnished with a reddish brown horsehair sofa and two horsehair chairs, all stiff and most uncomfortable; lamps with fringed shades; an area rug with big flowers that matched the sofa and chairs; and my grandma's upright piano and bench. The piano was brown oak. This room was used only when we had visitors or when Grandma played the piano.

That first year at Grandma and Grandpa's, every day was much the same. We knew when we came home from school Grandma would be there to greet us. Meals were ready when they were supposed to be. There was help with schoolwork. We knew what the rules were and what to expect if we didn't follow them. We had chores to do but were mostly expected to be kids and to play. I missed my parents in the beginning, but at our grandparents' home my brother and I were able to be kids and not worry so much about adult problems.

Free to play, imagine, and dream; free to be a child

Imagine life as a child without television, video games, Transformers, Legos, or Barbie. There were no play dates and no organized sports. There were no cell phones so the adults in your life could locate you if they wanted you to come home. They did not think it was their job to entertain you. They didn't worry that someone would try to hurt you. You had no social calendar. Kids did not wear backpacks to school and there was very little homework until junior high. At most you might practice your multiplication tables or your weekly spelling list. You probably had some chores to do around the house. But mostly as a child it was your job to entertain yourself and not bother the grownups.

Summer days were endless on East Philadelphia Street. Every week we made a trip to the library at Berston Field House, about ten blocks from home. When I was six, my cousin and I walked there on our own. I remember my first trip, when I walked into the library, looked at the shelves filled with books, and thought, *I'm going to read every book in this library.* The first book I checked out was Dr. Seuss's, *And To Think That I Saw It On Mulberry Street.* I took the books home and read them sitting on the porch swing and under my blanket at night using a flashlight.

There were song books. One was called *Hit Parade* and it had the words to popular songs of the day. My cousin Patty and I sat or stood on the porch and sang those songs as though we were starring in a movie. We used a broomstick as the handle to our microphone. In those days microphones stood on stands, there were no hand-held microphones.

Sometimes I took a blanket out in the yard, flopped down, and spent most of the day looking up at the sky and daydreaming. Mostly I thought about the stories in the books I read or the movies I saw. I imagined I was a princess or a cowgirl or a dancer or singer. Grandma grew flowers in the yard, peonies and hollyhocks and roses. We made dolls from the hollyhocks using toothpicks. The flower was the dress and hollyhock buds were stuck on the toothpicks for the head and arms.

Frequently on Saturdays we walked six blocks to the Nortown Theater on North Saginaw Street. There was always a full-length feature, cartoons, a newsreel, and a short feature, either a comedy or a cowboy story. Admission was fourteen cents. We had either popcorn or candy, seldom both. My favorite was Neccos, hard little wafers of different colors. I also liked Milk Duds and Jujubees. We loved Roy Rogers and Dale Evans, married in real life and sweetheart cowboy and cowgirl in the movies. We had holsters, guns, and cowgirl hats and acted out the scenes when we got home. Patty always wanted to be Roy and made me be Dale. Roy got to do more so I wanted to be him too, but she was the oldest and mostly got to do what she wanted. Dale sang with Roy and jumped on her horse to ride off with him. My horse was a broomstick.

Sometimes we were allowed to walk all the way downtown to the movie theater. It must have been at least a five-mile round trip. I can't imagine a parent feeling safe letting their eight- or nine-year-old child do this today. There were three movie theaters downtown, the Capitol, the Palace, and the Strand. The Capitol was especially ornate, with a ceiling that looked like a sky with clouds, stars, and floating angels. The Strand was a more modest theater. I remember seeing the deliciously scary Frankenstein movies there. After the movie we walked over to a little shop called the Honey Dell and got a caramel apple to eat on the way home.

Downtown Flint was a bustling place. Sometimes Grandma took us shopping at the big department store, Smith Bridgeman's. We dressed up and took the bus. The bus had a tether to an electric line that ran along the street. After shopping we got a hamburger at Kewpee's, now The Halo Burger, a Michigan chain founded in Flint. The hamburgers were good then and are good now.

In the evenings all the neighbor kids played outside, tag, hide and seek, Red Rover, and kick the can. There was very little traffic so we played in the street, boys and girls together. If my dad was at my grandparents' house and he wanted us to come in he whistled loudly. We always knew his whistle. Otherwise, we were to come home when the street lights came on.

Our neighbor, Mrs. Lane, held weekly Bible classes at her house for the kids in the neighborhood. She had a story board, an easel with a flannel-covered board across the top. There were flannel figures of the various people, animals, trees, stars, and more and she told a Bible story sticking the figures on the flannel board where they stayed in place. Sometimes on Sundays I went to church with Mrs. Lane. Our family did not attend church.

We had another neighbor, Mrs. Clark, who was strange. Sadly, we talked about her being crazy and stole rhubarb from her garden which upset her greatly. She ran out of the house and stood in the road yelling at us as we ran away laughing. We were scared but thought it was funny, too. Kids can be mean and I was no exception. Many years later, Mrs. Clark jumped off a bridge into the Flint River and died. By then, I was an adult and knew what mental illness was. I felt sad that we had treated her badly.

On rainy days, Patty, Dick, and I played in the basement. We played school, and Patty was the teacher most of the time--a pretty bossy one. We played house and Grandma let us put real tea in our teapot. Patty and I had baby dolls. There were no teenage dolls to dress in the latest fashion. We had a doll carriage and high chair, doll bottles, and doll clothes. One of our dolls would actually wet her pants when we fed her water with the bottle. We also had a white cat called Snowball and sometimes we dressed the cat in the doll clothes and pushed it in the carriage.

In the winter we went to school and in the evenings we played inside. We colored, played Monopoly, Tiddly Winks, and Pick Up Sticks. We had Tinker Toys to build things with. We listened to the radio. There were offers, things you could send away for, and once in awhile Grandma let us do that. I remember a ring that opened up to hide a secret message. On Saturdays we played outside building snowmen and making angels by lying down and moving our arms and legs in and out; we tried to get up without messing up the angel outline.

We had sleds. Philadelphia Street was on a downward slope from North Street to our house, about two-thirds of a block. We trudged up what we thought was the top of a hill, held our sleds up by the crossbar at the top, ran a few feet, and belly-flopped on the sled, coasting to our house and beyond if we could. Again, there were very few cars so it was safe to do over and over. I visited Philadelphia Street as an adult and was amazed that it was a slope and not a hill.

Prosenick's was a small neighborhood store on Industrial Boulevard about a block from home. Sometimes Grandma gave us a handful of pennies to spend there. Mrs. Prosenick was a short, gray-haired, rounded woman who spoke in broken English. Large glass containers on the counter were filled with penny candy. We chose what we wanted, and she put the candy in a small brown bag for us. She knew all the neighbor kids by name.

We did some silly kids things that annoyed our grandmother, but I don't remember us getting into any serious trouble. I do remember playing in a neighbor boy's basement one day. There was a small room under the stairs with shelves filled with home-canned fruits and vegetables. We opened a can of peppers and each took a bite. They were blazing hot. We started crying and ran upstairs. His mother gave us a slice of bread to press between our lips and said it would not burn for long. It seemed to me it went on for a long time. Another time when Grandma went out shopping, Patty and I decided to make peanut butter cookies, but we did not have the faintest idea how to do it. I'm not sure what we put in them but they were very runny, and we ended up dumping them in the toilet. The toilet clogged, and we had to confess. Patty decided she needed a haircut one day and she sat on the toilet while I chopped off clumps of her hair. I had difficulty getting it even on both sides so I kept on cutting. It ended up looking pretty bad and Grandma was more than unhappy with that particular prank.

I am grateful for those childhood times on Philadelphia Street, where the days lasted forever and there was freedom to explore and daydream and imagine and play. I felt safe, trusted to travel around the neighborhood and community, doing what I wanted to do in the moment, no plans. I worry that kids today have too many plans, too many schedules, and too little freedom and that their parents have too much fear. You don't miss what you never had and maybe they feel a different kind of freedom. I do believe they grow up faster and they know more than we did. Even if that is so, I'm still glad I had that time at my grandparents' house to just be a kid. It would be the most stable time in my childhood.

The nomadic life: You go where they send you, learn what you need to

Once I saw a cartoon that showed a large auditorium where the seats ascend from front to back. On the stage in front, a speaker stood at a podium. Strung across the back was a large banner with these words: NATIONAL CONVENTION OF SURVIVORS OF FUNCTIONAL FAMILIES. One person sat in the audience.

That cartoon may be a bit of an exaggeration, but the truth is there are many families with severe dysfunction like alcohol and/or drug abuse, domestic violence, child abuse, or untreated mental illness. And there are parents who fail to meet the needs of their children, physical, emotional, and/or spiritual, sometimes because the parents have no moral compass and sometimes because they don't have the skills, knowledge, and/or intellect to be good parents. But, in most families I think parents do the best that they can.

Mostly I think that kids are amazingly adaptable. If their basic needs for food, shelter, and health care are met, and they have someone present to assure them that they are safe, they will do okay. The degree to which they will do okay may vary. I believe that some of us inherently adapt to change more easily than others. I was one of the lucky ones. We got moved around like checkers on a checkerboard. I learned at an early age what it takes to adapt and survive.

My brother Dick and I were moved fourteen times in eight years from my parents' separation in 1942, when I was six and my brother was four, until 1950 when I turned fourteen and my brother was twelve and we finally lived with Dad in one place for two years. We went to eleven schools and had eight-plus caregivers. Each move meant there were more things to learn and adapt to than how to get from the new residence to school.

Our first move was the one to Grandma and Grandpa Hier's house on East Philadelphia Street in Flint. That was an easy adjustment. We knew and loved them and felt safe. We missed our mother but living without her soon seemed normal. Dad had always gone away to work and come home. His going away lasted longer now but time doesn't have a lot of meaning for young kids. Our cousin Patty became our leader and showed us just how far we could push the limits, which was not very far. I completed second grade while living with my grandparents.

My next move was the toughest. In 1944, the summer I turned eight, I was placed in the Whaley Home, just me, not my brother. It not only broke my heart, but fear settled in. I was young and did not understand why I was there. Deep inside I was sure that something was wrong with me. I was not lovable enough, I hadn't been good enough, and when you're not lovable and not good, people leave you. The fear stayed with me a long time. I changed. When I was old enough to think about it I described it as a separation of my emotions from my body. I often felt as though I was two persons in one. A part of me stayed outside of my body and watched the other me do whatever she did. The *outside of my body me* observed the *other me*, the one that interacted with others, was normal and happy, worked hard, and achieved. I don't mean I really thought I was two people. It felt like a protective device. The *outside of my body me* guarded all the feelings, she was detached, she watched and she waited to see if she could trust. I know it sounds a little crazy. It didn't feel crazy. I was only eight. It felt normal. I think the psychological description for this behavior is disassociation, and I'm sure I'm not the first to experience it. It isn't the kind of thing people talk about so I don't know. Later in life I described this as having one foot out the door, ready to run if I needed to, in my head if not in reality.

I went back to Grandma's after the Whaley Home and completed third grade. The next year my dad had a new wife,

Verla, and when I was nine years old and in fourth grade, the four of us--dad, Verla, my brother, and I--moved to Detroit. We rented a second-floor apartment on Continental Street, off Jefferson in a building that I think had four apartments. There was a living room, kitchen, two bedrooms, a bath, and an enclosed porch at the back of the house. I especially remember that instead of a refrigerator like we had at Grandma's house, we had an ice box. It was brown wood with three doors, two on the left and one on the right. The top door on the left was for the fifty-pound ice block that was regularly delivered to our door. We put a sign in our front window indicating we needed ice and the iceman, who had a cart pulled by a horse and every day traveled the route that led past our house, checked for the sign. He picked up the ice with a giant set of tongs, put it over his shoulder, and carried it up to our apartment.

A few months later Verla left. Dad advertised in the paper for a caregiver and hired Marian Betts, a nineteen-year-old with a nine-month-old baby, Patty. We liked Marian but after Verla, a world-class cook, Marian didn't measure up. Dad insisted we eat what she cooked or not eat at all. Once it was okra. When Grandma made okra it was in nice, firm, fried little patties. When Marian made it, it was runny goo. Eating that okra involved lots of gagging. Another time she made a tuna sandwich for my lunch. I did not like tuna and wouldn't eat it. I went without. It showed up on my plate at supper. I didn't eat it. Have you ever had a tuna sandwich for breakfast? I did.

Marian could be fun. I realize now she was still a kid. She was tough too, not afraid. I had a mean teacher at school who slapped her students. She took my ruler for some reason one day, put it on the chalk tray by the bulletin board, and would not give it back to me. Later I sneaked it back, she caught me, and she slapped me across the face in front of the entire class. The next day I refused to go to school. Marian figured out something was wrong and I told her what happened with the teacher. She walked me to school, went into the classroom, and told the teacher if she ever hit me again she would wish she hadn't. I could tell the teacher was frightened and I never got hit again.

Marian left. I don't know why. Dad took Dick and me back to Flint and put us in a children's home on Court Street right next to the school for the deaf. This was the second group home for me. It was a little easier to deal with than the Whaley Home because Dick was with me. I was ten and entering fifth grade.

Most of the children who were in the home had been removed from their homes because of abuse or neglect. Boys and girls were separated so Dick and I only saw each other across the room at meals, and at prayer meeting on Wednesday evenings. There were two live-in women caregivers at the home that I remember. One was a kind, older woman. The other was younger and had a teenage daughter who lived at the home with her. The younger caregiver was mean and so was her daughter.

The bigger kids, like me, were assigned a smaller child to help get dressed and make sure their teeth and hair were brushed in the mornings. They were three- and four-year-olds. When a child wet the bed, the mean caregiver made him or her strip the bed. Then she put the child in a cold shower and turned on the hot water in the bathtub, which somehow made the water in the shower colder. The poor little kids cried and cried. Then their big kid would wrap them in a towel and try to warm them and help them get dressed. Our hearts hurt for these little ones.

The Wednesday prayer meeting was led by the minister of a nearby church. It was one of the few times Dick and I could be close. He sat behind me and I reached my hands back so he could hold them. The mean caregiver's daughter told on us. After the meeting both Dick and I were spanked for inappropriate behavior.

I was angry, I wanted revenge, and soon I was able to retaliate. All of the kids attended the home's Halloween party. Apples were strung from the ceiling so they swung around. We each stood in front of an apple and when the lights were turned off we put our hands behind our backs and tried to grab a bite from the apple with our teeth. Everyone who got a bite earned a prize. We took turns, four or five kids at a time. The mean caregiver's daughter was in line to bite an apple and I wasn't. Before it got dark in the room I positioned myself so I could quickly get to and away from her. The lights went off. I stepped over, pinched her as hard as I could, and moved back into position. She started screaming and the lights went on. I did not get caught.

Dick was especially unhappy there. I wasn't happy but I liked school and easily made friends. He didn't and he ran away to Grandma's house. After this happened several times, Dad recognized Dick's unhappiness and moved us from the home.

Our next stop was a foster family home in Detroit. The parents were Mr. and Mrs. Tundis, Frank and Rose. They had two children, Madeline and Guy, about ages five and seven. I was in the last half of fifth grade. Frank and Rose were immigrants from Italy. The food was amazing. There seemed to be lots of people in and out of their home and sharing meals. I remember huge platters of spaghetti covered in a hot spicy sauce. They made pizza, but not the kind you get now. Their pizza was bread baked in a layer cake pan and covered with fresh tomatoes, green peppers, onion, and lots of garlic. Again, it was spicy. My mouth became accustomed to spicy food.

Rose provided our care while Frank worked during the day. He was pleasant to my brother and me but very strict with his children, especially his son. Once Guy took some money that didn't belong to him and his hand was held over the burner on the gas stove until it blistered. I can still remember his screams. Another time, Guy misbehaved and he was knocked down and kicked by his father, who was wearing heavy work boots. This was shocking to me and I'm sure I told my dad. We weren't there very long.

I liked school and did very well. One of my best memories was representing my school in the Detroit News Spelling Bee at the regional level. I won the bee at my school and moved to the regional bee that included students from fifth through twelfth grade. I spelled several words correctly, but missed a very simple word, carol as in Christmas carol. I spelled it *carrol*. I didn't like losing but I felt good that I had done as well as I had. One small thing marred my happiness. The night before the bee I was practicing my words and Dad told me I probably wouldn't win anyway. When I lost, I remembered his words. I believe he thought he could soften a loss by preparing me for failure. I find it odd that I remember that.

The next move was another foster family home, this time in Grosse Pointe Woods, Michigan. The parents were Mr. and Mrs. Jordan, Grace and Clint. They had two little boys, maybe three and one years old. I was still in fifth grade. I loved Grace Jordan. She truly mothered me, something I didn't even know I had missed. She let me cook with her, she took me shopping for clothes, she brushed my hair, and she hugged me. She told me I was smart and pretty, not something I had heard. She owned a flower shop and she liked to paint. Once she painted a portrait of me. I was happy there and made friends in the neighborhood.

But alas, it didn't last. In the summer of 1947, when I was almost eleven, I became very ill, running a high fever and vomiting. My dad took me to the doctor and I was diagnosed with polio. There were no vaccines for polio at that time and there was a terrible epidemic. Many young people were critically ill or dying. My dad put me in the back seat of the car and drove rapidly to Flint where my grandparents lived and our family doctor practiced. I was admitted to Hurley Hospital and put into an isolation unit. It was a separate wooden building, away from the main hospital, with screened windows that were often open and a screen door. Visitors came to the door and talked to whoever they were visiting through the screen. There were three beds. I was in the one closest to the door. I could not get out of bed. When I first got there I slept a lot. After a few weeks I felt better and was able to sit up but still not allowed to walk.

Dad brought me a radio to listen to and coloring books and paper dolls. Mom came to visit and talked to me through the doors. I remember she cried. I really had no concept about the seriousness of my illness. Once I felt better I happily entertained myself and visited with the two other kids in the room. After some time I was released and went to my grandmother's house. I had not walked in several weeks and when I tried to stand I could not balance myself and I walked on my toes. My dad had to help me to the car. It took awhile before I could walk normally, but I was fortunate; many polio victims never walked again.

In the fall, Marian Betts, the young caregiver with the little child, Patty, came back into our lives. Dad rented a tri-level house in Detroit and he, Dick, Marian, Patty, and I moved in. Marian must have been twenty-one at this time and Patty almost four. I was in the sixth grade.

I was intrigued with having a house with three levels. I had never seen one before. The living room and a bedroom with a bath were on the main floor. There were four or five steps down to a kitchen, dining area and utility room. There were also four or five steps up from the living room to more bedrooms and another bath. Marian and Patty slept upstairs as did Dick and I. Marian had magically improved her cooking in the two years since we last lived with her. I'm sad to say that I wasn't always nice to her. I was at a bratty stage and felt like she was too young to boss me around. I remember saying something very mean to her about having a child when she wasn't married. Sometime in the 1980s I called her and apologized and thanked her for her kindness to us because she was unfailingly kind. She never raised her voice, never spanked us, and corrected us gently if we misbehaved. She did not tell Dad, whose discipline would have been harsher. She often joined us in play. On Halloween she went with us door to door and hollered "trick or treat" as loud as we did. She was small and with a mask no one would have guessed she wasn't just another kid. It was traditional at that time in Detroit to tip over garbage cans on Halloween night and she joined us in tipping them.

At the end of sixth grade we moved again, this time back to Flint. Marian and her daughter, Patty, came with us. We rented the apartment above my grandparents' house on Philadelphia Street. It was 1948, I was twelve and entering seventh grade at Emerson Junior High and Dick was ten. Grandma had been diagnosed with uterine cancer and I'm sure part of Marian's job was to help her. Dad stayed in Detroit where he worked and visited on the weekends. Grandma and Marian liked each other. Grandma taught Marian how to grow flowers and she included her in the gatherings of neighborhood women. Dick was especially happy to be close to Grandma.

I had a good time in junior high. I took a city bus to school and carried my lunch. During the noon hour the words to songs were projected on a screen. A bouncing ball moved from word to word and the kids who ate their lunch in school gathered and sang along. I remember singing "Lavender Blue Dilly, Dilly," "Sentimental Journey," "Buttons and Bows," and "Five Minutes More." I had friends at school and in the neighborhood, and my cousin Patty was back in my life and providing plenty of excitement.

Sometime that year, my cousin Patty decided that at thirteen she was old enough to marry. She had a boyfriend, Freddie Lopez. My grandparents had forbidden her to see him so they decided to run away together, or at least Patty decided. It was a Saturday night. I stayed downstairs and Patty and I were sleeping on a pullout couch in the living room. Grandma was very sick and in a bed set up for her in the parlor. After everyone was asleep, Patty and I got up and she got the small suitcase we had packed together earlier in the day. We put pillows on her side of the bed and covered them to look like she was still in bed. I let her out of the house and went back to bed and even though I was excited, I fell back to sleep. The telephone rang sometime later. It was still dark. Grandpa got up and answered. He put down the phone, came to my bed and pulled back the covers, and discovered no Patty. It turns out that Freddie fell asleep and forgot to show up at the appointed meeting place. Patty then sneaked into his mother's house to wake him and his mother caught her and called the police. Evidently Freddie didn't think he was old enough to marry. They took Patty to the police station and called Grandpa. Patty was out of control, and not long after she was sent to California to live with her mother. When she turned eighteen, she hitchhiked across the country and married Freddie. They had three children. Sadly, my dear Patty died at age thirty-five.

Marian had reconnected with her child's father and they were going to marry. She would be leaving us. We moved back to Detroit and into another foster family home. I don't remember their names except their last name began with an M. They had one son, about seven. I was twelve and in the last half of seventh grade. Dick was ten. I attended Mumford Junior High School. I remember that I got braces while I lived there and the woman in the house took me to my dental appointments. I also remember that they loved to watch wrestling on television and their favorite was Gorgeous George, a husky, muscular man who wore a blonde wig in the ring. It was 1948 and television was new. Few families had a set. An evening's entertainment was inviting neighbors in to watch. Twenty-four hour programming and hundreds of channels were far in the future. A test pattern filled the screen after eleven in the evening. The signal came in through rabbit ears, a round silver ball with two antennas that could be moved around to pick up a signal. Later, towers were placed on the roof to draw the signal. There was no remote control and you actually had to get off the couch to change the channels.

In the last month of seventh grade, we moved back to my favorite foster care family home with Clint and Grace Jordan and their two boys. I continued to take the bus to Mumford until the school year ended. I started eighth grade at Grosse Pointe Junior High. At thirteen, I loved to read and go to the movies. I bought movie magazines filled with the latest gossip about the lives of the stars, cut out pictures, and pasted them in a scrapbook. I had two close friends who loved horseback riding and raised white mice for research. Their parents loved to bet on horse races. Both girls took gymnastics and I envied their ability to twist their bodies into all kinds of positions. I couldn't even do the splits. We went door to door in the neighborhood collecting playing cards with pictures on the back and spent hours trading them with each other.

Grosse Pointe, St. Clair Shores, Grosse Pointe Farms, and Grosse Pointe Woods were all suburbs of Detroit. The Woods was a middle-class community. Grosse Pointe, the Farms, and the Shores were all very wealthy areas filled with huge mansions. Class issues were apparent in the school, and the kids from Grosse Pointe Woods were not in the same cliques as those from the wealthy areas. There was some obnoxiously snobby behavior and I don't remember any particular friends from school, only those from the neighborhood.

In 1950, my mother lived in Pentwater, Michigan. For the first time in awhile, her life was stable. She had married her fourth husband, Fritz Stenberg, and she wanted Dick and me to live with her. We were surprised that Dad let us go. I attended Pentwater School for the last half of eighth grade. The school was in the center of town and divided into elementary, kindergarten through eighth grade, and high school, ninth through twelfth. Again, I made friends easily and I loved Pentwater. We lived in a big house across from Pentwater Lake. My stepfather's mother owned the home and she and her husband lived there too. She wasn't especially welcoming. I was a typical, day-dreaming thirteen-year-old, willing to help around the house if asked, but totally unaware of what needed to be done if I wasn't asked. She thought I was lazy and complained often.

Fritz and Mom were building a house and when it was finished the four of us, Mom, Fritz, Dick, and I, moved in. That was much better. My best friend, Shirley Coon, lived just a half block away from the new house on Pentwater Lake. Fritz was jealous of the time mother spent with Dick and me. He got upset and withdrew and did not speak to any of us. There were frequent arguments. Fritz especially didn't like Dick, and he tolerated me. We stayed through the summer and moved back to Detroit. I was fourteen and about to enter ninth grade. Dick was twelve.

Dad rented a house on Lauder Street, a half-block off West Chicago and not far from Seven Mile Road. It was a little Cape Cod and looked very much like every other house on the street. He hired a woman named Helen to cook and clean, wash clothes and iron, and to be there when we came home from school. I attended Tappen Junior High in ninth grade and for the first time ever got straight A's every marking period for the whole year. Helen left after a couple of months and Dad decided we could manage without help and that Dick and I were old enough to stay alone for periods of time. We stayed on Lauder Street for two years. Two years felt permanent after all those moves.

I have a friend whose father was career military and they moved often. I suppose our experience wasn't much different although geographically all the moves were between and within Flint and Detroit, and we had no idea why we were moved so frequently. I learned to adapt to differing rules from different caregivers, different food and cooking abilities, new schools and new friends. I learned when to flow with whatever was happening and when to stand up and not go along. I learned that I could not always depend on others. I learned that even a broken heart doesn't do you in. I learned that kids have little control over what happens to them. Those were hard but important lessons, and they may have been the training that got me through more difficult times to come.

Beginning a lifelong love of learning

I remember only a few things from kindergarten in 1941 while living on Court Street in Flint, Michigan. I have a vague recollection of walking to school with my friend Elaine, who lived half block away in a wonderful Victorian house. She had a huge bedroom with a sliding pocket door. I'd never seen a door like that. Her room was filled with toys. I envied her. I do remember that our job in kindergarten was to learn to interact with each other through play, to mind the teacher, and to sit quietly when told to do so. We were read to. I don't remember being taught to read but I did know how to read in first grade so I suppose we did have reading lessons.

My real attraction to school and learning started in first grade. We had moved to Fenton Lake and I attended a one-room schoolhouse, a wonderful experience. I loved my teacher. She treated each of us as though we were special to her. I lost my two front baby teeth and she affectionately called me *"toothless granny."* Every grade had specific things students were required to learn but each of us was allowed to learn beyond grade expectations. If you could keep up with something the second or third graders were doing, you were free to try. I tried. I read beyond grade level and I learned to tell time when the second graders did. The focus in early elementary school was on reading, writing, spelling, and arithmetic. In later elementary grades they added geography and history.

I attended fourteen schools in Flint, Detroit, and Pentwater from kindergarten through twelfth grade. School rooms were the same everywhere. Each student had a desk and bench/chair, both of which were bolted to the floor. The desk had a lid that lifted to store papers and books and in the upper-right-hand corner was an ink well, a round opening with a cup inside to hold ink. There were no ball point pens. The chair had a seat that folded up. The distance between the chair and the desk was the same for everyone and in the later

83

grades, if a child was a little too chubby, the desk was a tight fit. There was a blackboard at the front of the room with a wooden tray where the chalk and eraser were kept. It was a privilege to help the teacher erase the board and wash it with a damp cloth at the end of the day. In first grade I took a school bus to school and carried my lunch. This was my only school bus experience. In Flint and Detroit, we either walked to school or took a city bus.

The teachers were strict and the classrooms were orderly. I remember few times when a student acted out in class. If children misbehaved, teachers were allowed to discipline in whatever way they saw fit. A favorite method was a slap on the hands with a ruler. The teacher would ask the student to hold out his or her hand and would hit the palm with sufficient force to ensure a sting. Children were also asked to sit on a stool in a corner at the front of the class. I never had to do this but I did occasionally get a ruler slap, always for the same offense...talking. The *no talking unless you were asked to respond to a question* rule was always enforced. If you wanted to ask a question you raised your hand and waited to be recognized.

In elementary school social interaction took place at recess. In the fall and spring we played outdoors. The teacher often organized games or we played on the swings and slides. In winter recess was in the gym. In the later grades we had gym classes where we had to wear ugly uniforms: one piece, buttoned up the front, and short with elastic around the legs so the pants part ballooned out. All of the girls disliked them. We had to do things like climb ropes which I never could master, throw a ball to each other, and kick the ball and run after it. Gym was my least favorite class and I'm afraid it put me off physical activity for a long while.

We read in groups based on ability and moved to a more advanced group as our skills improved. I was immediately in love with reading. Our first reading book was the Elson-Gray reader which had several short stories including the Dick and Jane series. The characters were Dick and Jane; their baby sister, Sally; Mother and Father; Spot, their dog; Puff, their cat; and their teddy bear, Tim. Mother was a homemaker and I remember that in one story there was a mouse in the house and the mother jumped on a chair and screamed, leaving her little boy, Dick, to deal with the mouse. Evidently mom was not as brave as Dick. The family was middle class and father wore a suit. Of course, in first grade, we didn't know much about class issues. Eventually, these books lost favor because the characters did not represent the wide spectrum of people of all colors and classes in the United States. They also lost favor because they relied on repetition of words rather than phonics. Who in that era would ever forget "*See Spot run. Run, Spot, run.*"

We learned to write by practicing the Palmer Method of penmanship instruction developed and promoted by Austin Palmer in the late 19th and early 20th centuries. Students were taught to adopt a uniform system of cursive writing with rhythmic motions. It involved "muscle motion," in which the more proximal muscles of the arm were used for movement, rather than allowing the fingers to move in writing. Each student had a piece of lined paper and we were instructed to write a circle and retrace the same circle over and over, using the same arm motion from the shoulder. It was boring. I can't say that I ended up with good handwriting but I did learn to write quickly.

Spelling was a process of memorization. Each week we had lists of words we took home to practice. When we lived with Grandma, she would read the word and I spelled it. We had a practice test on Thursday and a final test on Friday. I'm happy to say I was a good speller.

Arithmetic was not my favorite subject but I didn't begin to have a problem until algebra in high school. At elementary level I moved easily from simple addition, to multiplication, subtraction, and division, short and long. We were required to memorize our multiplication tables.

Geography and history were interesting but it seemed to me that history was all about wars. Surely there were other important things that happened but we didn't seem to learn much about them. We did talk about current events and my elementary years, June 1941 through May 1948, were in an interesting time with the war, the nuclear bomb, and the death of the longest-serving president our country has had.

I loved school. I loved the orderliness and predictability, especially after my own young life became less stable. School felt safe. I loved the competition involved in learning faster and better than others, and the excitement of imagining myself in other places and doing other things through reading. Anything seemed possible. I loved new information, and that wonderful feeling of figuring something out, getting it! I loved the positive feedback I received because I was a good learner. I loved the social aspects, seeing and making friends every day. Love of learning took me through graduate school and continues still through reading and travel and creating as much adventure as I can in my life. If there is one thing I most wish for my grandchild and those who come after, it would be that they too love learning.

Living in Detroit, a world-class city

In 1945, we moved from Flint, Michigan's third largest city, to Detroit, the fourth largest city in the entire country, behind New York, Chicago, and Philadelphia. Dad had a new job, World War II was just ending, and the city and the auto industry were booming. Our first residence was on Continental Street off East Jefferson about six blocks from the Detroit River. We actually went swimming in the river several times, not something many people do today. I lived in Detroit most of the time for seven years from age nine to sixteen. We moved to different parts of the city. We lived on the east and the west side and in Grosse Pointe Woods, a suburb. Detroit was a world-class city during those years and it was an exciting time to live there.

Then as now, there is plenty to do in a world-class city. Dad loved sporting events, and when we lived in foster homes, which we did for much of our time in Detroit, our time with him was often spent watching games or listening to games on the radio. He took us to Detroit Tigers games at Briggs Stadium on the corner of Michigan and Trumbull. We sat on bleacher seats, up high. Young men carried metal crates with a strap attached that looped over their necks, and walked up and down the steps, hollering, *"Peanuts, popcorn, candy."* Other vendors sold hot dogs and cold drinks. Our menu never varied, hot dog and pop before the game and popcorn at the seventh inning stretch. We all stood and sang the National Anthem, our hands over our hearts. As soon as the song ended, the crowd clapped and yelled, *"Go Tigers!"*

The stadium was the last one in the country to install lights for night games. The first year we were in Detroit the Tigers won the World Series. My brother and I knew the names of the big players, Dizzy Trout, Hank Greenberg, and Hal Newhouser. The radio announcer for the games was Harry Heilman. He was from the south and his distinctive voice added excitement to the game. Later, around 1950, I remember watching George Kell, Hoot Evers, and Vic Wertz. I loved the name Hoot and George Kell was one of the best players in the league.

Through his work Dad got tickets to Red Wings hockey and to lacrosse games at Olympia Stadium on Grand River Boulevard. It was called the big red barn because of the color and size of the building. Gordie Howe was the star of the Red Wings, and he played with Sid Abel, Terry Sawchuck, Red Kelley, and Ted Lindsay. In the early 1950s the team was red hot, winning the championship Stanley Cup in 1948, 1950, 1952, 1954, and 1955. I can't remember who played lacrosse. It wasn't as big a sport. I do remember wondering how it would feel if a player got hit by that hard, wooden ball they tossed using a small net attached to a long handle, about the same length as a hockey stick. Dad also loved wrestling and we attended matches a few times. Seldom were there other young kids at wrestling matches. Later, Dad watched wrestling on television. He played football in high school, but he never seemed to have that much interest in the Detroit Lions.

Dad took us to Bob-Lo Island. We caught a ferry at the boarding dock at the end of Woodward Avenue. The island is eighteen miles southwest of Windsor, Canada, about a half-mile wide and three miles long. At that time it was primarily a place to relax and have a picnic. Later an amusement park was added with a Ferris wheel and roller coaster. Each time we went to Bob-Lo, and sometimes without going to Bob-Lo, we stopped at the Vernors Ginger Ale bottling plant where we were able to take a tour and sample the product. A large menu hung on the wall above the soda fountain describing all of the flavorings or ice cream floats available. I took my time and tried a variety of combinations, but my favorite was simple: ginger ale with vanilla ice cream. It came with a straw and a long spoon. The ginger ale fizzed and bubbled when the ice cream was dropped in the glass.

In the summer we visited Belle Isle, an island park in the Detroit River designed by Frederick Olmstead, who also designed Central Park in New York City. We crossed over a bridge leaving the noisy and hot city behind, and entered a place of leafy green with the sounds of children shouting, radios playing, and grownups laughing. We walked to the conservatory and botanical gardens, stopped to view the beautiful fountain, visited the marble lighthouse, or stopped by the band shell if a band was playing. Sometimes we took in part of a ballgame at the sports field, or sat by the river watching the boats moving past the island. We packed a lunch and ate in one of the picnic areas or grabbed a hot dog at one of the food stands. Dick and I loved these times; we had Dad all to ourselves and he listened to whatever child tales we wanted to share. We were a family.

Twice we visited Greenfield Village and the Henry Ford Museum in nearby Dearborn. The museum houses Henry Ford's personal collection of historical artifacts. The village included nearly a hundred historical buildings and depicts how Americans worked and lived from the country's founding. Significant buildings that have been moved to the village are the Wright Brothers bicycle shop, Thomas Edison's Menlo Park laboratory, Henry Ford's birthplace and garage, and the Illinois courthouse where Abraham Lincoln practiced law. Several craft buildings offer demonstrations such as glassblowing, pottery making, and tin shops. Transportation around the site includes horse-drawn buses, a Model-A bus, and a steam locomotive. It's nearly impossible to see everything in one day. I remember being particularly fascinated that they had moved entire homes to the site, completely furnished in the period in which they were built.

It was also a treat to travel to downtown Detroit. I remember my stepmother Verla, and later our caregiver, Marian Betts, taking me downtown to shop at Hudson's Department Store for school clothes. We went by streetcar. A double set of steel tracks ran the length of Jefferson Street, one going each direction. The pole atop the trolley was attached to copper electric wires strung overhead. We got on the streetcar at the front and paid our nickel. The conductor closed the accordion-style doors. We sat on wicker seats running along each side of the trolley. The streetcar driver used a large lever with a wood handle to pull back to a notch, which started the trolley. Then he stepped on a button to activate the bell warning that the trolley was about to move. It was very loud, clang, clang, clang. He then moved the lever to other notches until the streetcar was moving at the appropriate clip. When the streetcar got going it swayed from side to side, which made it hard for riders to stay in place. When we got to our stop we exited at the rear. It was pretty exciting. The last streetcar was replaced by a bus in 1956.

Hudson's was on Woodward Avenue. At the time, it was the tallest department store in the world at thirty-three stories, and the second largest store in the country after Macy's in New York City. Like Macy's, Hudson's had an annual Christmas parade escorting Santa Claus into town. Whenever we went to Hudson's, we dressed up in our best and wore gloves. The grown-up women wore high heels. After we shopped, we visited the famous Sanders Fudge and Candy Shop on Woodward and Gratiot Streets next to Grinnell's. We sat at their marble top soda fountain and, of course, ordered hot fudge sundaes. Hudson's closed in 1983. Sanders went through an expansion and built several shops in the Detroit area but they have all closed within the last few years.

The city I described here is not one most people think of when they think of Detroit. People see it now as a city struggling to survive and a high percentage of its people live in poverty. Just prior to our move, from 1941 to 1945 during World War II Detroit was known as the most important production center in the country. It was dubbed the *Arsenal of Democracy*. Major defense employers recruited African Americans from the south to work in the defense plants.

Those who came were given jobs but not housing. Whites in Detroit guarded community dividing lines and the 200,000 black residents were all crammed into sixty square blocks on Detroit's east side, an area called Paradise Valley. The Ku Klux Klan was active in Detroit and there were continuous incidents of intolerance. Two years before we moved to Detroit, the city experienced a race riot that began on Belle Isle and resulted in the death of twenty-five blacks, seventeen killed by white police officers, and nine whites; widespread looting; and property damage. After three days, federal troops were called in. Riots had occurred that same year in Los Angeles, California; Mobile, Alabama; and Beaumont, Texas. Things settled down but race problems never ended.

In the 1950s whites began to leave the city and relocate in the suburbs. In 1967, there was another major race riot. The city has not yet recovered and there are many parts of the inner city that still bear witness to that very difficult time. Michigan's poor economy in this, the early 21st century, has affected all of Michigan, but Detroit has been hit harder than most other areas. There are and have been ongoing efforts to restore Detroit to the world-class status it enjoyed in the years I lived there, and some progress is visible, particularly in the downtown and near-downtown area along the riverfront.

Recently, the Michigan legislature enacted a law allowing the governor to appoint an emergency manager in cities that are in debt and cannot meet their obligations, a highly controversial move that takes all decision-making power from elected officials placing it in the hands of the manager. Detroit was recently assigned an emergency manager who has filed bankruptcy, the first major city to have done so.

I have fond memories of my time in Detroit and I hope that it can be rehabilitated. It will be a long struggle and it's difficult to see how such devastation can be turned around. I doubt it will happen in my lifetime.

A typical 1950's teenage girl

The interests of most teenage girls in the early 1950s were not much different than I imagine they are today and will continue to be...boys, music and dancing, clothes, movies, friends, what I want to be when I'm grown, having money to do things, cars, and learning to drive. Today some girls might add sports but there were few organized sports for girls before Title IX became law in the 1970s.

Let's start with boys, because quite frankly my teenage mind was often occupied with thinking about them, starting with crushes defined as romantic imaginings usually focused on one boy at a time. My imaginings were not graphic. They involved our eyes meeting, heightened awareness and a lightness of body and mind, a compelling need to move closer, close my eyes and kiss the object of my crush, losing myself in the kiss. Words weren't much of a part of these imagined encounters; any words I thought of were the same as those I heard in the movies.

The real path into dating and romance was much different from my imaginings. The facts of life message doled out to teenagers in the early 1950s was not particularly helpful. Girls were told, usually by their mothers although in my case by my father, that boys would desire sex and it was the girl's job not to excite boys too much and definitely not to give in because our reputation would be ruined and no decent man would want to marry us. Boys, at least the ones I knew including my brother, got the talk from their dads. They were told there were good girls and bad girls and they were to respect and not take advantage of the good girls. And they were told that if they found themselves in a situation where they were going to have sex they should make sure they were protected. They were warned against getting a girl pregnant because if they did, they would have to marry her or at least support the child financially. Sometimes they were handed a condom and told how to use it and where to buy them. You can see the conflict these divergent approaches based on gender might inspire.

I had vague crushes on various boys from age six when I thought Bobby Allen who lived near me in Lake Fenton was so-o-o cute. He called me sometimes on the phone and I was giddy. I didn't have thoughts of kissing. At age nine, I had a crush on a twelve-year-old boy who lived in our apartment building in Detroit. He treated me like the nuisance his little sister was, but I sure thought he was cute and followed him around every chance I got.

At twelve and thirteen, my girlfriends and I talked a lot about kissing, mostly how to do it and when it would happen. My first real kiss came at age fourteen when I lived on Lauder Street in Detroit. I had a large circle of friends, boys and girls. Some of them paired off as a couple but most of us did not. Everybody sort of liked or was attracted to several different people in the group at different times. We often hung out in our basement, especially when my dad was out or at work. Someone suggested one time that we play spin the bottle. It didn't take me long to find a bottle. We sat in a circle and when it was your turn you laid the bottle on the floor and made it spin. When it stopped you were to kiss the boy nearest to where the bottle pointed (or nearest girl if you were a boy spinning the bottle). We went into a small, dark storage room for the kiss. Of course, we always hoped the bottle would point to our latest crush but it really didn't matter. A kiss was a kiss. The boy would come out of the room either fake-fanning himself with his hand or trying to look nonchalant.

It was also a safer time than it seems today. We never heard about kidnapping or rape although probably both occurred. We had no fear. So, we also practiced our kissing techniques at the local movie theater on Saturday afternoon. My girlfriends and I went to the movies, and so would a group of guy friends. Before the movie started, the guys

93

started a conversation with the girls sitting in front or behind. If there was interest, seats were swapped so the guy could sit next to the girl he was attracted to. When the lights dimmed, the newly formed couple kissed throughout the movie. There were ushers in those days, usually young men who carried a flashlight. They walked up and down the aisles to ensure there were no problems. Sometimes they shined the light on a couple kissing and told them in a loud whisper to break it up. It was quite embarrassing if it happened to you, but the break in kissing never lasted long. When the movie was over, we said goodbye and went our separate ways. The girlfriends would jabber about the encounter all the way home. No date was made. We were not allowed to date.

My first date was at age fifteen. His name was Al. My girlfriend Diane Ryder, a precocious fifteen-year-old who had boys standing in line to spend time with her, met him and gave him my phone number. He thought it was hers. She told me what she had done. Neither of us thought he would call, but he did. I don't know how old he was, but I would guess eighteen or nineteen. We talked on the phone over a couple of months and then he asked me to go swimming with him on a Saturday afternoon. My dad said yes. That was a miracle. He came to the house and walked up to the door. That was required. No sitting outside and honking the horn. He was introduced to Dad and told when to have me home.

I remember that he wore chartreuse bathing trunks and my suit was neon orange, both popular colors at the time. He hugged me as we stood in the water but did not try to kiss me. When he took me home he walked me to the door and kissed me good night. He asked me to go to a drive-in movie with him the following weekend. I said I would have to ask permission and he could call me. I knew getting Dad's permission would not be easy. I waited until after dinner when I thought he'd be in the best mood. Dad was sitting in a chair in the living room reading the paper and listening to the news on television.

"Dad, I need to talk to you," I said. He looked up and waited. "Al asked me to go to the drive-in Saturday night. I know the rule is to be home by nine, but I would really like to go." Dad didn't say anything for what seemed like a long time. "No," he said. "You're only fifteen. The rule was that you couldn't date until you were sixteen, and now you want to push the limits on time. No. Find something else to do that will get you home at nine." He picked up his paper again, and I walked away. I was not happy, but with Dad I knew I had to formulate a strategy if I was going to change his mind. The next night, again after supper but before he picked up the paper, I said, "Dad, I've been thinking about my date this weekend. I promise to come home as soon as the movie is over." He answered, "I said no." My strategy was to wear him down. I begged a few more times and finally, the night before Al had agreed to call, I approached Dad again. The look on his face told me that he was tired of my begging, but I started my speech anyway. "Dad, I know you said no, and I've tried hard to think of something we could do on Saturday night that would get me home at nine. I don't understand why you won't let me go. I'll be sixteen at the end of the summer. Al treated me like a lady on the first date, and I expect he will on the next one. If I have to be home at nine, we can't go to the drive-in and I can't think of anyplace we can go, so I'll have to tell him to go park somewhere and there won't be a movie to distract us." To my surprise, he laughed and said, "Okay, Sis, you win, but I want you home at exactly midnight, not a minute later."

Al called, we went to the movies, we kissed during the movie, and he took me home. He walked me to the door and told me that he liked me, but that there was too big an age difference. I don't remember feeling bad about it. In fact, I was a little relieved. I also thought there was too big an age difference.

I moved to Pentwater the summer I turned sixteen. I knew that, as long as I lived with Dad, dating would be a problem. Mom was much more realistic. She talked about the things that could be a problem and told me not to get serious about any boy that was not respectful. It was an interesting thing in Pentwater that mostly we girls did not date boys we went to school with. It was a small town, and the kids our age were like brothers and sisters. So, the guys we dated were from nearby farm communities or Hart, a small town ten miles south of Pentwater. Dating a farm boy was different. They mostly drove pickup trucks, and no one in the big city of Detroit where I had lived drove a pickup. They seemed less worldly and they talked about their job on the farm. They were more serious and they were definitely respectful, although not cool in my opinion. Sometime that next winter I

 met the man I thought I would marry. Willard Fetters (left) was a farm boy. What did I know at sixteen? I thought you fell in love and if he said he loved you back you got married. He and a friend were downtown and my girlfriend knew his friend. They were in a car and we were walking. They stopped to say hello and asked if we wanted to take a ride to the beach. My girlfriend and I hopped in the back seat.

We drove to Ludington and walked on the beach. I had not worn boots and it was cold. When we got back in the car he got in the back with me, took off my shoes, and rubbed my feet to get them warm. What sixteen-year-old girl wouldn't think that was swell? And besides, he was tall, blonde, and handsome.

He asked me out and soon asked me to go steady, and soon after that he told me he loved me. He was my prom date. I met his parents and his mother didn't like me all that much. It wasn't personal. She barely spoke to me. He told me that when I gave him a framed graduation picture of me, he put it on the table that night at supper and said he had invited his girlfriend to dinner. His mother told him to get *that* girl's picture off the table, and he told her that she better get used to me because he loved me. He was her youngest boy and I don't think she wanted him to ever leave home. His dad liked me, though, and teased me, most often about things a city girl wouldn't know. I remember he asked if I knew that the spouts on a cow's udder produced different kinds of milk, one was cream, the other chocolate, and two held white milk. Even a city girl knew that was not true.

Going steady did not mean I spent all of my time with my boyfriend, Willard. He was older, twenty-one, and worked. I was in school and did all the things you do when you're in school. I went to the basketball games, hung out with my girlfriends, had a role in the school plays, and sang in the chorus. I had part-time jobs working in restaurants, and in the summer I found time to hang out at the beach. I daydreamed about marriage and having six kids and was disappointed when Willard did not give me an engagement ring at high school graduation. One of my best friends, Doris, got an engagement ring from her steady. Instead Willard broke up with me at the end of that summer. He didn't give a reason and I was pretty sad for a short time. I moved to Muskegon and began life on my own. There was too much new and exciting about being on my own to stay sad. And there would be many more boys in my future.

I can still sing along to the music of the fifties
and love to dance

Grandma Hier loved music. I learned the words to all the songs of the early 1900s from her. She played piano even though she never had a lesson. We gathered around her and sang. We also listened to the radio and there was an era of silly songs like "Marezy Doats." Translated that is, *"mares eat oats"*. Another was "Chickory, chick, cha-la, cha-la." There's no translation for that one.

My mother also loved music. One of my earliest memories is hearing her sing the songs of the thirties and forties. In 1929, and the early 1930s, people were struggling after the stock market crash and during the Great Depression, and the songs reflected the tough times, songs like "Brother Can You Spare a Dime," "Happy Days are Here Again", and an amazing rendition of "God Bless America" by Kate Smith, who had a big, big voice.

In the 1940s, big bands were popular and Mom's favorites were Glenn Miller, the Dorsey Brothers, Tommy and Jimmy, Benny Goodman, and Harry James. It was an era of crooners like Frank Sinatra and Bing Crosby. Crooning was a mellow, understated delivery of songs. Mom liked "I've Got You Under My Skin," "You'll Never Know," and "White Christmas." World War II had a major impact on music. The radio played "Boogie Woogie Bugle Boy," "I Don't Want to Walk Without You," and "I'll Walk Alone." We had a record player that played seventy-eight RPM records, one at a time. They were about ten inches across, and they broke and scratched easily.

But, lucky me, my teenage years brought rock and roll. Dad bought me a portable radio with batteries. It weighed a ton but I loved it and could take my music to the beach. My first strong memory of rock and roll was "Rock Around the Clock" by Bill Haley and the Comets. And every girl I know fell in love with Elvis Presley, who, by the way, was older than I am by a couple of years. When he appeared on the Ed Sullivan television show in the early 1950s my eyes were glued to the screen and I was turned on. His dark hair fell over his eye and he looked directly at the camera when he sang. It felt like he was singing to me. We didn't see his hip-swinging dance moves until later because they only televised him from the waist up. It was thought his dancing was too suggestive. Hard to believe in today's age when the dancing on television, and lots of other places for that matter, is more than suggestive. I have to admit that the inability to see Elvis move to his music required us to use our imagination, which turned out to be pretty darned exciting.

You couldn't sit still and listen to rock and roll and we didn't. In the beginning, our dance to rock and roll was similar to our mother's jitterbug. We called it the finale. At the school dances the boys stood on the sidelines while the girls danced together. Later, dancing to rock and roll evolved into what we see today, just letting your body move in any way the music takes you. For some it's all in the hips, for others the shoulders, and for still others only their feet are moving. Some put their whole selves into it. More boys started dancing once there was no special set of dance moves.

I was always one of the first to learn a new dance as a teenager. I could bop, knew the camel walk, and loved the twist. I bounced to the frug and the swim. I watched them all on television and copied the moves. I danced alone through the house, and I danced with a broom and a mop or whatever was handy. Later I learned the Latin dances, cha-cha, rumba, and merengue.

My mother and father both loved to dance. The fox trot was Dad's favorite. I never saw his parents dance, but my mother said her mother loved to dance. My daughter, Julie, loves to dance. As an adult, she has taken ballroom dance lessons and tap dancing. You can see the joy when she's dancing. I'm thinking it would be okay when I'm very old to dance my way out of this world and into the next.

A five-minute driving lesson

Becoming old enough to drive is always a big moment in any teenager's life. In August, 1952, I would turn sixteen. At the beginning of that summer, as soon as school was out, I told my mother I wanted to learn to drive and that my boyfriend had agreed to teach me. At that time, there was no driver's training. Young people were taught by another licensed driver, and parents were required to give permission for their daughter or son to get a license at age sixteen. At age eighteen, you could get the license on your own after taking a driver's test.

Like many women of her time, my mother, and both of my grandmothers before her, had never learned to drive. I thought she would be thrilled to have me learn. I was wrong. She was terrified and said without hesitation that she would not sign for me to apply for a license and I would have to wait until I was eighteen. I was not happy but nothing I said would change her mind. So I did what most sixteen-year-olds would do. I drove anyway.

My first driving lesson lasted about five minutes. My boyfriend, Willard Fetters, bought a car in a town about twelve miles from his home. He came over to pick me up in his father's car and said, "I want you to drive my new car home, and I'll drive my dad's car." I said, "You know I don't know how to drive." He said, "Yeah, but I'll show you. It's easy. You won't have to drive that far, and most of it is on a country road with no traffic. "His assurance didn't ease my mind, but I did want to learn how to drive.

His car was a 1947 Ford sedan with a stick shift which meant, of course, that three pedals have to be managed: the clutch, the brake, and the accelerator. When we got to the car lot, he got in the driver's seat and I got in the passenger's seat, and he showed me how to shift from first, into second and then into third, and how to ease up on the clutch with my left foot while taking my right foot off the brake, placing it on the accelerator, and slowly pushing it down. Simultaneously, I was to hold onto the steering wheel with my left hand and use my right hand to shift from first to second. Then, I was to engage the clutch again and shift to third to get up to full speed. This was a whole lot of coordination to learn in a few minutes.

I took the wheel to drive, albeit not smoothly. With several jerks of the car, I managed to get the car into third and move forward. Then we talked about steering. He told me not to go over the line painted on the middle of the road. He also told me that if I was going to turn left and there was a car behind me, I should slow down, stick my arm out the window and point left, and make the turn when there were no cars coming from the other direction. There were no turn signals in the car. That was my driving lesson.

He moved out ahead of me and I stalled. Finally, after several jerky starts, I was moving forward. At the first and only left turn, there were no cars behind me and no cars coming from either direction. The Lord was, indeed, looking out for me. I was going along pretty smoothly thinking I was doing swell when a car approached from the other direction. There wasn't nearly as much traffic on the road in those days as there is now. I clutched the wheel as tightly as I could. I was scared and not at all sure the other guy wouldn't cross over the line and hit me. Unfortunately, I learned that the car you're driving goes where you look and I was looking at the car in the oncoming lane. My car started veering slightly left. I jerked it back and veered off the pavement on the right. My foot came off the gas and the car stalled. Then there was the whole process of starting over, again jerking and jumping until I could get it into third gear. By this time, my trusting boyfriend was way ahead of me. I was quite grateful that he didn't see my lack of grace and coordination.

I pulled into the driveway of his house and stopped. He said thank you and I said whatever the equivalent of *piece of cake* was in those days. I wanted to look cool and composed and, perhaps, earn a chance to drive again. He let me drive sometimes, and I conned my grandfather into letting me drive sometimes. It was easy when he was drunk. I'd tease him and tell him I was his favorite granddaughter, and even if I didn't know how to drive, I would do better sober than he did with a few shots under his belt. Eventually I gained the coordination and confidence to get my license at eighteen.

I would be twenty-two and married before I had my own car, actually a marital car, to drive. I bought my first car on my own when I was divorced at age twenty-seven. It was a one hundred-dollar junker and all I could afford. Junkers continued to be all I could afford for a long time until my dad bought me my first new car, a 1978 blue and white Oldsmobile Cutlass Calais, when I was forty-one. Unlike the first car I drove, it had turn signals and automatic shifting. It was a classy car and marked the end of my junk car era, although I converted the first new car I paid for myself, a 1982 Honda, into a junker. I drove it for eight years and racked up nearly 300,000 miles, until it died and was towed from a theater parking lot in Greenville, Michigan.

Pentwater, Michigan: A place of good memories

Pentwater is a wonderful small town in western Michigan. As I said earlier, Mom's house was on Pentwater Lake. I had visited her the last three summers, loved the town and had friends there. Several times Mom asked Dad if my brother and I could live with her. My dad always said it was up to us and we said no. We knew very clearly that Dad would be hurt if we did. But the summer of 1952, when I was eager to date and Dad was eager to limit my dating, she asked again and I said yes. My dad was hurt, but my desire to have more freedom beat out any guilt I might have felt.

What a change! Detroit was the largest city in Michigan. Pentwater had fewer than seven hundred permanent residents. McKenzie High School in Detroit had more than a thousand kids. There were fifteen kids in my class in Pentwater, nine girls and six boys. The entire town supported the school. Two hundred people or more turned out for the boys' basketball games. When a class had a fundraiser, the same number would attend. Everyone knew everyone else.

My dad sent very little money for my support so I worked during the school year and summers in local restaurants: Harbor Inn, the Dairy Bar, and Lakeside Inn. One summer I worked for my stepfather, a commercial fisherman, selling smoked fish from his market. I bought my own clothes and paid for my entertainment with the money I earned.

I took all of the required courses in school and my electives were typing, shorthand, and bookkeeping. We didn't have a wide selection to choose from. There were no language classes. English was my favorite class and my best friend, Shirley Coon, was frequently irritated with me because she slaved over a paper and I dashed one off in the morning before school and got a better grade than she did. School was pretty easy for me and in ninth and tenth grades I had all A's.

In eleventh grade I decided to major in fun. My social life was much more important. I got good grades, mostly B's and some A's. Mr. Steilstra, our superintendent of schools, frequently told me that I had *so much potential.* It was obvious that he didn't think I was living up to it. I seldom got in trouble in school, and if I did it was for talking during study hall. Mr. Steilstra would come up to me, pinch me on the muscle just behind my collar bone, close to my neck, and quietly say *Miss Hier, there is a no talking rule in study hall.* The pinching hurt so much I couldn't breathe or talk. It didn't take too many pinches for me to quit talking in study hall.

Sports were primarily for boys. We had a girls' basketball team, half-court, and few people attended the games. I played on the girls' softball team in eleventh grade until I got caught smoking at an out-of-town game. There was no gym in the school, so we used the one in the community building downtown for our school dances, basketball practice and games, and spaghetti dinner fundraisers. My girlfriends and I often drove north to Ludington, a slightly larger town, to dance in a little place that had a jukebox.

The school did have a music teacher, Mr. Styles, who had played marimba professionally in Chicago. He taught band and boys' and girls' chorus. I joined the chorus, and in my senior year I was part of a quartet of girls who sang harmony. We sang at local gatherings and at the senior prom. I had the deepest voice so I sang bass.

Mr. Styles paid for my first airplane ride. DeDe Ardrey and I were good friends. She had a wonderful contralto voice. He gave her private lessons, and in our senior year he took us to Chicago where he had arranged an audition for DeDe with a voice coach. Her parents required a chaperone and she chose me. I felt quite grown up when I got on the small plane at the Muskegon airport. My stomach dropped as the wheels left the ground, but I soon got comfortable and marveled at being able to fly into and above the clouds.

Girlfriends who had a large enough house had pajama parties and every girl in the class went. Because there were so few of us, no one was left out. There were no cliques. I never knew of any bullying. Some kids were elected prom king and queen, some were star basketball players and school cheerleaders; there were kids who were class president, vice-president, secretary, and treasurer; kids who had the lead in school plays and kids who played solos at band concerts; and the valedictorian and salutatorian of the class. There were enough honors for anyone who sought an honor.

In summers when I wasn't working I spent time at Lake Michigan's beach. We prided ourselves on jumping in the frigid water on Memorial Day, a thirty-second dash in,  and a dash out almost as fast. When the weather warmed, we took our lunch and movie magazines, spread our blanket on the sand, rubbed ourselves with baby oil, and stayed most of the day. I burned the first couple of days, but then turned tan and could stay uncovered longer. The beach was full of resorters, people from Chicago, Detroit, and other places whose families had cottages and stayed the summer, or who rented cottages by the week. The town boys dated resorters, but the town girls did not, probably because we knew they'd be gone by the end of summer.

Mother had very few rules but in a small town like Pentwater she had no trouble finding out what I was up to. One day my friend Shirley Popps and I skipped school and headed to the beach. We sat on the breakwater wall and two older boys we knew came over to talk. One said, "Hey, we have some beer in the car. Want to go for a ride and have one?" I didn't like beer all that much, but Shirley and I didn't have a plan for the day. We looked at each other. "Sure," we said. They got into the front seat, we got into the back and the boy in the passenger's seat passed a bottle to each of us. I took a few sips, and before the driver could start his car, the Pentwater sheriff, Don Lamb, pulled in behind us. Don knew Shirley and me. His house was near mine. I was nervous. Someone in the car said, "Now we're going to get it."

Don got out of his car, walked up to us, and looked in the car. He called Shirley and me by name and asked, "Do your mothers know you aren't in school?" We said no. He said, "They will now." He told the boys, "Put the beer in the trash while I watch and then leave. They did as they were told. Now I was really worried. Would he tell our mothers? He looked at both of us and said nothing for what seemed an eternity and then said, "I'm going to let this pass this time. If I catch you again, I will personally take you home and have a talk with your mothers." We thanked him and left. I was grateful that he had let us leave instead of taking us to his office and filing an official complaint.

I pushed limits often. Today, I am embarrassed at the way I sometimes defied my mother. Once I asked to stay at a girlfriend's house. Mom said no. My response to my much smaller mother was, "What are you going to do to stop me, tie me to the bed?" She cried. I knew she was doing her job and trying to protect me, and I felt terrible that my sassy response made her cry. I decided not to go.

When I went to the junior prom, Mom told me I had to be home by one in the morning. Several couples decided to go to the beach for a party, and I got home at five in the morning. Mom said, "If you can stay up all night, you can stay up all day." I sat at a chair at the kitchen table and every time I rested my head on my arms on the table, she shook my shoulder and said, "Don't you dare go to sleep. Wake up." This went on until about noon when she gave in and let me go to sleep. I know she couldn't sleep while I was out. When I came home after she was in bed, as I passed her room on the way to mine, she coughed lightly three of four times to let me know she knew what time I was getting in. Although I never would have told her, I liked it that she cared enough to worry.

I graduated from Pentwater High School in June, 1954. My yearbook would tell you that I had a good time in high school. In the mock elections, I was voted Class Clown and Class Flirt. I had clear priorities and they weren't academic.

Although I only lived two years in Pentwater, it was where my mother lived until she died and a place I frequently went back to visit. It will always be a special place, not the place where I was born, or even the place where I spent most of my school years, but a place where everyone knew me. I

was part of a community of people who looked out for me. We had only two reunions in the years since graduation, but I am in contact with Shirley, my closest high school friend, and I still have family there.

Pentwater is not the small, sleepy little village that it was when I lived there. It has been discovered. People from the big cities moved in, tore down many of the charming houses in the village, and built large homes that take up the entire lot and have no yard. Downtown is filled with kitschy little shops and on summer weekends the sidewalks are crowded with people. My family complains there isn't a parking place to be had. It's good for the economy, no doubt, but those who lived there when it was a sleepy resort town do not like the condominiums that crowd Pentwater's lakeshore. The house where my mother lived has been moved off the lake away from town and replaced with a very large two-story house. But even with all that, when I turn off the highway at the Pentwater exit, pass the bridge that separates the Pentwater River from Pentwater Lake, and the Catholic Church, and turn the curve that begins downtown, it still feels like home.

Young and single in Muskegon, Michigan

I moved to Muskegon in 1954 when I graduated from Pentwater High School. It was a place of opportunity then. A recruiter from Muskegon Business School, now morphed into Baker College, came to Pentwater to tell us about the school. I had taken secretarial courses and decided to enroll. My high school best friend, Shirley Coon (above), moved with me, and the school found us an apartment within walking distance, right downtown at 431 West Webster Avenue. We shared the apartment with Carol and JoAnne, two *older* women in their twenties. Our apartment on the first floor was the largest in this old converted Victorian. The front door opened from the verandah-like porch into a large room. A wide stairway led to a door, locked to prevent entry to our space by second- floor tenants. A grand piano sat in a bay window facing the street. None of us played piano. The even larger living room to the right featured a fireplace and another bay window. The bathroom was tiny and under the stairwell. It took some planning to arrange a bathroom schedule for four women getting ready for work and school in the morning. The only bedroom was across from the bath, both reached by a hallway leading to the kitchen at the rear. There were two double beds and a dresser for each of us. There must have been closet space, but I don't remember how much. The kitchen was small but adequate. A door in the kitchen led to an apartment in the rear of the house.

I remember four apartments on the second floor. A young doctor lived in one. I dated him once, and he asked if I knew I had lovely breasts. He hadn't even seen them. I thought that was pretty rude and any interest I might have had quickly disappeared. Perhaps I was too hard on him; perhaps it was a clinical observation. Right! I wonder if the woman he married had lovely breasts.

Also on the second floor was a woman whose name was Thora. When my lifetime friend, Evelyn Stiver, moved into the building she became Thora's roommate. Another young woman, Patricia, had the third apartment. She was dating a local attorney, Tom O'Toole, who later became the attorney for the City of Muskegon. An older man lived in the fourth apartment. I remember two third-floor apartments. Margaret Peterson, the tenant with the most seniority, lived in one, and woman named Hazel in the other. Evelyn and I thought Hazel was *loose*. An older man visited a couple of times each week, and she told us he paid her rent.

The business school arranged a part-time job for me at W.B. Taylor Realtors on Terrace Street, in a white clapboard house within walking distance of the school and the apartment and directly across the street from the Muskegon County Courthouse. The real estate office was on the second floor and Muskegon Agency Insurance was downstairs. My boss, Burt Taylor, lived on Fifth Street around the corner from my apartment. He and his wife, Grace, invited me for dinner occasionally. I worked half days, sometimes mornings and sometimes afternoons. I answered the phone and typed letters and forms. Two salesmen worked there. One was not particularly fond of me, probably because he wasn't much older than I was and I saw him as an equal rather than someone I worked for. The other one was too fond of me and tried to corner me in a closet where we kept office supplies. When I noted that he was old enough to be my grandfather, it cooled his ardor.

School and work were not my major interest, I must confess. My first priority was partying and boys. We primarily met boys *cruising the avenue*. Young people drove a three-block-wide, one-block-deep route from Jefferson Street west on Western Avenue to Third Street, one block south to Clay Avenue, three blocks east on Clay to Jefferson, and one block north back to Western. My friend Evelyn had a car. Before the car, we walked downtown. A favorite stopping place, Occidental Candy Shop, located on the ground floor of the Occidental Hotel, was famous for its hot fudge sundaes. Some nights Evelyn or I would get an ice cream craving, roust the other from bed, put our coats on over our pajamas, and walk east on Webster, to Fourth Street, across Hackley Park to Third Street and Clay Avenue, and up Third to the hotel. We were never afraid of roaming the streets after dark.

Downtown was a real downtown then. There were several blocks of stores: Sears, J.C.Penney, Federal's, Grossman's, Hardy-Herpolsheimers, two five-and-ten-cent stores, Neisner's and Kresge's, banks, movie theaters, restaurants, small dress and shoe shops, Walgreen's drug store, doctor's offices, and more. It was fun to live so close to all this activity.

I dated several young men, but my first boyfriend after high school who lasted more than two or three dates was Jerry Fulwider (below), who worked next door to the real estate office at Lucky Auto Seat Covers. One warm day, when the windows were open in my office, a breeze kicked up and a message I had taken for Mr. Taylor drifted out the window and landed on the roof of a shed just below. I was frantic, grabbed a broom, hung out the window, and tried to knock it

off the roof onto the ground so I could go get it. It didn't work. A very cute young man, with dark hair that hung over his eye, making him look a little like Elvis Presley, and a grin that would melt anyone's heart, hollered up at me and asked if he could help. I told him what I was doing, and he climbed onto the roof of the porch, rescued the message, and came up

110

the stairs to my office and delivered it. I thanked him and he said his reward would be a date that evening. Well, of course.

Evelyn and I had also been meeting and dating young men who were stationed at an army base in Claybanks Township, about twenty-five miles north of Muskegon. A bus brought them to town every night. Evelyn mostly dated a nice guy whose name was Mac, and I dated all of Mac's friends. We often stayed out all night and drove our dates back to camp, getting us home in the wee hours. Sleep was not a high priority and I was exhausted most of the time. Each day after work we slept for a couple of hours, got up, and headed out for more fun. Weekends we tried to catch up.

Sometime during the first year, Carol and JoAnne moved out. The business school placed other roommates. Our landlord was a more involved landlord than you might see today. He had keys to our apartment and a couple of times I woke up to find him standing in our bedroom door watching us sleep. That was startling, but I had no idea what to do about it. He also was upset and scolded us after a neighbor told him a black man had visited us. Eventually the parties got me evicted. I was dating Jerry at the time, and his grandparents took me in. It was only for a short time and Joe agreed to rent to me again. I must have promised I would behave. Jerry and I broke up soon after. With all the soldiers in town, my disappointment didn't last long.

In 1956, I met Bart Geyer, the man I would eventually marry. The partying continued. This tested my landlord even further. Shirley moved back to Pentwater to marry her high school sweetheart. Bart's family invited me to stay with them.

I remember my two years of single life in downtown Muskegon as a time of learning to manage freedom. I suppose for those times, Evelyn and I would have been considered wild. By today's standards, maybe not. It was an innocent fun. We liked to party, and we liked boys. Who doesn't at that age? I learned to be successful at work. I learned to love Muskegon and the city where I would live most of my life. It is the place I say I'm from when anyone asks. I still have many friendships there. I learned to be a community leader there. I think I made some difference for good there. And, in Evelyn, I made a friend for life.

LOVE, MARRIAGE, BABIES

"In our sleep pain which cannot forget
Falls drop by drop upon the heart until
In our despair against our will comes wisdom,
The awful grace of God."
Greek poet, Aeschylus

AND
MY CAREER AND WHAT SHAPED IT

"I swore never to be silent whenever and wherever human
beings endure suffering and humiliation. Neutrality helps the
oppressor, never the victim. Silence encourages the tormentor, never
the tormented."
Elie Wiesel
Nobel Prize Acceptance Speech (1986)
Reprinted with permission from The Nobel Foundation

Women and love, marriage and babies in the 1950s

In 1956, when I turned twenty, life for women and girls was very different from what it is today. Our expectations for how we would live life were shaped by the expectations of our family and by the cultural norms of the time. Most young women expected they would marry and have children, in that order. Some would go to college before marriage and might work outside the home before they had children, and again after the children started school.

There were a limited number of sports girls could play in high school, and considerably more money was spent on boys' sports. There were sports scholarships for boys but not for girls. In the schools I attended there were gender-segregated shop classes for boys and home economics classes for girls. In college there were no co-ed dorms and the girls' dorms had stricter curfews than boys' dorms. Girls did not ask boys for a date and in many homes girls could not call a boy they liked. The boy had to call them.

There was also a double standard related to sexuality. Boys were expected to sow their wild oats before settling down and girls were expected to remain virtuous until marriage. The girls that the boys sowed their wild oats with were bad girls or *wild*. Some couples who went steady did *go all the way*, the phrase for having intercourse. There was no reliable birth control method so sometimes a girl got pregnant. When that happened, her choices were to marry and pretend the baby came early or to leave town to take care of a sick aunt and give the baby up for adoption.

In the small high school I attended, of the twenty or so girls who were juniors or seniors, two girls quit school and married in eleventh grade because they were pregnant. A third quit school in her senior year, went away to have her baby, and came back to graduate in my class, the class behind hers. A fourth girl bound her stomach and wore *fat* clothes so that no one would know she was pregnant. She had a baby within two weeks of graduation. The baby was adopted out. There was gossip and shame. I never heard blame placed on the young man who obviously played a part in the pregnancy. If the couple had been going steady, most young men accepted responsibility or were pressured by their family to marry the girl. If they did not marry, there seemed to be no stigma, no lasting stain on his reputation.

If pregnancy was the result of a casual coupling or even rape, the girl bore the responsibility and carried the stigma. If a girl was raped, there was frequently discussion about what she had done to encourage it. Was her behavior too provocative? Were her clothes too revealing? Somehow the idea was conveyed that men had drives they were not able to control, so it was up to women to make sure that they didn't tempt a man beyond that ability.

Young women lived their lives *until:* that is, I will work *until* I get married, or I will work or go to college *until* my husband finishes college and can support us, or I will work *until* I have a baby. If your husband could afford to support you, chances are you would stay home and take care of the child. It didn't matter how much education you had. If your husband could not support the family with his wages you might continue to work but his job would always be considered more important than yours.

Married women could not get credit in their own name. A married man could take out a loan for a car without his spouse's signature; a married woman could not. It was expected that if you married, the husband was the head of household and you were financially dependent. Oh sure, in some households women managed the money but there was no doubt that the man was the one who earned it. It was not uncommon for women to get allowances, just as children did, money above and beyond household expenses that she could spend any way she wished. Men would sometimes joke that they had to take their paychecks home and hand them over to *the wife*, and maybe they did.

Most women did not dream beyond what was possible. Most did not yearn to break free of those expectations and limitations. Most women did not know that one day women would have many other options. Some were content with the way things were; some were not. Often that depended on whether they were married to a kind and generous man. If they were not, if the man was abusive, there were no programs or any societally sanctioned structures or mores to help. If the police were called, it was generally accepted that the man's home was his castle and he could not be forced to leave. If she and her children were not safe, she was the one who had to leave.

It is part of the American culture to be competitive to one degree or another. There was little possibility for women to compete on an even playing field with men in the workplace or with other women in sports. There was some opportunity to compete equally on an intellectual level, but women got the message that if they wanted to get a man, it didn't pay to act like you were smarter than he was. Girls were encouraged to get a boy to talk about himself so that they could gain his interest. Talking about oneself was discouraged.

Women often professed that they didn't like other women. It was not unusual to hear a woman say she would never work for a woman; she might criticize another woman as being *too pushy*. Women put each other down and sought male approval. They valued the qualities they saw in men but not those they saw in women. I would often say to women that when they attributed negative stereotypes to women they had forgotten that they were applying those stereotypes to themselves. There was a sense that your future must be marriage, and if you were to marry you needed to know how to attract men.

Later, when some women began to identify and speak up about the ways in which their lives were limited by gender expectations, other women were often their most outspoken critics. *I'm not a feminist,* they would say proudly. To be a feminist was viewed as being anti-men, and to be anti-men raised the specter of being rejected by men. Since men held most of the economic power, to separate you from them could have repercussions. The fact was and is that feminism has nothing to do with being anti-men, and everything to do with being pro-equality for women. Feminists are people, women and men, who actively work so that women and girls can have every opportunity unencumbered by artificial barrier. The goal is to create a world where your future is not defined by your gender--what it is okay for women to do and what it is okay for men to do--but instead is defined by your gifts and abilities and how hard you are willing to work to achieve your dreams.

In the middle of my life, expectations changed. The list of what was possible grew, the world changed for women, and more things are possible. It is a different world for my daughter. It will be a still different world for my granddaughter. There will always be struggles, barriers to overcome, but there will be far fewer based on whether you are a woman or a man, and far more based on what you dream and what you're willing to do to make those dreams come true. Today, thanks to a lot of hard work by a lot of women and some men we have a choice. The culture, our gender, our family background can shape our future, but we can learn, gain wisdom and grow, and shape the future differently for our own children, and for other women and their children. Hallelujah and amen!

Coming of age: My perspective on women and work in 1956

In the 1950s and earlier, career choices for women were limited. If you didn't go to college, you were most likely an office worker, a waitress, a nanny, a bank teller, a store clerk, or a factory worker. When I was young, doctors, attorneys, engineers, plumbers, carpenters, police officers, firefighters, college professors, scientists, bank presidents, soldiers, and professional athletes were all men. Newspaper help-wanted ads were divided by "Help Wanted Male" and "Help Wanted Female." Of the nine girls in my graduating class, two went to college to become teachers, two went to business school to become secretaries, three married immediately, and two worked in a factory. If a woman had a career, it was likely she was never married or, if married, had no children.

Pregnant women were required to quit their jobs when their condition became obvious. There was no maternity leave, nor did you have a right to your job if you wished to return when the baby was born. There was little opportunity to do the same job a man did, but if you did--teaching, for example--you made less than a male teacher and it was not illegal. The idea was that men had families to support. Things were not equal and there were few jobs for women that could adequately support a family. There were no stay-at-home dads.

Sexual harassment was not unusual, and if you objected, you were far more likely to lose your job than the man who harassed you. Promotional opportunities were limited; there was a ceiling beyond which you knew you could not go. There was no equal pay legislation and little recourse if you were fired. The only exception was if you had a union job.

Women were called girls no matter how old they were. A boss might say about his secretary, *I'll have my girl get us coffee.* There was an unwritten dress code if you worked anyplace except a factory or as a nurse or caregiver. You wore a dress or skirt and blouse, not slacks.

When women first started to move into executive positions, or professions where they had not been, such as firefighters or police officers, there was considerable resistance. The reason given, no matter what the job, was that somehow women were not suited. They weren't strong enough if the job was physical. They would have to depend on their male co-worker to protect them and that would distract him from his job. If women and men worked together as a team, wives would be upset. There were many excuses, few of them valid.

There were almost no women in political office. 1972 was the year in which more women were elected in my community. I was elected to my city's governing body in 1978 and only one woman preceded me. There were few women senators or representatives, and Congress is still nowhere near representative of the fifty-plus percentage of women in our country. Today, there are three women Supreme Court justices. In the 1950s there were none. We have yet to elect a woman president, although a few have run, with Hilary Clinton coming the closest to a major party nomination in 2008.

Young women today can do anything they aspire to. What is true, though, is that women still bear most of the responsibility for the work at home. Some husbands *help* with housekeeping chores and child care but women still put in much more time at managing the family than do men. There are a few, very few, stay-at-home fathers. This adds considerable stress to women's lives and it is small wonder that many young women are concerned about balancing their work and personal lives. More and more women are becoming small business owners so they can better manage their schedules. More young women opt to put family first and not climb the promotional ladder. More are choosing to stay home after a child is born if they can afford it. In fact, this work balance issue may be the next biggest civil rights issue. Either that, or women will continue to be limited in what kind of work they do and how far they will progress.

My first job as an office girl

In 1954, at age eighteen, when I graduated from high
school, I believed my career choices were nurse, teacher,
factory worker, or office worker. I liked the idea of teaching,
but nursing and teaching required more education than I
could afford. Factory work held no appeal. I had taken
secretarial courses in high school, shorthand, typing, and
bookkeeping, and I knew I had the aptitude to do office work.

Muskegon Business School in Muskegon, the nearest
bigger city to Pentwater, was ahead of its time in marketing.
They sent a professionally dressed woman, Ethyl Stark, to
schools around the state to talk to potential students about
advanced training for office work. She said that a degree from
Muskegon Business School would get you a better job and
more pay. She said they would find you a place to live that
you could afford and a part-time job to help pay the cost of
school and living in Muskegon. I applied. At the time I still
hoped my dad would help with college, perhaps, to get a
degree to teach, but when that didn't happen I moved to
Muskegon, started business school, and got my first office job.

I worked in a real estate office mornings and took
classes afternoons and some evenings. I liked having to dress
up to go to work. Office *girls* in those days wore dresses and
skirts, nylons and high heels. Your hair looked nice and you
wore lipstick. The work was easy. I answered the phone and
made appointments for my boss, Mr. Taylor, and our
salesmen. I greeted customers when they came in. Mr. Taylor
didn't like to dictate. He wrote his letters in longhand and I
typed them. I filled out a lot of forms which are required in
real estate transactions.

There were two problems with this job. The first was
that my social life at this young age took priority over work
and school and I was tired most of the time. This tends to
affect efficiency. The second was that one of the salesmen, for

reasons I didn't understand then but understand better today, did not like me.

After a year, I realized that my salary would not cover my expenses for school and living, and with no help from family, I quit business school and Mr. Taylor hired me full-time. A year or so later, my least favorite salesperson went to Mr. Taylor and told him that we didn't need a full-time person. He was probably right. I didn't have enough work to keep me busy, and as tired as I was from my social life, I never complained that I wasn't busy enough. Mr. Taylor had a hard time telling me he had to let me go; he kept apologizing, but he did let me go.

I found another job immediately in the office of West Michigan Foundry. It was 1956, and I was twenty. I was a secretary in the engineering department and filled in on the switchboard. I reported to an office manager, a man, as did all of the other women who worked there. My work assignments came from the chief engineer, a nice man who was happy as long as I showed up every day and did my work with as few mistakes as possible. One of the rules was that women could not smoke at their desk; however, men could. The president of the company did not like to see women smoke. His father was the company founder and he and his brother ran the company. The brother didn't seem to do much and although they were wealthy he never carried any money. He continually borrowed from the *girls* who worked on switchboard to buy a cup of coffee, and he didn't pay them back.

In 1957, I married. I continued to work at West Michigan Steel Foundry until my first pregnancy became noticeable at seven months.

We met and we married

I met Barton Geyer, Bart for short, on a Thursday night the first week of June, 1956. I was still living in the Victorian apartment house in downtown Muskegon, but I had run out of money, quit business school, and began working full-time as a secretary in the W.B. Taylor Real Estate office. One of my roommates, Shirley Homrich, and I went for a walk in the early evening. A car pulled alongside us, and the driver, Ken Byer, a young man she knew, asked if we wanted a ride. Bart was in the passenger seat. Ken had dark wavy hair and was very good looking, so I was initially interested in him. After all, I was young, and good-looking mattered.

After about two minutes it became apparent that he was not the brightest bulb on the marquee and I began a conversation with Bart. He had dark black hair that he wore in a brush cut clipped short. His eyes were his best feature, bright blue under dark black eyebrows. He had a straight nose, nice enough lips, and his face was covered in dark freckles. It was unusual to see someone with dark hair and that many freckles, to say nothing of those blue eyes. He was in good physical shape, about five feet, ten inches tall with wide shoulders, and he would tell me later, a twenty-nine inch waist. He had a sarcastic wit and he kept us laughing. When we introduced ourselves, he made fun of our rhyming last names, Byer, Geyer, and Hier. We drove down to the lake and headed back when Shirley and I said we had to be at work the next day and needed to go home. Before I got out of the car, Bart told me he had graduated from high school the week before and asked if I would give him a graduation kiss. He was attractive, so I said yes. It was a nice kiss, and we made a date for the following night.

123

He picked me up in his father's car. There were two six packs of beer in the back seat. We stopped at a party at the house of someone he knew. He took the beer to the party. I didn't really like beer all that much so I sipped on one and he had several. After we left the party, he told me it was his birthday and asked for a birthday kiss. I told him I thought that was clever but I didn't believe him since the night before he'd asked for a graduation kiss. He pulled out his wallet and showed me his driver's license; it was indeed his birthday. He got the kiss. It was close to midnight and he suggested that we go to his house and his mother would fix us something to eat. I said, "You're crazy, we shouldn't wake your mother.

It's the middle of the night." He said, "She always gets up when she hears me come in." I thought, *Oh, well, he knows his mother better than I do.* On some level I was probably flattered that he wanted his mother to meet me. I should have been thinking, *what guy asks his mother to feed you instead of taking you out to eat?*

The house was dark. Our entry did wake his mother, Elinor, pictured here with her husband, Herb, and she came into the living room in a nightgown and robe. Bart said, "Mom, this is Bev. We're hungry. Will you fix us something to eat?" She nodded at me, no smile, and went to the kitchen. My mother would have told us to feed our own damned selves. I was embarrassed. She made a pitcher of lemonade, put it on the table, and said, "Here, drink this. It's better for you than what you have been drinking." Whoops! I was pretty quiet the rest of the time there. She fixed sandwiches, we ate, and Bart took me home. Just before I got out of the car he told me his mother suggested he bring me back the next evening so she could meet me while she was still awake. He did, and much later she told me that when I had the nerve to come back and face her, she knew I was okay.

I dated Bart exclusively. He would not have been at all comfortable dating someone who dated others. Six months after our first date we were engaged. I can't say we were enthusiastic about marriage. There was a baby on the way, and at that time you had two choices: marry, or go away and have the baby and give it up for adoption. Some girls had illegal abortions, but it was dangerous. We chose marriage.

On March 9, 1957, we were married at St. Francis de Sales Catholic Church. I wore a white, street-length, silk brocade dress with a boat neckline, three-quarter- length sleeves, and a small white flowered hat. Bart wore a dark suit and tie. I was twenty; Bart was nineteen. Bart's friend, Pete Huss, and Bart's sister, Gloria, were our witnesses. I have a picture of Bart and Pete standing by the door ready to leave for the church. His face registered resignation and fear. I was feeling none too hopeful myself.

We had a small reception at his parent's house. His mother prepared the food. My mother and stepfather, Nola and Fred Stenberg, and my father and stepmother, Lynn and Pauline Hier, were the only guests I invited. My brother was still in the navy. Bart's guests were his older sister and two younger brothers, his maternal grandmother, and several aunts, uncles, and cousins.

We began our married life in a black and white, thirty-seven-foot trailer purchased with money Bart had saved. The bed was tucked between three walls, and I had to climb on it to make it. The bathroom was so small I could scrub the entire floor without entering the room. A built-in dresser and small open space big enough for a crib were across from the bath. There was no room for privacy. We parked it at Dunes Trailer Park on West Sherman Boulevard in Muskegon.

Bart worked in the water and sewer department for the City of Muskegon, the same place his father worked, and I now worked at West Michigan Steel Foundry as secretary in the engineering department. We had problems almost immediately. Bart controlled all of the money. He insisted that I give him my paycheck and he gave me fifty cents each day to carry to work. He expected me to have forty cents when I came home or to explain where it was spent. The ten cents was for coffee. He went to the grocery store with me and if I put something in the basket that he thought was unnecessary--in one case a tube of lipstick--he took it out and put it back on the shelf. Once I needed a new bra. He would not give me the money so I charged it. When the bill came he was furious. He had a bad temper which I had not seen prior to marriage, and I was afraid of him.

He hit me for the first time when I was seven months pregnant. He got dressed to go out and I asked him where he was going. He told me it was none of my business. I said it was, I was his wife. He doubled up his fist and punched me on the side of my head. I was stunned and started to cry. He walked out the door and came back much later, very drunk. The next day he pleaded with me not to leave and promised it wouldn't happen again. I stayed. Where would I go? I was pregnant and had no money of my own.

I was able to work longer than the usual five months allowed because I didn't show until I was seven months pregnant.

The baby is born

On my first visit to Dr. Jesson to verify my pregnancy,
he estimated my due date would be August ninth. Brad
Stephen Geyer was born on September 9, 1957. The doctor
was off by a month. I did not look pregnant for the longest
time, then around the seventh month, boom, my belly stuck
out so far in the front I had to lean backwards to balance
myself. From the back I didn't look pregnant at all. In fact, I
was pleased when one day in my seventh month I was
walking down Lakeshore Drive and the driver of a car
approaching from behind tooted his horn and whistled his
approval. The look on his face when he actually got a look at
the front of me was priceless. We both laughed.

About two weeks after the due date, in the heat of
summer, I was impatient to meet this new little person, and
tired of being pregnant. I tried a few things to speed it along
like taking a motor boat ride over waves in Muskegon Lake. If
you've done that you know there's a great deal of hard
bouncing. But babies will come when they're ready. The
evening of September eighth, Bart, and I went to the drive-in
movie theater. I ate a huge box of popcorn. We got home
around midnight. We were staying with Bart's parents
because we didn't have a car, and when the time came, we
wanted to be able to get to the hospital quickly. I started labor
shortly after we got home. We woke Bart's mother, who six
months earlier had given birth to a baby herself. She timed
the labor pains. They reached five minutes apart very quickly,
so we grabbed my little suitcase that had been packed for a
month and headed to the hospital.

Like any first-time mother I had no idea what labor felt
like. No one talks to a first-time mother about labor pains.
Mine rapidly started coming every two minutes and I retched
up all the popcorn. That was not fun. The nurses checked to
see how far I was dilated and said that not all the pains were

real labor pains. *There is something called false labor pains,* I thought? Let me tell you they all felt very real to me.

In those days fathers were not allowed in the delivery room during the birth. It was thought that they might get upset, you know, at the blood and stuff, and then the doctor would be distracted by having to deal with them. They could be with you during labor. Bart was in the waiting room and the nurse asked me if I wanted him to come in. My response was *hell, no, he did this to me.* I completely ignored the fact that I was complicit in the act that led to the pregnancy. I can only say that pain makes me irrational.

Obviously I survived. The baby was born in the morning at 8:31. He had a head full of black hair and he was the prettiest baby ever born. "He's a miracle, he's a miracle," I kept saying. I could not have imagined the immediate, overwhelming love I felt for this little boy. They weighed him, eight pounds and three ounces, and took him away to clean him up. I was wheeled down the hall to my room and Bart joined me. The nurses brought the baby to us, and I was alarmed to find that his right arm was in a sling. The nurse explained that his clavicle, his collar bone, was broken during delivery, and that this was not uncommon. They said he had broad shoulders and I had a narrow pelvis.

There were not many tender moments with Bart. His usual response to anything tender was to crack a joke. He told me once that he felt funny when he said anything nice. But our first moments after Brad's birth were tender. I scooted over in the bed, Bart sat next to me, and together we opened the blanket that swaddled Brad. Bart ran his finger along the baby's arm and said, "Feel how soft his skin is." We checked to be sure he had all of his toes and fingers, and marveled at how perfect they were, exactly like grown-up people's fingers, only very tiny. My family has an inherited trait, crooked little fingers, and I said, "Look, his little fingers on both hands are crooked like mine and my mother's." I asked Bart if he wanted to hold him. I rewrapped the blanket and held him out. Bart took him carefully, as if he would break. It would take some time before he figured out how to cradle him in his arms, but the look on Bart's face said that he was as taken with this little boy as I was.

We decided to name the baby Brad Stephen. One of my wishes was that my children would not have nicknames and Brad doesn't lend itself to one. I also wanted a name that began with B as did both his father's and mine. Stephen was chosen from a list of male saint's names in the Catholic tradition. Bart went off to call family and tell them that Brad had arrived.

I was going back to work in six weeks, and in 1957 women did not pump breast milk or have someone bring the child to nurse. The nurse brought a bottle and showed me how to feed and burp the baby. I was just as awkward as Bart as I cradled the baby in my left arm, lifted the bottle to his mouth, and tried to get him to suckle. His face squinched up and he squirmed and moved his mouth away from the bottle, but finally he took in the nipple and drank. I couldn't take my eyes off his face and tears welled up. Did I have what it takes to care for this little person? How would I keep him safe, make sure he got what he needed? I hadn't had much mothering myself, and I wanted to give this baby the love and attention I'd missed.

I am not being just a mother when I say that Brad was beautiful. People stopped me on the street and told me he was beautiful. Total strangers came up to me and said he was such a cute baby. It happened so often that I began to think they were surprised that Bart and I, who were average looking, neither beautiful nor homely, would have such a good-looking child.

He may have been beautiful, but Brad was not an easy baby. He had colic and I was up every hour and a half all night for four and one-half months. I was exhausted, especially after I started back to work, and I had an inkling about why people abuse their babies. Not that I could ever do it, but I do see how it could happen. It never entered Bart's mind that he should share the nightly feedings. His father had little involvement in the care of Bart or his siblings, his mother provided all of the baby care, and it was assumed it was my responsibility. I don't know how Bart could sleep through it. In our small trailer, the baby's crib was maybe six feet from our bed. After Brad started sleeping for five- or six-hour stretches, Bart finally offered to get up with him one night.

Brad was an easy baby to take care of after he got over being colicky. When I went back to work he had the company of his Grandma Geyer and his youngest uncle, Gil, who was  only six months older. That arrangement lasted for a few months until Mom Geyer had to give it up. Caring for two infants understandably became too much. But Gil and Brad did remain playmates.

When Brad was three, we gave him a mixed blessing, a baby brother. He had had his parents to himself and sharing the spotlight didn't sit too well. Brad would gently pat the new baby, look at us for praise because he was being so nice, and when we turned our attention away, his gentle pats got considerably less gentle and the new baby started crying. Actually, this was a preview of what would come later with Brad and his siblings.

Brad started morning kindergarten at Bunker School in Lakeside in 1962, the year his little sister was born. Our house on LeTarte Street was seven or eight blocks from school. I didn't go back to work immediately after her birth, so I was home one mid- morning when Brad walked in the door. I asked him what he was doing home and he told me that all the kids had gone outside. I figured out it was recess, and somehow Brad thought it was time to come home, so he did. No one called from the school to say he was missing, which was scary. I piled the kids in the car and took him back to school. He was embarrassed and didn't want to go back. I took him anyway. He was not happy, but he joined the kids while I talked to the teacher. The kids hadn't noticed he was gone and obviously neither had she.

When Brad was in first grade, we lived close enough to school for him to walk. That winter there was a lot of snow; winters were a lot snowier then. One morning after a huge snowfall, I bundled Brad up in his snowsuit and boots, took him to the front door, and told him to walk to school. I could hardly see ten feet ahead, the wind was whipping the snow around, and neither Brad nor I could find the steps on the small front porch. Nevertheless, he bravely stepped off the porch and sank into snow up to his hips. I decided I had to drive him because never missing school was one of my rules. Of course, we got to school and it was closed. I haven't forgotten that I was willing to send my six-year-old child to school in a blizzard. Brad has chosen not to have children, but it would have been a great story to tell them about how, when he was six years old, his mother made him walk to school in snow drifts nearly up to his neck.

When Brad entered second grade we moved to the Oakview School neighborhood on the east side of town. When he entered third grade, we moved again, this time to the Moon School neighborhood. At this time he had seven siblings, two biological and five stepbrothers and stepsisters. You'll hear more about that later. Instead of being the oldest child in the house, now he was right in the middle. There were three older, one the same age who was cognitively disabled so not at the same level, and three younger.

Brad was shy anywhere except at home, so I assumed he would be the same in school. He wasn't noisy, but like many boys he had difficulty sitting in place. That changed in fifth and sixth grade when his teachers were both men. When

I went to parent-teacher conferences both told me how well behaved he was. I said thank you, but I did wonder if they were talking about my son Brad. At home Brad was the boss of the younger kids. If they were doing something he decided was not what they should be doing, he saw it as his job to take care of it. This started when his father and I separated. I consistently told him that he was not their parent, I was, and that I would handle the discipline. His response was that somebody had to make them mind, and evidently he was convinced I was not meeting his standards. His favorite action to get his younger siblings in line was to put their head in the crook of his arm and rub the top of their heads very hard with his knuckles. It is amazing to me that his younger brother not only speaks to him today, but that they are great friends.

Brad, his brother Brian, and stepbrother Clint were inseparable. Brad had other friends, but with these two he was the leader. He had a bike, they roamed the neighborhood, and I never worried about them. At some point, maybe when he was twelve, he had a paper route. I'm sure it was my suggestion, but Brad liked the idea of having his own money. I liked the idea that working meant he would learn responsibility. He was responsible in doing the job, but when he went to visit his dad, the paper route became my responsibility. I especially hated collecting the money. Today people are billed and send a check to the newspaper. Back then the paperboys, and they were boys, gave every customer a card and when they collected their money they punched the card. That was the receipt to show that customers had paid. Well, the older customers wanted to talk when I went to collect and others hid so they wouldn't have to pay. I could see a car in the driveway but no one would come to the door. I decided to end the paper route.

I worried about Brad when he went into seventh grade and junior high school. His dad had a terrible temper and Brad had a temper too. It was mostly directed at his younger siblings. I really didn't know how to deal with it. I took him for counseling and the counselor told me three things: that Brad was very smart, that he was completely honest, and that he was, indeed, angry. Brad was attending Steele Junior High School and there were race issues. Black kids and white kids self-segregated. A few boys, still in junior high, were sixteen and seventeen to Brad's thirteen. These bigger students bullied the smaller kids and the administration did little to control it. The counselor had no suggestions about school. There wasn't another option because kids were required to attend school in the district they lived in. He suggested that I figure out what Brad was interested in, engage him, and provide stability.

How does one provide a stable home when dealing with an alcoholic husband, working full time, and caring for eight children ages seven to eighteen. I sure didn't know how. I loved Brad beyond words. I ached to find a way to calm whatever it was he was dealing with in his growing up, to see him at peace. I feared because he had some of his father's personality traits, the teasing and riling and the frustration, and it scared me. I had not been parented well and had hardly been mothered. My father was very strict and not always fair in his discipline. I didn't want to be that kind of a parent. I didn't know what kind of parent I needed to be. Each child was different and needed something different.

The counselor suggested we all go on a vacation together and include the kids in the planning. We bought a big tent, maybe more than one, and went camping. The kids did like it, but it didn't solve any problems. I also enrolled the boys in a bowling league and found that Brad was an excellent bowler.

In 1971, Brad started high school. He still didn't like school, but he did well enough. He was now the oldest kid at home and he thought he was in charge of the family. He stirred things up, and when his siblings started arguing (at this point there were four including him), he sat back and

133

smiled, job accomplished. The kids never seemed to mind but I had difficulty with the chaos. Once I was so frustrated that I locked him out of the house until I could get myself under control. He tried climbing in a window. Shortly, there was a knock on the door; I looked out the window and saw a police officer holding Brad by the arm. I opened the door and the officer said, "I saw this young man trying to get in your window. Do you know him?" You have no idea how much I momentarily wanted to say no. We've had some good laughs over that.

As he got older my worries got bigger. Like many teenagers Brad was experimenting with drinking and so were his brothers. With my family history, and his father's alcohol addiction, I had good reason to worry. I moved with the four kids, Brad, Clint, Brian, and Julie, all teenagers now, from the apartment to a house in the Bunker School district. At this point, Brad was not alone in creating chaos. I had become the staff leader at Every Woman's Place, worked long hours, and sometimes brought home women who were in danger. I struggled to raise enough money to keep the agency open, and it was my responsibility to make sure we did. I was torn between a very responsible job for which I had a passion, and finding enough time to give my children the supervision they needed.

Respite came when my stepson's father insisted he live with him, and my three children visited their paternal grandparents in Florida. Thank God for my friend and former mother-in-law, Elinor. Brad had an uncle and three cousins in Florida who were close to his age, and his Aunt Gloria was an excellent parent, good at setting limits and ensuring they were kept. She invited Brad to stay with them through the school year, and he wanted to stay. He started eleventh grade. Gloria was a stay-at-home mother who established rules and Brad and his cousins followed them. She set expectations for school and he met them. He got a job, and she helped him learn to manage money. She sent me letters telling me what a good kid he was and how much she loved him. I went to visit and he was a different kid. He had what he needed, structure, something I never was able to provide. I had been in survival mode most of Brad's life. He was never a bad kid, just a very bright kid who was frustrated at living in a chaotic environment. Brad at heart likes a calm environment even though he was often the one to stir it up. He needed a grown-up who could create that environment. It wasn't me.

He came home to Muskegon to graduate from high school. He got a job and started college but college was not for him. He was a cook in a regional chain restaurant and worked hard. He was promoted to assistant manager, and then manager, and then he was sent to other restaurants in the chain to turn them around and create a profit. He did this by setting expectations for employees and establishing discipline in every aspect from purchasing to preparation to service.

When his younger brother, Brian, left for college, Brad took over the land contract on a house I was buying. He owned his own home by the time he was twenty-one. I never knew whether or when he dated. I never met anyone, but at age twenty-four he married. I made a fool of myself at the wedding and cried. I didn't just wet my eyes with tears, I sobbed. I couldn't stop. I'm not sure why even today.

Time has passed. Brad's marriage ended and he was single for a long time. He left the restaurant business and started a home security business. His early training in being in charge of his siblings must have been part of the training. The business is successful. In his forties he married again and chose exactly the right woman for him. Donna clearly appreciates and loves Brad. They have much in common and she encourages him to have fun. Her grown children like Brad, and that gives him family. They own a lovely home on a small lake in a very quiet place at the end of a road in Hesperia, Michigan. He likes to play poker, visit the casino, and hunt. He manages his money well and has enough. My fears have not come to pass. Drinking does not create

problems in his life, and he is not violent. I asked him not long ago if he was happy and he said, "I am happy, Mom." That makes me happy.

Brad has grown to be a person of good character. He is honest and hard-working and wise. He surprises me sometimes with his wisdom. He makes good choices, and he is a good person. I love Brad unconditionally and without measure. I am grateful that I was chosen to be his mom.

A bad boss and a good boss

When Brad was six weeks old, Bart insisted I find a job because if we ever wanted a house we would need the extra income. Bart's mother offered to take care of Brad. There wasn't an opportunity to return to my former job at City Hall, so I went to work in the purchasing department of Brunswick Corporation. They made bowling equipment and other sporting goods. I was secretary to one of six buyers and the only secretary who was married and had a child. The purchasing agent, the top guy, sat in the first office, the largest one. His secretary sat right outside his door. Each of the buyers had a cubicle with a large window that faced the desk of his particular secretary. If they needed you, they often tapped on the window to get your attention. The office was in a big warehouse kind of building with many departments on each floor.

There were no women bosses. Every woman was an office worker. Every secretary in our department thought the big boss, the purchasing agent, was a jerk. He told the secretarial pool that they were expected to wear high heels to work because their legs looked better in heels. He sent them home to get them if they didn't. I was smart enough to keep a pair in my desk for those winter days when walking in heels would have been treacherous.

I did not attend the annual Christmas party. One of my co-workers had worked there for more than one Christmas party, and reported that some of the guys drank too much, and the women office workers were fair game for fondling. My husband would not have allowed it, and I would have suffered his wrath had I overridden his decision. The first work day after the party the big boss stopped at my desk, put his foot up on the side so he and his crotch were in my personal space, and asked me why I didn't attend. I told him the truth, and he said all employees in his department were expected to attend company events.

137

The women in the department helped each other and shared information, including the fact that every time the big boss cheated on his wife and came home late, his secretary was told to send flowers to his wife. Shortly after the Christmas party conversation, my boss called me into his office and said that the big boss had asked him to let me go. He said there was nothing wrong with my work, but there was a woman in the personnel department the big boss wanted to move into our department and I had the least amount of seniority. *Damn, I was fired.* I was angry and I felt powerless. For a short while, I wished a terrible fate for the big boss, that he would get killed in a car accident, or at the least, get fired himself. Of course, that didn't happen and I did get over it. It certainly taught me that secretaries had zero power.

My next job was as a deputy clerk in the Clerk's office for the City of Muskegon. My husband and his father both worked in the city water department and those were the days when it was easier to get hired if you knew someone. I had to pass a civil service test but that was not difficult. I loved the job and I really liked my boss. He respected people in general, and gave me some of the best work advice ever. The first day at work he said, "I'm not the boss you need to worry about. Our jobs, yours and mine, are paid for with tax dollars, so every person who walks in this door is our boss, and we are to treat them as we would treat a boss." His philosophy carried over into the way we treated each other. My co-worker, Rose Lovejoy, had been there a long time. She was a perfectionist, and I learned a lot from her. We shared our workload and our life stories.

Rose's story touched my heart. She was in love with a man whose name was Aaron. When her dad was dying, he asked Rose, the oldest daughter, to promise to take care of her mother financially. In Rose's mind, that meant she could not marry and have children. She broke off the marriage plan with Aaron. They remained friends and he married her sister.

I asked her, "Weren't you angry at your sister?" She said, "No, I loved my sister, and if I couldn't have Aaron, I wanted her to have him." It was, and still is, hard for me to imagine what that must have been like for Rose. Aaron and the sister stayed married until the sister's death, and then Aaron married Rose. Rose's story about having to choose between working, and caring for her mother and marriage, was not unusual at the time.

Meanwhile, Bart's controlling behavior continued, and often erupted in violence. One night he came home after drinking, punched me in the face, and I went to work with a black eye. Rose asked me what happened and I told the usual lie about running into a door when I got up during the night. His violence was a part of my life story I hadn't shared. I was ashamed. I often had bruises that couldn't be seen. I lived in fear, but I had no idea how I would support myself and my child on a weekly salary of fifty dollars. I asked my father to help, but he said I had made my bed and now I had to lie in it. I was resigned to staying in the marriage.

I left my job at City Hall in my fifth month of pregnancy for my second child, once again with no maternity leave. What I had learned so far in my world of work is that the public sector provided the opportunity to serve a bigger world, and the private sector the opportunity to serve one man. What I had learned about marriage was that it wasn't the romantic notion I had daydreamed about in high school and maybe Rose was better off having not married until much later in life.

My family increases

Oddly enough, the due date for my second child was the same as my first, August ninth. Bless his heart, he arrived two days early. Brian Thomas Geyer, another B name and another saint name, was born on August 7, 1960, weighing eight pounds, eight ounces. He also had a broken collar bone. Labor was long and hard, thirty-six hours. Again those false labor pains and again the wonder at how anything that hurt that much could not be real. Bart had taken Brad to my mother's house in Pentwater where he would stay while I was in the hospital. This time I was better prepared emotionally for birth and so I answered yes when the nurses asked if I wanted Bart to come in while I was in labor. Again, after Brian was cleaned up and brought to my room, we checked him from head to toe and declared him perfect. He also has the crooked little fingers.

Every birth is a new experience. Every child born is different from the one before. I wondered if I would feel that same awe at being the bearer of this miracle, this tiny perfect little boy. Turns out, I was just as much in love with Brian as I was with Brad, just as deeply and unconditionally. I had several days of rest in the hospital, and it was a wonderful luxury to have this new little baby boy all to myself before going home and jumping into life with two little ones.

Brian was a calm and happy baby, easy to take care of. Within a very short time he slept most of the night. Before he was born we had a single bed built into the back of the trailer for Brad, removed our bed, and put a crib in its place. Bart and I slept on the pullout couch. We knew that we would have to look for a house soon.

As an infant, Brian loved to be wherever there were people. He had a stuffed clown doll that laughed infectiously when it was squeezed. We squeezed it often just to hear Brian laugh. He loved taking baths and the entire kitchen was wet when the bath was over. He loved his big brother even though, until they got older and could actually play together, Brad was not too happy about having Brian around.

I went back to work again when he was six weeks old. Our child care person, Yvonne German, had come to our trailer to look after Brad while I worked, and she was willing to care for both of them. She was around twenty, reliable, and loved kids, always important when you have to leave babies to go to work.

We moved into a home in Lakeside, a Muskegon neighborhood, when Brian was about a year and a half. The house had two bedrooms; one would be Bart's and my room, and the other, right next to it, would be for the new baby on the way. Bart built a family room and a bedroom for the boys in the basement. Both rooms were warm and carpeted. We had a big back yard for the kids to play in.

I was laid off from work and collecting unemployment insurance, so I was able to stay home, making it possible to spend much more time with Brian as a small child than I had with Brad. I loved that time of being with both of them. I took them for walks in an old-fashioned baby buggy, big enough for the two of them. We visited friends who had little children so they could play with other kids.

I had two scary times with Brian. He could move fast. Once I went to the bathroom and he got out of the house. I looked everywhere and couldn't find him. I called his dad and the police. I was hysterical. We scoured the neighborhood and then we spotted him holding the hand of a woman who had seen him wandering alone and was trying to help him find his house. He escaped one other time while we lived there. We looked everywhere and again called the police. After an hour of frantic search, he wandered into the backyard rubbing his eyes. He had crawled in the dog house belonging to the next door neighbor and taken a nap. Our yelling his name finally woke him up.

Brian had an active imagination. One time he was playing with an imaginary ball, tossing it from hand to hand.

141

He came into the house to use the bathroom and cracked me up when he put the imaginary ball on the table and picked it up again on his way back outside. Brian started kindergarten at Moon School. I walked him to school that first day, and like many children he cried and didn't want me to leave. I left and by the time I got home from work that night, he was bubbling over telling me all of the things he had done that day. He would be the only one of my children to stay in one elementary school through sixth grade.

The elementary school kids walked eight blocks to Moon School, and came home for lunch with a neighbor who fed them. They walked back to school after lunch and back home after school. That was a lot of walking for a kindergartner. Once a week on their way home, each child at Moon School whose journey came close to Ryke's Bakery was given a free butter cookie. This is a favorite memory for all my kids. A while back when Brian and his daughter, Tessa, were visiting, he drove her by the house where we lived, the bakery, and  the school. He said the distance seems much shorter now than it did then, and shorter than he had been telling Tessa it was.

Brian was an excellent student and loved school except for the time in junior high when he experienced the same bullying that Brad had. He took music instruction and played the cornet beginning in elementary school. He was in the band in high school. He liked sports and played whatever brand of football little kids play at grade school age. I remember a school play, I think in first grade, when he spoke his lines loudly like he was told to do. He spoke somewhat louder than anyone else and the audience laughed. He was embarrassed because he always wanted to do the right thing. When he got to junior high with those large sixteen- and seventeen-year-olds he was too small to make the team. He and Brad were Cub Scouts and they both spent a week in the summer at the YMCA Camp Pendalouan. I still worked full-time, but I had a boss who understood and gave me time off for anything having to do with my children.

Brian was always tenderhearted and affectionate. Once, when he was maybe six or seven years old, he bought me a cameo pin for my birthday. He asked me what I wanted after he bought it and I said, without thinking, that he didn't have to buy me anything, I didn't want anything. He was heartbroken and started to cry. He gave me the present and I told him I was so sorry, that I didn't know he had bought me a present and just thought he should save his money for something he wanted. Of course, I also praised him and told him how much I loved the pin, making sure to wear it a lot.

The same fears about drinking that I had with Brad cropped up again, when Brian was a teenager. On his stepbrother Clint's seventeenth birthday, when Brian was fifteen, they got beer from somewhere and were out riding their bikes. I got a call from the police asking me to come down and pick him up at the police station. It seems they had stopped in front of someone's house on Lakeshore Drive to relieve themselves and the homeowner called the police. Clint mouthed off so they put him in the cruiser. Brian, in loyalty to Clint, said, "You can't take my brother unless you take me." They responded, "That can be arranged," and shortly Brian and both bikes were with Clint in the cruiser. When I got to the station house, the boys came out wheeling their bikes, and Brian right away said, "I can explain, Mother." Through gritted teeth I said, "Do not to talk to me until I get over being mad. I am so mad, I am afraid I might kill you." I know lots of parents go through these things, but again, with my background, my response was not just anger, it was intense fear.

Brian had a high school sweetheart named Nancy. They began dating when he was in eleventh grade. He graduated from high school with honors and scholarships, and the following fall he attended college at Michigan Technological University in the Upper Peninsula of Michigan. He lived in a dorm the first year, and rented a house with a group of guys after that. It was a long distance away, so he only came home during school breaks, Thanksgiving, Christmas, spring break, and summer. The weather was often treacherous on the winter trips. I visited a couple of times. Nancy and Brian broke up in his first year away. Later, he had a college girlfriend, Julie, and that relationship ended when college ended.

Brian's degree is in mechanical engineering. He worked summers for Consumers Power Company. After college he was hired by General Electric to work in the nuclear energy field, traveling the country to various nuclear power installations. He worked with several other young men who became close friends. He traveled home at holidays and I visited him in Minneapolis and San Francisco. He was having a great time. Women like Brian and there seemed to be lots of dating and good times. I met his college girlfriend, and I met another girlfriend, Bonnie Illies, in Minneapolis. I'm sure there were more.

When Brian was around twenty-seven, I met him in Chicago and was introduced to a new girlfriend. I could see this relationship was serious. Her name was Donna Jabour. She had a little boy, Austin, who was under a year. Brian met her while working in the south, where Donna lived. He had been transferred to Indiana, bought a house, and she was visiting. Some of the guys he worked with rented from him. Soon after we met, Donna and Austin moved into Brian's house, and I grew close to Austin, who called me Grandma. When Austin was two, Brian changed companies and started work at the nuclear power plant in South Carolina on the Georgia border near Augusta. He and Donna bought a house in the Bobby Jones subdivision where I visited often and had wonderful fun times with Austin. I was ready for a grandchild, and Brian was definitely a dad to Austin.

144

Brian and Donna decided they wanted a baby, so they married. They asked me to help with wedding arrangements because the wedding would be in Muskegon where Brian's family lived. Donna had only her dad, mother, brother, and two stepparents. Brad was the best man, Donna invited a girlfriend to be her bridesmaid, and Austin was the ring bearer. He was adorable in his little tuxedo. Nine months and maybe a week after the wedding, Tessa, my only biological and perfect grandchild, was born. I was a frequent Georgia visitor after she was born, and both children visited me each summer.

When Tessa was still very young Brian and Donna divorced. I was heartbroken and disappointed. As a child of divorced parents, and divorced myself, I so much wanted it to be different for my children. It was none of my business but I wanted them to try harder. That didn't happen. The marriage was over, but they have been and are the best co-parents I know. Tessa comes first with both of them. They have never lived far apart and Tessa has always stayed in whichever house she wanted to. They both attended every sports event she was involved in and that was a lot of sports events. Both attended parent-teacher conferences, and they have been together every birthday and holiday. Neither has remarried.

Brian went on to get a master's degree in business administration and he has been successful at work. Nuclear energy work is highly confidential so I don't know what he does except that he works to find better answers for storing nuclear waste. In addition to his work, he invests in real estate, buying houses that need some work but not too much, fixing them, and putting them on the market. He also bought and lives in a seven-bedroom, five-and-a-half-bath home, some of the time with Tessa and some of the time alone. Each spring when the Augusta Open golf tournament is held in the first week of April, Brian rents the home and makes a lot of money. I go to Georgia the week before and help him organize and clean the house. Tessa's birthday falls in that

145

week too. I love going because it gives me time alone with Brian and with Tessa. I get to cook for them and be a full-time grandma for a week. Austin is grown and on his own so it's just the three of us. I treasure that time.

Brian has some of the same qualities that his older brother has. He is honest and hard-working and successful. He also likes golf and gambling. They enjoy doing both of those things together when they can. Brian is more social, like I am, and has lots of friends. There has generally been a woman in his life, sometimes more than one. He dated one woman for several years, and when marriage didn't happen she moved on. Today he is again dating Nancy, his high

 school sweetheart, long distance because she lives in Muskegon. Brian will not marry at least until Tessa is fully on her own. I am deeply moved by his commitment to his daughter, and with all the affection she gets from both of her parents she is a sensible, confident young woman. For sure, she's not seeking attention she doesn't get at home.

I get emotional when I think about my children. My sons are not as good at staying in touch as I wish they were. Other mothers of sons in my circle say that is also true for them. I initiate most of the phone calls. When I call them they both are happy to hear from me. Brian always answers the phone saying in a delighted voice, "MOMMMM!" He carries on a conversation; Brad is more likely to respond and wait for the next question.

I talked to Brian recently and asked him what was new. He told me he had gotten a raise, one he hadn't asked for and wasn't regularly scheduled, but was given with his boss telling him it was for doing an outstanding job. He enjoys feeling competent. When I ask him about Tessa his voice changes and I can hear the emotion. At her recent high school graduation the look of pride and joy on his face was amazing. Seeing him with so much feeling for her overwhelmed me with love for and pride in him. I can't thank him enough for the gift of grandchildren. It's always each child's choice, but most parents hope for a next generation.

When I think about Brian and who he is, I do realize that with all of the drama in my own life when I was raising children, I still managed to raise a child who knows how to be a good parent. Sometimes children benefit from what you don't do as well as you might have, and not just from the things you did well. I can't take credit for all the good in my children, but I may be able to take credit for teaching them survival and unconditional love.

Back to City Hall and, later, the boss from hell

In 1960, six weeks after my second child, Brian, was born, I was able to come back to work temporarily in the City Treasurer's office during tax season. For the first time I had a woman boss, Rose Smith: too bad the job was temporary; she was terrific.

In early 1961, I went to work full-time as secretary to the sales manager at Norge, a national refrigerator manufacturing firm. This job was another eye-opener. The woman who preceded me stayed a week to train me. She told me that the man I would work for was difficult to deal with. I asked in what way, and she said he made inappropriate sexual comments. I was momentarily taken aback, but then I thought, naively, that he must have been attracted to her and I wouldn't have that problem. I needed the job and I was sure I could handle anything he might do. I never asked her for specifics.

I sat in a separate office contiguous to the boss's office. My desk faced his office and there was a bank of filing cabinets behind me. After about two weeks on the job, he came into my office to get something from the files. After he got what he was looking for, I got something I wasn't looking for. He took hold of my shoulders and rubbed his crotch into my shoulders. I was too shocked to say anything and he was out of my office and into his in a flash. Momentarily I wondered if I had imagined it. Nope, it happened. Thereafter, I was on high alert. Anytime he moved toward the filing cabinets, I swiveled my chair to face them and asked if I could find something for him, and I didn't swivel back until he was in front of my desk.

The next inappropriate incident happened when he called me from a motel while he was away on business. After asking if there were any calls and from whom, he told me that he was thinking about me and wishing I was there with him in his room. What do you say to that? I said nothing. He then said goodbye as though he hadn't shared his wish. After I had been there a month or so, when he called me into his office to take dictation, I again had a lesson in the need to be quick and clever. His office had two doors, one to the hallway to the main office area, and the other to my office. He shut the hallway door, and told me to move my chair close to the desk so he could feel my legs while he was giving dictation. I did not move my chair closer. Instead, I got up, opened the hallway door, went back to my chair, and lifted my steno pad, poised to take dictation. There were no repercussions when I didn't respond to his unsolicited attention, but the attention never stopped. I talked about it to women co-workers. They were sympathetic but could not suggest a solution other than to keep evading him. We called him the dirty old man, because he seemed old and he definitely was lecherous. When I look back he was probably in his forties.

As if that wasn't enough, there was a man who reported to my boss and frequently dropped into my office. He had been in prison for child molestation, and when my boss wasn't there, he sometimes started talking about young girls, how tempting they were, and how much they liked to be touched. No one in those days talked about these perversions, nothing on television, nothing in magazines. It was a taboo subject. I said nothing when he said these things. I was horrified, but didn't know what to say. As soon as I could, I would make an excuse to leave the office. There was nothing about my boss that made me think he would do anything about this guy's behavior. It never entered my mind to go to anyone above these men. I felt unsafe and slightly soiled, but not for one minute did I think that if I complained anything would be done about it. In fact, I believed I would lose my job.

Finally, after about six months on the job, and many requests for fondling by my boss, I was called in to take dictation and he asked again. I started to cry and this is what I told him. "I live in hell at home, I have a husband who hits

149

me and controls everything I do. I have two little children I'm responsible for, and I come to work and have to deal with you making advances that I never asked for. It's making a wreck out of me. How can I be expected to do the best job I can, the kind of job I want to do?" He stopped and never did it again. Obviously, I found the right words.

Shortly after that conversation, I learned I was pregnant with my third child, Julie. One might ask why I got pregnant three times with the marriage as it was. I can only say that birth control pills had not yet been invented, and saying no to a violent man doesn't work particularly well. The company announced it was moving to Fort Smith, Arkansas, before my pregnancy became apparent. My boss was promoted to the corporate office in Chicago, and I was laid off and eligible for unemployment insurance. It was a great relief to leave and still have an income. I collected until my fifth month when it was assumed I was not eligible for employment and, therefore, not eligible for unemployment compensation.

It's a girl!

I had plenty of time to get ready for my third child. I wasn't working, and I was as relaxed as possible given the state of my marriage. She was born on April 4, 1962, and weighed seven pounds, three ounces. Again I tried to give her a name which would not easily become a nickname, but I gave up on the B idea. I could not think of a name I especially liked that started with a B. Back then there were not all of the various unusual names there now are. I thought of Barbara, Brenda, and Bethany, and also April because that would be her birth month, and while there is nothing wrong with those names, they just didn't feel right. And then I had a great idea. My grandfather was Julius and Bart's grandmother was Julia. There were no grandchildren on either side named after the great-grandparent generation. She would be Julie, plus Ann for Saint Ann.

I went into the hospital between five and six in the evening and she was born about five hours later. No false labor pains this time. Her father had taken her brothers to my mother's house in Pentwater and he did not make it back in time for the birth. He only missed by a few minutes. When he got to the hospital, I had been wheeled to my room and she was being cleaned up by the nurses. He walked in and the first words out of my mouth were, "I got my girl!" He asked, "Do you want me to call the family?" "Absolutely not," I declared. "She's my girl, the first girl grandchild on both sides and I'm calling." And I did. I was to the moon happy. Third time, two boys, and this time I really wanted a girl.

The nurses brought Julie into the room and we checked tiny fingers and toes, and once again there were the crooked little fingers, just like her brothers, my mother, and I had. She had dark hair, not as much as her big brother Brad, but not bald like her big brother Brian. She was beautiful, a calm and happy baby. We took her home to our new house. What fun I had dressing her in her cute little dresses with matching ruffled panties. She would be a girly girl. Hah, once she started making her own clothing decisions, around junior high, I didn't see her in a dress until sometime during her college years.

As a child, with my parents in and out of my life, I had a difficult time feeling loved. When I lived with my grandmother I was sure she cared more for my cousin and my brother. That is probably why I wondered if I would be able to love my children equally. I know it sounds silly, but it worried me. Then, after the birth of my second child I learned that each child is different, and as a parent you are different with each child, but you love them equally. When I first met each of my babies I was overwhelmed with loving them and felt that I had taken part in a miracle. That beautiful, tiny baby girl, so dependent on me to keep her safe, won my heart immediately. She wasn't planned, but she was absolutely welcomed and unconditionally loved.

I realize that I've left my children's father out of my talking about my love for them. He loved them too and still does. The tender moments we had are all related to our children. He isn't demonstrative when it comes to loving, but they know he cares. I've left him out because, in fact, I raised them and I did it almost completely alone. I was there for the victories and the difficulties. I feel fiercely that they are MY babies and always will be. He's their dad, but I earned the parent stripes.

Julie was adventurous as a toddler. Before she was two, she learned how to slip the hook on the screen and get out the door. Our child-care person was Emma, a woman with nine children of her own. She had endless patience. The neighbors told me that she took Julie for a walk and followed along behind her. When Julie got tired of walking, she sat down on the ground and Emma coaxed her up instead of taking her arm and pulling her up. Sometimes it took several minutes. One Sunday morning Julie got the screen unlocked and trotted off dressed only in a diaper. Within a very short time I realized she was gone, and knew she could not be far away. There was a church two doors from us. A neighbor across the street saw me and told me she had gone into the church. Oh, Lord, no pun intended, I went up the steps and peeked in. The pews were filled, the preacher was talking, and Julie was walking down the center aisle about a third of the way to the altar. I darted in, grabbed her, and headed out trying to ignore the smiles on both sides of the aisle. A funny thing, Julie ended up attending this same church as an adult--fully clothed, of course.

Julie was more attached to me than either of her brothers. She hated it when I left for work and cried every morning. When she was three or four, the babysitter, another Emma, tried to distract her until I got out the door. One morning she followed me about a block down the street, where I met the people who gave me a ride to work. I didn't see her, got into the car, and we drove off. The woman whose house she was standing in front of came out and picked her up and held her. By that time the babysitter caught up to her, took her home, and called me. It was sad to know that she was so upset at my leaving. Her need to be physically close continued until she was twelve or so.

In the home where we lived when I had eight children, Julie shared a room with Susie, who was eight. Susie's side of the room was always messy. Julie was born tidy, and even at three she was greatly upset by the mess. From the time she was old enough to put her clothes away and make her bed, she did. The two older girls, Janice and Paula, also shared a room. Paula was messy and Janice was neat. I had paired the girls by age. I moved Julie into Janice's room, and now they were paired by a desire for neatness, which worked out much better.

In addition to the tidiness Julie liked to help. She pulled a stool up to the sink and helped the big girls do dishes. Once she pulled the stool too close to the counter and leaned over the stove to get something when a burner was on.

 She was in a little slip and panties and her slip caught fire. Paula was there and whipped the slip off before Julie could get a burn. Thank God and Paula.

Julie was good at everything she tried. When she was five she could jump rope continuously, not stopping between each rope swing like most little kids did. The first time she got on a two-wheel bike she took off pedaling without tipping over. It upset her brother Brian, because he had to make several attempts before he could balance his bike. The first time she put on ice skates she set off skating, no wobbly ankles.

Julie's place as the youngest in the family was not enviable. Her stepsisters were good to her, but her brothers and stepbrothers relentlessly picked on her. They were the bane of her existence for a long time. It was frustrating and it justifiably made her angry. We had rules about teasing, and the boys were punished, but it never stopped. My husband's response was to yell at them, which didn't work. Time-outs and privileges withheld didn't work either. Mostly this went on when I was at work. Our child care person, the second Emma, didn't manage the children well. I kept her because she never missed work, and she did keep track of the kids.

Julie went to Moon School from kindergarten through fourth grade. Her best friend was Tina King and they were in the same fourth grade class. At a parent-teacher conference her teacher said that the two of them would not mind and it made her cry. I asked her what they did and she said they talked and whispered and giggled in class and wouldn't stop when she told them to. I thought her crying about this was a little over the top. She should have lived at my house.

We moved to the Marquette school district when Julie was ready for fifth grade. One of the boys in class liked Julie and told her he wanted her to be his girlfriend. Two large girls in her class didn't like it and they were aggressive with Julie, taunting her and calling names when she was on her way home. She began to have stomach aches and didn't want to go to school. I talked to the principal, who refused to address the issue. I talked to the mother of the boy and she talked to her son, who verified my story, and we went to the school together. The principal still did nothing. At the end of that school year I moved and enrolled Julie in another school. She had enough to deal with at home without dealing with this discord at school.

And then Julie became a teenager. I was unprepared for the mercurial disposition of teenage girls. She pushed as many limits as she could. I worried often about her safety, but in spite of the difficulty of teenage years, Julie is the poster child for how well kids can come through it. She graduated from Muskegon High School and later from Ferris State College, where she majored in hospitality management, with a minor in marketing. She paid her way with loans and by working in a travel agency. Her first job after college was in a hotel near Chicago. Later she moved back to Michigan and worked at a hotel in Grand Rapids. She tired of the schedules hotel workers are required to keep. It's also a field without a lot of stability; people come and go. People without a degree can do as well as those who have one. She recognized that her skills were in marketing and sales, and at the very beginning of the cell phone boom, she landed a job at Verizon. She found that her best qualities made her successful. She is highly organized and understands that excellent customer service works. She is a perfectionist; things must be done right.

She sold a lot of phones and worked hard to help her customers. Unlike Julie, some salespeople make their money by selling to new buyers, not by taking care of the ones they have already sold a phone to, even though those customers can be a strong source of referrals. Julie continued to sell and serve for quite a while, but as she got more customers, she found she was always working and had little time for herself. She quit Verizon and took a job as a pharmaceutical salesperson. The wages and benefits were good and her time could be better controlled; however, she quickly learned that it wasn't a job of selling. What she was required to do was bring food to the doctor's office, make a presentation, and leave free samples. She never knew whether her work ended in a successful sale.

A friend who worked in the mortgage business suggested that Julie might like that kind of work. She applied, got a job, and was very successful. Banks were lending money easily, and people were buying who earlier could not get credit. She didn't sell directly to home buyers; her company bought mortgages from mortgage companies that did. Then, the bottom fell out of the housing business and banks quit lending. Nearly everyone was let go.

She was out of work only a short time when she was recruited by a financial management firm. She studied successfully to obtain her license as a registered financial planner. The job required cold calling and working evenings and weekends. Once again, just as happened at Verizon, life was all work. She wanted balance, so she was back into job-seeking. Fifth Third, a regional bank with offices throughout the Midwest, initiated a new program in Grand Rapids designed to build relationships with their business clients. Julie's work success had always been through relationship building, so she had high hopes. The idea was a good one, but the execution was not. The job quickly morphed into getting points for selling new products rather than building relationships that would lead to the purchase of new products. She waited a year and transferred to another job in the bank where she has regular hours and time for other interests. She is content with her work, and her life has balance, exactly what she wants.

Julie has been married and divorced twice, both times to the same man, Brian Linstrom. He is a good person, but they have very different interests and personalities. There are no children. They decided to separate, this time it appears for good, and they have become good friends. They share a chocolate Lab, Jasmine, and Julie is the world's best doggy mom.

There is much more that can be said about who Julie is besides the fact that she is conscientious and a hard worker. The most important thing about her is her generosity, caring, and hard-won wisdom. In her childhood years, she continually had to defend herself as the youngest child. She needed my presence much more than I gave it and that was difficult for her. She struggled to find her way until her late twenties, and then she came to a place where she understood that she had to take charge of her life. She has worked harder to manage her life in a productive way than anyone I know. She gained wisdom, and she became strong and able to understand what worked in her life and what didn't. When something wasn't working, she accepted it if she couldn't change it, and changed it if she could. She is generous to a fault, one of those people who pay for dinner for strangers in a restaurant just because she can. She is the one grandchild out of nine who regularly visited her grandmother in the nursing home. She stays in touch with her stepsister Susie, who is cognitively impaired, and takes her out to lunch and celebrates birthdays and Christmas with her. Julie is a loyal friend and tries hard to honor her friendships. Like her brothers, she is honest to a fault and straightforward in her response to everything. She plays no games. She has high standards and expects a lot of herself.

I wasn't a perfect parent, but I know I did some things right. There were some strong messages I gave my children. I set an example for honesty and hard work. All three share those values. I told them that they were going to go to college and I would do all I could to make that happen. It was never *if* you go to college, it was *when* you go to college. I preached responsibility and they are responsible. I said it was

 unacceptable to have a child before they were in a position to take care of that child physically, emotionally, and financially. Two chose not to have children, and the third waited until he was in his early thirties. I have wished many times I had been a more present mother during those years when children, girls especially, are so fragile. Those years were more difficult for Julie than they should have been, but she survived and became the strong woman I hoped she would be. She was the one who did the work, and she gets the credit for who she is today.

I love Julie, not just because she's my daughter, but because she is such a wonderful person. I am proud of what she has accomplished, and even more so about the caring and generous person she is. Thank God I was chosen to be her mother.

Enough is enough

One night, shortly after I found out I was pregnant for Julie, Bart again came home drunk. "Get me something to eat," he ordered. I refused and he started punching me, cursing and yelling, "I told you to get me something to eat, dammit." The more he hit the angrier he seemed to get. He ran to the bedroom and grabbed his shotgun and headed to the basement where he kept the bullets. This was the first time he had threatened me with a weapon other than his fists. I ran out of the house, pounded on the neighbor's door, and shouted, "Call the police." I stayed with them until the police came, terrified because my sons were still in the house. The police took his guns and asked, "Where can we take you and the children?" I asked, "Can't you make him leave? The kids need to be in their own beds." The officer said, "No, it's his house, we have no authority to make anyone leave. We suggest that you and the kids leave for your own safety. Tomorrow, he'll be sober and calmed down." I took the kids and went to his parents' house, because I had no family in Muskegon. I was ashamed to go to friends. The violence continued throughout the pregnancy, and I called the police several times. I wasn't working and had no access to money. There were no domestic violence programs, no shelters for battered women.

Three weeks after Julie was born, she was sleeping and Bart came home drunk. "Put the boys to bed downstairs," he said, "and go to the bedroom." Brad was five and Brian was twenty months old. Brad went to bed quietly, but Brian stood in his crib and cried. He wasn't ready to go to sleep. Bart said again, "Go to our bedroom. Let him cry, he'll get over it." Brian kept crying. Bart was furious, jumped off the bed and headed to the basement, with me running behind him. Bart stopped to get a two by four board from under the steps and I ran to Brian's crib and stood between Brian and his father. Bart lifted the board over his head. I looked him in the eye

159

and said as calmly as I could, "If you raise a hand to this baby it will be the last time you hurt anyone." He looked at me defiantly for what seemed a long time, put down the board, cursed, and left in the car.

That week, while Bart was at work, I answered an ad in the paper for a secretarial job at Daniels Office Supply store. I interviewed the next week and got the job. I told Bart I made less money than I actually did, and started to set money aside to file for divorce. Shortly before the papers were to be served, I confided in my mother-in-law, and asked if the children and I could stay with her for a short while after he was served. The papers ordered Bart out of the house, but I knew that the time immediately after he was served would be dangerous.

She tried to talk me out of a divorce, but I told her if we stayed I was sure Bart would kill me or harm the kids. I would move back to the house when I was sure Bart had calmed down. She knew the violence had escalated, and she said yes. It wasn't easy for her. Her marriage had always been difficult, but she never felt she had any choice except to stay. In the past when we talked about Bart's violence she asked me to see our parish priest, which I did. Nothing changed. Her love for her grandkids moved her to protect us and I will always be grateful.

On the day the papers were served, after Bart went to work, I called my workplace and told them I wouldn't be in. I packed clothes for the kids and headed to her house. He was served just as he left work, came home, found we weren't there, and drove to his mother's. When he arrived, she and his dad intervened and convinced him that violence would create further problems, and perhaps jail time.

He moved out of the house, and the kids and I moved back in. Brad was five, Brian was two, and Julie was under six months old. I didn't know how I would make it financially. I made $75 a week, and paid $25 to a babysitter. The court ordered Bart to pay $21 weekly in child support, not quite enough to cover the sitter. He complained mightily. "I'm not paying on a dead horse," he said, but he paid.

We stayed in our house for a while. I had been awarded ownership, but Bart was so angry that I worried he would continue the violence. That fear drove me to sell him the house and the kids and I rented a house not far away so Brad was able to stay in the same school district. He was six, Brian was three, and Julie under a year.

Mine is a common story, but not a pretty one. Marriage is supposed to be a safe place, a place where you are loved for who you are. That's not what I got. What this marriage did give me are three amazing children, the loves of my life; a strengthened warrior spirit; a determination not to allow myself to be treated this way again; and a commitment to never be in a position where I was unable to take care of myself and my children. It taught me compassion for women who have been undervalued and mistreated. It was the foundation for the work I would later do.

My children have a relationship with their father. He has never abused them, although they learned early that he lacked the capacity to give them much emotionally. As adults they seem to understand his fears and low self-esteem, the basis for his violence against me and others who came after me. For my part, it took me a long time to recover emotionally. I knew as a child of divorced parents how important it is to children that the parent they don't live with, whatever his or her shortcomings, is not criticized. Sometimes that meant I said nothing at all. Bart is not all bad. He worked hard, was thrifty with his money, paid his bills, and loved his children to the best of his ability. When he was sober, he had a good sense of humor and could be fun to be around. His best attribute is his ability to laugh at himself.

I am not the first woman in my family to have survived domestic violence. My maternal grandmother and my mother share that history, but the cycle appears to have ended with me. My sons are not abusive and my daughter did not marry an abuser. Other women are still living the nightmare, although things are some better and there are safe places to go. Today, police, prosecutors, judges, and others who work with women who are battered have a much better understanding of the dynamics and rarely blame the victim. Domestic violence is no longer a dirty little secret that nobody talks about. More people understand and fewer people ask why a woman stays. The statistics indicate that while women are still abused, they leave sooner than they used to, exposing their children for a shorter period of time. It is my hope that someday all violence will end, that no woman and no child will have to live in a home that isn't safe. No, it's not a pretty story. It's the story of a survivor.

My second marriage, what was I thinking?

On August 25, 1965, I became the mother of five more children, bringing the total child count to eight. I didn't birth them or I would have made the nightly news. I didn't adopt them, I married them. Well, actually, I married their father, Clinton John Perigard, and they were a bonus. Joseph, Janice, Paula, Susie, and Clint Perigard joined my biological children, Brad, Brian, and Julie. Joe was fourteen, Janice thirteen, Paula eleven, Susie eight, Brad eight, Clint six, Brian five, and Julie three.

I had just purchased a four-bedroom house at 532 E. Dale Avenue in Muskegon from Mitchell DeYoung, my mom's neighbor in Pentwater. On my salary, and with three kids to support, I could never have saved for a down payment. Mitch raised his family in this house, his kids were grown, and he struggled to find good tenants. He offered me a land contract with nothing down and a monthly payment of $65. It truly was a gift, and the kids and I moved in.

Clint and I had dated for about a year. There was no plan to marry when I bought the house. I had been divorced for nearly two years, and he had a lot of baggage, not the least of which was that he drank too much and had a lot of debt. His three daughters were living with his mother-in-law and he and his two sons were living with his mother. His first wife, the children's mother, was mentally ill and had been in and out of Traverse City State Hospital several times, most recently for the past four years.

In June, 1965, Clint's mother-in-law called and said she could not care for the girls any longer. There was no room in

163

his mother's house, so he asked if I would take them until he could arrange something else. With some hesitation--not because of them, I'd met them and they were good kids who had been through too much in their young lives--I said yes. I was the child of divorced parents and twice spent time in group homes for children. These separations from family were the most difficult times of my childhood. My heart told me I could not say no.

The girls moved in. Two months later I was married and Clinton and the boys moved in. The Perigard kids and the Geyer kids became brothers and sisters. They all have said they remember the years we were together as fun. There was always someone to play with, never a dull moment. In some ways it was easier for me because the kids looked out for each other. I was only twenty-nine, so I had a lot of energy and I was lucky enough to have a boss who had no problem with the kids calling me at work, or giving me time off for school conferences, field trips, and emergencies when they came up.

Holidays were amazing. Imagine presents for eight kids under the Christmas tree, most of them purchased and wrapped by me. The kids pored over the Sears catalog and talked endlessly about what they wanted from Santa. The little ones wanted the most popular toys; the big kids, clothes. There were visits to Santa and shopping trips to the nearby variety store so they could buy presents for each other. The night before Christmas they set out cookies and milk for Santa and carrots for his reindeer. On Christmas morning we told them they couldn't wake us until seven. We heard the little ones on the stairs whispering and giggling, waiting until we got up and they could see what Santa brought. They woke us and we sent them to wake the big kids. There had to be some order with that many kids, so everyone picked a spot and sat, waiting for one of the big kids to pass the presents. I tried to make sure each child had several packages, usually one main toy and several smaller ones. One of my sons told me he would always remember how many gifts were piled under our tree, more than forty, for sure.

Imagine how big the Thanksgiving turkey was--large enough to feed the ten of us and whatever family showed up. We went through a lot of boxes of sparklers on the Fourth of July. But, the holiday the kids liked best, maybe after Christmas, was Easter.

The first Easter, I purchased eight baskets, eight packages of Easter grass, a lot of jelly beans, several packages of foil-wrapped chocolate bunnies, plastic Easter eggs and trinkets to put inside, and eight packages, three to a package, of bright yellow marshmallow Peeps. I hid all of this in my closet, high on a shelf, covered with a blanket.

The night before Easter all eight kids and I gathered around the yellow Formica-topped kitchen table to color eggs. A leaf expanded the table to make room for every child to have a chair. Two coffee mugs, each with a different color dye, sat on the table in front of each chair. It was understood that the kids had to trade cups from time to time. I poured hot water and a little vinegar in each cup because someone had told me it helped with the color. I hard-boiled four dozen eggs, six apiece, and each child had a little wax pencil to write on an egg before coloring. Wherever there was wax, the color did not take. While they dyed eggs we talked about the Easter Bunny and how he left candy for all the good little girls and boys.

Easter night, after the kids went to bed, eight o'clock for the little ones, nine for the big kids, I put the baskets together while Clint hid the eggs. Just like on Christmas, the kids were told they couldn't wake us until seven a.m., but also like Christmas, before seven a.m., we heard the little ones sitting on the steps whispering to each other, "I wonder what the Easter Bunny left?" We got up and the little ones were hopping with excitement. First, came the egg hunt. They had instructions that they could only find six eggs each. The big kids were great about helping the little ones search, and waited to find the eggs that were harder to locate. A lot of delightful "I found one" shouts rang out.

Next, what they all were waiting for: finding the basket the Easter Bunny left. The night before, after the baskets were filled, I designed a treasure hunt for each kid to find an Easter basket. The little kids were handed written clues that would lead them to their basket. The big kids were each assigned a little kid to help before they could search for their own baskets. They loved the hunt.

Top L to R: Jan, Paula, Brad, Susan,
Bottom L to R: Joe, Clint, Brian, Julie

There were other good times, too. Summers we went to the beach and a couple of times we went camping. Winters the kids had saucer sleds, and we packed hot chocolate and sandwiches and went sledding. Some of the kids had ice skates and skated on rinks at nearby parks. Sometimes we went to the roller skating rink. When I look back, I'm not sure how we managed. I know I had more energy then. All in all our big family had six years of holiday celebrations, not so many, but enough to make good memories.

Realistically, however, it wasn't all fun. Clint's drinking had progressed; he tried to hide it, but I found empty bottles all over the house. There were fights over the drinking and struggles over money. His son Joe had serious emotional and behavioral problems that we assumed stemmed from his uncertain childhood but realized later were far more serious, and that created problems with the other kids. I lost any hope that things would change.

By 1971, the three oldest Perigard kids, Joe, Jan, and Paula, had graduated from high school. Joe and Jan had jobs and moved out on their own. I had been unhappy in my marriage almost from the beginning. I asked Clint to leave, and he did. His daughter Susie, who was fourteen, had cognitive disabilities and moved into her aunt's foster home. My children, Brad, Brian, and Julie, and Clint's children, Paula and Clint, Jr., moved with me to a townhouse in Oakwood Village in Muskegon. Paula was with us for nearly a year until she married. As soon as I could afford it, I filed for divorce.

Every person who divorces has a story about why. I couldn't blame Clint. Like my first husband, he was an alcoholic, and I knew before I married him that I did not love him. I married anyway, but I married because I loved the kids and not their father. My years with them, although harder work than I ever imagined when I took on the responsibility, were also filled with fun times, and I know that these kids might have had a much rougher road had I not gone with my heart.

Life for the Perigard children has not been easy. Joe, who was diagnosed with schizophrenia in his early twenties, was killed in an automobile accident while walking in the middle of the street. Paula lives in Alabama, has two grown children, and has been diagnosed as bipolar, the same illness her mother lived with. When her mother was diagnosed, people with mental illness were institutionalized. Paula does well with medication. Jan lives in Florida and has married three times. Paula tells me she is happy in her last marriage. Neither she nor the youngest, Clint, Jr. has children, a decision they made based on the illness and alcoholism in their family. Clint, Jr. also lives in Florida, is happily married and doing well. Sadly, Jan, Paula, and Clint do not stay in touch with each other. I have talked to Paula by phone, and I communicate with Clint, Jr. on Facebook. I had a lovely visit with him and his wife, Barbara, this year. Susie continues to live with her aunt, and my daughter, Julie, sees her regularly. I'm glad they had those years when we were together, years when they could just be kids without the burdens that would come later.

When I look back on the time in my life when I parented eight children, I marvel and ask myself, "How in the world did you do that?" or maybe a better question, "Why in the world did you do that?" I come up with two answers. As a child, I had never felt wanted, and I hoped I could raise children who never doubted that they were loved by someone. The second is that the result of feeling unloved pushed me to seek approval and I grew up to be an adult who needed to be needed. Both could be true, but finally, I'm grateful that kids are so flexible. Whatever my parenting was or wasn't, all of the kids, with the exception of Joe, have made a life, a life with struggles, for sure, but a life where they have taken risks, made mistakes, loved, and survived. They have done things that brought them grief, but they have done very little to cause grief to others. Not a bad result. Isn't that what life is all about?

Another opportunity at City Hall

In 1964, when I was twenty-eight, friends at Muskegon City Hall called and said there was an opening in the planning department. I applied, took the test, and got the job. I loved working for the city. As I said earlier, working in the public sector was different than working in the private sector because people were focused on service. The office staff did not have a union, but we had the same benefits as those who did. Loyalty was a high priority and if you did your work you were valued. My boss, Bob Lighton, was a family man and he understood my home responsibilities as a single parent.

I stayed in the planning department for five years. I remarried and became the stepmother of five more children, a total of eight counting my three. In 1969, four years into the marriage, I realized we needed a larger income. A big family is expensive, so I looked for a job where I could make more money. Government jobs have a pay scale for every job classification. I was at the top of my scale with only one position available above the one I was in, the city manager's secretary. She would be there for her work lifetime.

I found work as a secretary in the sales department at Anderson Bolling Manufacturing in Spring Lake, a family-owned business started by the senior Mr. Bolling. His son, Warren, was head of sales but he was on medical leave, so I reported to the sales manager, Glenn Eaton. My husband worked in Coopersville and dropped me off for work every day, which meant we saved on gas. I was making more money, and it was a good place to work. Again, there were no opportunities for women beyond office work; there were no women in the shop but, at that time, no one thought there should be. I liked the people I worked with. I was there for a year.

Office work has changed as technology has changed. Today it often involves higher-level decision-making, and more often today, the boss is another woman. Laws now provide recourse if a woman is sexually harassed or treated differently than her male co-workers. I cannot imagine a woman being asked to go home and get high heels, or being fired because she won't attend a Christmas party. In most offices people get their own coffee. Things are better.

In early 1970, Bob Lighton, my old boss from the city planning department, called to tell me there was an opening in the Community Development Department, and that they were doing some exciting work that I might enjoy. My marriage to Clint was never good, but it was beyond bad and I knew I would soon divorce. I was waiting until his three oldest children graduated from high school within the next year and a half. I didn't want to be working in Spring Lake when that happened. This decision was the beginning of an entirely new career path for me, but I didn't know it at the time

Meeting the love of my life

I first met Jose Olivieri in 1955 when I was almost nineteen. He was the driver of the bus that shuttled soldiers from Camp Claybanks to downtown Muskegon where my friend Evelyn and I spent a lot of our social time. Evelyn's most frequent date was Mac, who worked in the motor pool with Jose. I had frequent dates with soldiers too, but had not settled on one in particular. My theory was why limit yourself to one entrée when you have access to a smorgasbord.

Jose was short, five feet, six inches, and had dark hair and warm brown eyes. It was summer; he was tanned and fit. His upper body was muscular, but from the waist down he was skinny. I thought he was shy, and maybe he was, but the real barrier to a conversation was that he spoke Spanish and I spoke English. I glibly said, "Nice to meet you," and moved on, no sparks, so many options. And, I was so young.

The next time I met Jose, in 1964, I was dating his brother-in-law, Clint. Clint and I were at a neighborhood bar, and when we left the car wouldn't start. Clint said, "I'll call Jose. He can fix anything." I was introduced again. I didn't remember the first meeting until later when I realized he had been stationed at Camp Claybanks. By this time, he spoke fluent English. Jose started to work on the car, and it was apparent that he was not particularly happy to be doing so. I didn't know either Jose or Clint well enough to understand why. Later I would know. I just thought that he had worked all day and was probably tired.

In 1965, when I married Clint, Jose was the best man at our wedding. In the six- plus years I was married to Clint, I got to know Jose better, and saw him as a gifted mechanic and a hard worker. We were in-laws in the same family, so our contact was at family gatherings, and he and his wife, Ann, sometimes played cards with us. I knew there were problems in his marriage; he seemed perpetually preoccupied and disapproving of his wife, but we never had a personal conversation, so I didn't know why. Sometimes we would joke about the nutty family we had married into, but those were just passing comments. He was always friendly, and we liked each other as relatives sometimes do.

Jose and Ann separated in 1969, and, in the next year, I saw him once. It was early summer, 1970; Evelyn and I had taken our kids to a skating rink and Jose was there with his kids. We were pleased to see each other, and we chatted pleasantly for a few minutes. He looked relaxed and happier than I remembered him. He had grown a mustache and had sideburns, which were popular at the time; he also had added a little weight and was no longer skinny. He had on a fashionable top coat with the collar turned up, and the warm brown eyes I remembered from the first time I met him were still warm. In fact, when he left the rink I looked at Evelyn and enthusiastically said, "He looks good!" I thought he was attractive, a thought that had not occurred to me before. He was just Jose, my brother-in-law.

Clint had moved out in early June, 1971, and I still lived in the house we had shared. On July thirtieth, a Friday night, I was home alone. My kids were visiting their grandmother in Florida, and young Clint was with his dad. I was going out with a girlfriend, Melanie, that evening and wore a short dress, mini-skirts were in style, and had just fixed my hair and put on makeup when I heard a knock at the front door. It was too early for my friend. I opened the door and Jose was on my front porch. He said he lived about three blocks away, had driven down my street on the way to wherever he was going, saw my car, and on the spur of the moment decided to stop and say hello. I was surprised to see him but pleased too. I asked if he'd like a cup of coffee and invited him in. We drank our coffee and chatted, and he said his kids told him that Clint had moved out and we were divorcing. After a half-hour or so, he said he'd better go; he and the kids were leaving the next morning for a week of camping in Michigan's Upper Peninsula. "Nice to see you," I said. And, indeed, it was.

The following Saturday night, August seventh, without phoning ahead, he stopped by again. Being a reasonably bright woman, I figured he was no longer looking at me as his former sister-in-law. I invited him in for more coffee, and although I was somewhat out of practice, I tried to send signals that I was no longer thinking of him as my brother-in-law--lots of smiling, chatter, and holding eye contact a beat longer than necessary. After an hour or so, he said he guessed he better leave. What? Did he miss my signals? I walked him to the door and we stood on the porch talking. He said he had just bought a new quadraphonic

 eight-track tape player. I knew less than nothing about what a quadraphonic player was, but, giving it one more shot, I was pretty enthusiastic about it. "Oh," I said, "I'd love to hear it." He said, "The Coast Guard Festival is going on in Grand Haven. Would you like to take a ride over and listen to the player?" I said, "That would be fun," but I was thinking, *I thought you'd never ask.*

We drove to Grand Haven, and I listened to Carol King's *Tapestry* and Tony Orlando and Dawn albums in quadraphonic sound the whole way. We had dinner at the BilMar Restaurant overlooking Lake Michigan, and on the way home we stopped at a night club to dance. In between we talked and caught up on each other's life. He talked mostly about a recent visit to his family in Puerto Rico where he was born. As we got closer to home, he asked, "Would you like to stop by my place to see the pictures from my Puerto Rico visit?" I said, "Sure, that would be nice," and I thought, *Oh, baby, now we're getting someplace.* The next day I drove to Pentwater to visit Mom and told her I'd finally met a man I was attracted to who wasn't an alcoholic. We did have a good laugh over that remark. Later he told me that all he thought about while camping with his kids was my legs below that mini skirt. Let's hear it for youthful legs and miniskirts.

I was not at all interested in marriage, nor did we choose to live together. I had three kids to raise, one of Clint's children still living with me, and a lot of debt from the marriage. Jose was trying to rebuild financially after an expensive divorce and worked two jobs to make ends meet. Given our respective responsibilities, we were happy to spend as much time together as possible, and were not concerned about commitment beyond having an exclusive relationship.

We continued that relationship for twelve years. I was your basic couch potato and did not see myself as an outdoor person. Jose loved outdoor adventure. He had snowmobiles, and we spent hours on weekends riding through the woods. His first gift to me was a snowmobile suit, boots, and gloves. He had a camper, and we camped with and without the kids, his and mine. Fortunately, his kids liked me and mine liked him. He joined a four-wheel drive group, and I rode in the passenger seat. Later, we took up cross-country skiing.

Although I was born and raised in Michigan, I never liked the cold. Winter is long, and playing in the snow was something that ended for me when I laid in it on my back, spread my arms and legs, and made an angel figure when I was about eight or ten. As an adult, I drove to everything, went inside where it was warm, got into my car, and drove back to where it was warm. But let's face it, this was a new relationship, he was a handsome guy, and I wanted to impress him. So, when he asked me on a snowmobiling date I threw my shoulders back, lifted my chin, looked him in the eyes, and lied through my teeth. "I'd love to go snowmobiling. It sounds like so much fun. What should I wear?"

We were scheduled to ride on the following weekend with several of his friends who owned snowmobiles, both of us on his sled. We would meet them somewhere in North

Muskegon, travel to Hart, stay overnight, and head back the next day. The answer to what should I wear could be found at a sporting goods store on Ottawa Street. I needed special warm boots, a snowmobile suit, a helmet, and gloves. My suit was dark blue with a red stripe, the helmet was red, and I looked as good as one can look in a snowmobile suit. I was nervous, but I was ready for the big adventure.

At that time, hair pieces that added body to your hair were in style. We were all going out to dinner after the ride, so Saturday morning I got dressed in the suit first and then the boots, fastened the hair piece on my head, and put on my lipstick. A woman has got to look good when impressing a new man. Jose arrived with the snowmobile on a trailer behind the car and we set off to meet the other riders. I noticed that many of the women had their own sleds. I rode behind Jose.

I was introduced, the drivers gathered to talk about the route, a lead rider and one to take the rear position were selected, and we were ready to go. I put the helmet on, carefully so I wouldn't displace the hair piece, slid my hands into my gloves, got on the snowmobile, and put my arms around Jose's waist so I wouldn't fly off.

It wasn't fun. I'd like to say it was, but it was mostly bump, bump, bump. I couldn't see much because I was behind Jose; much of the time we were going fast and I was hanging on tight. The good thing was that the sun was out and the special snowmobile suit, boots, and gloves kept me plenty warm. In fact, I was sweating. That was a surprise. We stopped often to let the laggers catch up, and Jose always thoughtfully asked if I was doing okay and if I liked it. Even though I didn't particularly, of course I smiled my best smile, and said I love it, with enough enthusiasm in my voice that I'm sure he believed me.

We finally reached our destination after what seemed like fifty stops and hours of bump, bump, and more bump. We had a half hour until dinner, and went to our room where

I took off my helmet and realized I was not going to look good. My hair was soaked with perspiration and the hair piece? Let's just say it looked like a dead kitten. What the heck, I was into this being a good sport thing, so I did the best I could with my hair, slapped on some lipstick, and off we went. The lucky thing was that Jose seemed to be as smitten as I was, so I don't think he even noticed.

The trip back on Sunday was mostly uneventful except the guys tried a new trick, new to me anyway. They decided to ride a hill, a steep one. The idea was to go up really fast, make a U-turn, and come back, never letting up on the speed. Up we went, but when we got to the U-turn part, another sled was heading toward us. Jose went higher on the hill to get out of the way, and our sled started to tip to the left. I tried to bend to the right to counter balance, but Jose couldn't hold the sled. He yelled jump off and he did so, I followed, and crawled as fast as I could down the hill. The problem was that the snowmobile was rolling down the hill right behind me. Everyone was yelling, "Get out of the way, move to the side." I looked back and quickly saw what a good idea that would be. I barely escaped being pinned by a very heavy snowmobile. I hoped Jose wouldn't ask me right at that particular moment if I was having fun. Continuing with my good sport attitude, I quickly stood up and said, "I'm fine." I wanted to say, *What the hell did we do that for?*

Jose decided to buy a new and bigger snowmobile, keep the smaller one, and teach me to drive it. It was more fun than riding on the back. My best friend, Evelyn, and her husband also had snowmobiles, and we spent several weekends on our sleds roaming the woods near her family's farm in northern Michigan. I liked best the moments when we stopped in a stand of evergreens laden with snow, plopped down on our backs, held hands, and filled with awe gazed at the million stars visible because there were no city lights. The sled engines were off; there wasn't a sound. Our suits and boots kept us warm no matter how crisp the air. A lovely and romantic time, made even better because I was in love.

I have learned over the years that Jose gets bored if he focuses on one activity too long. Snowmobiling got old. He heard about a group of folks who had formed the Port City Four-Wheel Drive Group and went to a meeting. By this time we had been dating for three or four years, so while I was game to go along, I wasn't as gung-ho as when we started snowmobiling. Jose had a Chevy Blazer, and later he had a souped-up Ford Bronco. The Bronco was brown with white trim, sat high off the ground, had an air scoop on the hood, and drew attention wherever we traveled.

The group members were all couples, the men drove, and the women were passengers. We traveled on two-track trails and sometimes no trail at all, climbed over rocks and fallen trees, forded streams, and did donuts in mud bogs. Sometimes the women drove, but never on the most difficult terrain. The guys got so revved up that giving up the wheel was not something they welcomed. The ride for the passenger was not pleasant. It was necessary to hang onto the grab bar much of the time, and I was thrown from one side to the other, as well as up and down. I found it boring, usually brought a book, and tried to read while bouncing. Jose was a little annoyed because when I'm reading, I'm not paying attention to what's going on. I was supposed to co-pilot and help watch for impediments. *Why?* I thought. *He loves impediments. He doesn't want to avoid them, he wants to conquer them.*

I did enjoy the couples we rode with and we became good friends. We made longer trips to the Upper Peninsula, visited, and enjoyed communal meals. It was a pretty traditional group and the men, who of course were tired from all that fun, visited and drank beer while the women prepared the meal, and then, and this really aggravated me, did the dishes after. I did my part to rally a revolt, but these women were not easily led into revolt. I did manage to irritate the guys.

The memory Jose and I talk about the most is funny in hindsight, but was not so funny at the time. On an Upper Peninsula trip, after a full day of driving, we pulled up to a river with a boat ramp to wash the mud off the car. Jose backed onto the ramp a few feet, and suddenly I realized water was coming in around the shift console. I said, "We're sinking." Jose said, "We can't be," and put his hands over the gear shift to try to stop the water from rising. I was not going to argue about it—we were sinking. The windows were down, it was a warm day, and the roof vent was open. I wanted to be as high up as possible, so I climbed right over Jose, out the roof vent, and headed to shore. I was looking out for me, but I was glad to see he bailed out too. The Bronco sank in nine feet of water, and all you could see was the top of the whip on the back.

Some of the guys had winches on the front of their vehicles. People get stuck in mud and need to get towed, but not many have their vehicles end up at the bottom of a river. Jose dove down, hooked up the winch cable to the front of his car, and one of the guys pulled it out. Meanwhile, we rescued our stuff, including Jose's wallet, which was a miracle. The vehicle, of course, could not be driven. It was towed to a local garage, the engine was dried and the fluids were drained and replaced. They worked to get the water out of the upholstery, but there was no way to get the seats completely dry. We drove home with plastic bags on the seats, cut holes in other plastic bags to put our head and arms through, and wore the bags on our bodies. Jose was not happy with himself. He doesn't like doing things he thinks are dumb, so for the rest of the weekend there was little conversation. It wasn't dumb; it was, indeed, a very short ramp, which no one realized. The Bronco was restored without any problems and ran fine after that. Our relationship survived and we lived to four-wheel again. Eventually, Jose got tired of four-wheeling. This was right around the time we ended our dating relationship in 1983, and went our separate ways.

Moving up instead of on

Each time I moved out of a job and into a new one, it was either because I was pregnant and forced to leave, or I found a better opportunity in work at the same level of responsibility. I either earned more, had better benefits, or more freedom. In 1970, I went to work for the newly formed Community Development Department in the City of Muskegon, actually a spinoff from the planning department. The new department was headed by Joe Knowles, who was charged with implementing three urban renewal projects, one downtown and two in deteriorating neighborhoods on the eastern side of the city. I reported directly to him. He had an executive secretary who worked only for him, and I did the secretarial work for all of the other men in the office. Urban renewal projects were federally funded. As the name suggests, the purpose was to rebuild and sometimes reinvent areas where there were increasing vacancies and a declining tax base.

Each project had a development plan. The downtown plan called for building a mall around individually owned stores and businesses currently occupied, and new stores that would be owned and leased by a mall development company. All would be connected by a common area as is found in all indoor malls. There would also be complementary development downtown including a hotel, parking ramp, and office space. The Marquette neighborhood, the second project area, and home of Muskegon's community college, would be focused on single-family homes and apartment housing for lower-income and middle-class individuals and families. An important goal was for the neighborhood to remain racially balanced. In the third project area, Froebel neighborhood, homes were older and many were beyond repair. Those that were substandard would be removed and the lots sold at affordable prices to private low-income buyers for rebuilding. Each neighborhood would have improved infrastructure, underground wiring, new or spruced up parks, and so on. The men I worked for were to implement the plan, buying and selling property, getting bids from contractors for infrastructure work, and communicating with people in each neighborhood.

One day when I came to work, I found a note Mr. Knowles left on my desk. It said, *"I want you to write a grant to fund rehabilitation of the Freddie Townsend Neighborhood Center in the Froebel neighborhood."* I looked at the note and my mind went blank. I had never written a grant in my life and didn't know where to begin. I approached him with some dread and asked, "Could I talk to you for a minute?" He lifted his eyes from his work, looked at me, nodded his head briefly, and waited. "I've never written a grant and I don't know how to do it," I said. Another pause, and without any expression on his face he said, "Frankly, I'm not interested in what you don't know how to do, figure it out." He went back to work and I went back to my desk to figure it out.

I went to my former boss, Bob Lighton, who had written many grants, and asked how I might get started. He gave me copies of grants he had written and told me how to look for funding sources. Motivated by fear, I wrote the grant, sent it to a funding source suggested by Bob, and, miracle of miracles, it was funded. I had no idea then how unlikely it is to have your first grant funded. I felt competent in a whole new way. My desire to continue learning was sparked.

Mr. Knowles was impressed and offered me a promotion. It was a government organization, so any new job classification and the salary attached had to be presented to and approved by the City Commission. At the same time, my boss was going to present a job offered to a young man who worked for the department summers while in high school. He was eighteen; I was thirty-four. His new position would pay only three hundred dollars yearly less than mine. The City Commission reviewed the job positions and salaries, and they approved his with no comment. In my case, they said there was an unwritten rule that no woman at City Hall can make more than the city manager's secretary. A light bulb went off; not a word was said about creating a job for only three hundred dollars less for a man fifteen years my junior who had never held a full-time job. How could any woman move forward with those attitudes? Mr. Knowles persisted and eventually they approved the position and the salary.

After shedding some tears and ranting to my friends about the unfairness, I realized I had a new job that would allow me to gain new skills and, I hoped, show others that I deserved the higher pay. The promotion put me in closer contact with co-workers who were college graduates, all men, all younger, and all more open to the idea that women were capable of more than they had been allowed to do. Most had gone to college during the 1960s when the second wave of the women's movement had its start. They respected my skills, they encouraged me, and my confidence increased. I dared to dream again about college.

Education, the dream that came true

In September, 1971, at age thirty-five, I took my first college class. I was a single mom, my children were fourteen, eleven, and nine, and I worked full-time. I was scared that I would not be able to keep up with young people right out of high school who were used to studying and sure to be much smarter than I was.

I had always dreamed of college. Why did I wait so long? The seeds for the delay go back a way. When I graduated from high school in Pentwater, Michigan, in 1954, the kind of financial aid and scholarships available today did not exist. I worked from age fourteen and saved some money, but not enough. Dad believed that college would be a waste of money and said I would only get married anyway. I was disappointed, and felt he still resented my decision to live with my mom. Mom did not have access to money of her own. Dad's prediction was right. Three years later I was married and had the first of my three children. The dream of college seemed a long way off. The most I could do was read, read, and read. That was my learning plan.

I applied for and got a small scholarship from the

 Women's Center in nearby Grand Rapids, just enough for one class. I enrolled in a political science class at Muskegon Community College. Like many older students, I discovered that my life experience put me on a par with and, perhaps, gave me an advantage over my much younger college peers. My confidence increased and the dream of a college degree was reignited.

It took seventeen years, one class at a time, while working full-time, raising my children, and volunteering in the community, to get a bachelor of science degree with a major in public administration. In 1988, my three kids attended my graduation ceremony at Grand Valley State University. There were tears of joy on that day. I did it!

The confidence I gained during my years in college led to other accomplishments. I was elected president of our local National Organization for Women chapter, a founder and first executive director of Muskegon's women's center, and a pioneer in Michigan working for women who are survivors of domestic violence and sexual assault. And, in 1977, I was elected to the City Commission, the same governmental body that a few years earlier had decided I could not make more money than the city manager's secretary. In 1990, I earned a master's degree in Public Administration, and from time to time I dream about getting a PhD.

The year that changed my perspective forever

When I dreamed my teenage dreams I was going to graduate from college, work until I married, or marry right after college and work until I had my first baby. Maybe I would go back to work when my children were grown. The magazines and books I read, the stories I saw on television, the messages I got all pointed to marriage and babies as the path to happiness. Never mind that I had plenty of living examples in my family that should have given me some indication that this might not be completely true.

I encountered a few women who were considered career women but for the most part they were unmarried or, if married, they had no children. I didn't know any married women who had a job that could fully support a family. I didn't know any men who didn't, unless they were too old or disabled.

Reality forced me to examine my dreams in my middle years. By the time I was thirty-five, in 1971, I had married two men with serious alcohol problems and divorced both. I had birthed three children and raised five stepchildren. A light bulb went off. I woke up and realized that my best course of action was to stay single until I was absolutely sure that whatever spurred me to make bad choices was fixed.

I had worked at a series of secretarial jobs, quitting some as required when I was pregnant, and others when I found a better financial opportunity. As a single parent responsible for the support of myself and my children, my need for more money became acute. My children's father paid just under eleven hundred dollars yearly in child support, hardly enough to live on. It looked like I'd be working until I died. I had always been a quick learner, a hard worker, and willing to do what needed to be done whether it was in my job description or not. I appreciated a challenge.

1971 was the year I was given an opportunity, met the challenge, and for the first time, was promoted out of the secretarial pool. It didn't happen easily. My boss had to fight for the promotion and the salary that went with it. I was angry and it became clear to me that when it came to opportunity, the playing field was different for women than for men. There were no women in management at any level. Another light bulb went off. I was limited by my gender. No matter how hard I worked or how quickly I learned, unless the entrenched sexist practices of most employers were changed, as a single woman with children to support I would live in poverty with little hope of doing better.

1971 was also the year I overcame my fear and started college. I had been walking through life looking straight ahead, doing what had to be done, surviving difficult marriages, taking care of my children, and showing up for work. I didn't have much time to lift myself above the daily grind to see what was going on in the bigger world. In college classes, for the first time, I was exposed to issues like civil rights for people of color, feminism and the women's movement, poverty and how poverty is dominated by women and people of color, economic power, who had it and who didn't, and what a difference it made. A zillion light bulbs went off.

My first reaction to these exploding light bulbs was to be mightily pissed off. I stayed pissed off for quite a while. That's not fair, I railed. People should not be limited by the color of their skin, their gender, their sexual orientation, their social class. Everyone should have the opportunity to move beyond the artificial barriers that permeate our culture and limit groups of people based on qualities they can do nothing about. I kept hearing my father's voice in my head every time I said something wasn't fair, asking, "*Whoever said life was fair, sweetie?*" No one, I thought, but it sure as heck should be. I had no idea what to do with all the emotion, all the energy emanating from the blazing light bulbs in my head. Mostly people do not react well to a lone, pissed-off woman. Where could I focus all this energy? How could I do something to change the way things were? Gloria Steinem said, *"The truth will set you free, but first it will piss you off."* That was most certainly true for me.

Fortunately, I was able to limit my railing to college class discussions and conversations with friends, women and people of color, who were pretty much as pissed off as I was. Well, that's not exactly true. My kids tell me I did quite a bit of railing at home. But also fortunately, college classes taught me that there were people banding together in organizations and collectively making change. Where were they in Muskegon, Michigan? I wanted to know. No, I *had* to know. It had become an imperative. I had to put that light-bulb energy to work in a productive way. I was driven to get involved.

An education in civil rights

I was raised by a father who was a racist, and I suspect he was also raised by a father who was a racist. My father was a supervisor in the A.C. Spark Plug factory in the early 1940s and some of the people he supervised were black. I can remember him saying, *"The only good nigger is a dead nigger."* He told stories at the dinner table, *"I told those lazy niggers to get off their lazy butts, there* was *work that needed to be done."* He called Jewish people kikes, Italians were dagos, and Hispanics were spics.

As kids we counted to decide who would be first in a game. We said, *"Eenie, meenie, miney, moe, catch a nigger by the toe."* We called brazil nuts *"nigger toes."* When we lived with my grandparents, we had Hispanic and black neighbors. I don't remember ever playing with the children in those families. No one ever said we couldn't, and I'm pretty sure I didn't even connect the word *nigger* with our neighbors.

I was eleven years old and in the sixth grade before I became aware that the way my dad felt about race was wrong. We lived in Detroit and the schools were very crowded. Our desks were wide and we sat two to a seat. My seat partner was Irma. We were friends, playing together at recess and sharing snacks. We sometimes got in trouble for talking during class. One Friday, we made a plan to visit the library together the next day.

I will never forget what happened. Irma came to our house Saturday morning and knocked on the front door. Dad went to the door and Irma asked, "Is Beverly home? We're going to the library together." My dad said, "You aren't going anywhere together," and shut the door. I asked, "Dad, was that Irma? We're seatmates at school. We're going to the library." He turned to me and in an angry voice said. "You're not going anywhere with that nigger and I don't want that girl showing up here again." I started to cry and said, "Daddy, she's my friend," and he said, "White people and niggers are not friends."

I knew there was something terribly wrong with what he was saying. For the first time, I was ashamed of my father and what he said to my friend. I didn't know what I would say to her Monday at school. I knew, though, that I wanted her to continue to be my friend but we would only see each other at school. It felt very unfair but there wasn't any way I could defy my father. Irma and I continued to play at recess, but she never asked me to go anywhere with her again, nor did I ask her.

Sadly, it would be a long time before I had another friend who was black. I lived in white neighborhoods. There were black kids in my classrooms when I attended schools in Flint and Detroit, and we were friendly at school, but afterwards we lived in separate worlds. In Pentwater where I spent my last two high school years, there was only one black family in the entire town. The father in the family sometimes came into the restaurant where I worked. One time when he came in, I waited on a white couple who asked me if we were going to serve *him.* I said, of course. They asked to see my boss. I told her what was going on. She came out of the kitchen, walked up to the white couple, and said she understood they were concerned about whether we are going to serve one of our regular customers. They said they weren't going to eat in a restaurant that served *"people like him."* "Indeed we are going to serve him, and if that is a problem for you, I suggest you go somewhere else for dinner," she said. They stood, walked toward the door, and said loudly that they were *"not eating with any niggers."* My boss went up to the gentleman, who by this time had lowered his head and was staring at the table, and apologized for the behavior of the couple. It made me wish my boss had been there when Irma came to the door.

Until 1970, at age thirty-four, I had never worked in a racially integrated workplace. When I look back on that, I am astounded that I hadn't even noticed. In the City of Muskegon's Community Development Department, a third of the staff was black, including three of the six clerical staff I was a part of. All of us were friends; we had lunch together and pitched in to help each other. One, Jeanette, became a friend with whom I spent social time. We shared our personal stories as friends do.

These friends talked openly about their frustrations, about wanting to get ahead, and ways in which they felt limited. They liked me and began to educate me about the subtle ways in which blacks were treated differently. For example, Joanie, a white clerical worker, was late for work every day. No one ever said anything about it. Ruthie, a black clerical worker, sometimes didn't have enough to do. In order to occupy herself, she read at her desk. I was Joanie and Ruthie's supervisor. Several of the white male employees complained to me that Ruthie was reading at her desk. No one complained about Joanie showing up late. I talked to Jeanette about it and she suggested that, perhaps, black employees were watched more closely than white employees. My solution was to teach Ruthie to read without the office guys seeing it.

My friends liked me enough that they confronted me if I said something that was ignorant. Once I said that I didn't understand what the problem was with race, blacks are just as smart as whites. Paul, a black man I worked with, quietly asked, "Might it even be possible that some blacks are smarter than some whites?" He then asked, "Do you think white people could survive the kind of discrimination faced by blacks from the time of slavery until this very day?" I thought about it. He suggested I needed to get educated. I began to read, think, and observe. I surely did not want to follow in my dad's footsteps. By this time, I knew that his thinking was warped. His attitudes were the attitudes of many whites at that time, and sadly some whites still today.

In 1954, in my first job after high school, I was a secretary in a real estate office. I remember being told that blacks were not to be shown property west of Peck Street, a main street dividing the town. There were no blacks living west of Peck Street. I lived west of Peck Street. In the 1950s and '60s, I was aware that things were changing in our country. In 1955 Rosa Parks, tired after a day's work, refused to give up her seat on the city bus to a white person as required by Montgomery, Alabama, law; she was arrested and the incident set off a bus boycott. I knew about the integration of Central High School in Little Rock, Arkansas; sit-ins at Woolworth's lunch counter in North Carolina in 1960; and the murder of NAACP's field secretary, Medgar Evers, in 1962. In 1963, television news showed civil rights demonstrators terrorized by police dogs released to attack them and knocked down by powerful sprays from fire hoses. That same year I heard Martin Luther King's "I have a Dream" speech, in which he said he *"looked toward the day when his children would be judged by the content of their character and not the color of their skin."* I watched the television news reports about four little black girls killed at Sunday school when a bomb exploded at their church, a popular location for civil rights meetings. I thought all of this was horrific, but in my ignorance I thought it was taking place down south and things weren't so bad in the north.

I knew that President Lyndon Johnson had signed the Civil Rights Act of 1964 prohibiting discrimination based on race, color, religion, or national origin and that the federal government had the power to enforce desegregation. I knew that blacks and some whites were marching from Selma to Montgomery, Alabama, in support of voting rights and that Congress passed the Voting Rights Act of 1965 making it easier for southern blacks to register to vote. There had been literacy tests, poll taxes, and other requirements to restrict black voting. I knew that in 1968 President Johnson added the Fair Housing Act to the 1964 Civil Rights Act, prohibiting discrimination in housing. In 1971, when I worked in the Community Development Department, the Supreme Court upheld busing as a means for achieving integration of public schools.

I heard lots of whites express their fears that their children would be bused into a black neighborhood. I supported all of these laws but I still didn't get it. Again I thought, if I thought of it at all, that the north was much more open and that blacks could get any job they were qualified for. It was just that most didn't have as much education so the jobs they got would, of course, not pay as much. I thought that blacks preferred to segregate themselves and might not necessarily want to go to white schools, but, of course, if they did they should be able to.

Sure, I knew there had been slavery, and while I couldn't imagine the pain of being treated as less than a person, I had no idea what the long-range effect of slavery was in the black community. I had no idea what *white privilege* was or what *institutional racism* was. I knew there was a civil rights movement, but until my friends started my educational process it did not become personal. I had no idea how people right in my own town were limited in myriad ways by their color. I was an eager learner. My heart still hurt over the way my dad treated Irma. Slowly, with help from my friends, my eyes were opened and the very next year I would have an opportunity to work in an organization whose mission was to work to make a difference for people of color who lived in Muskegon. And I would learn that when the lives of any group of people are improved, life improves for us all.

An opportunity to make change in my home town

The United States Congress passed the Civil Rights Act of 1964, and subsequently President Johnson signed Executive Order 11246 requiring equal employment opportunity on federally funded construction projects. Any federally funded contract required affirmative action to ensure racial integration in the work force in every entity contracting with the federal government. Additionally, contractors were responsible to ensure affirmative action by everyone with whom they sub-contracted using federal funds. The Office of Contract Compliance (OFCC) was the federal department charged with enforcement of contract requirements.

All three of the City of Muskegon's urban renewal projects, the work of Muskegon's Community Development Department where I worked, were funded through contracts between the city and the federal government. In fact, the County of Muskegon and other local governmental units in Muskegon County all contracted with the federal government for various projects. They, too, were subject to affirmative action requirements.

According to the 1970 census, minorities were about 12 percent of Muskegon County's population. Local government units, other than Muskegon Heights where the minority population was 90 percent or more, were not integrated. My boss, Joe Knowles, the City of Muskegon's Community Development Director, recognized that his department was not in compliance with the affirmative action requirements in the contracts for which he was responsible.

He connected with Dr. Paul Grunstein of Case Western Reserve University in Cleveland, Ohio, to develop a *home-town plan* to recruit and place qualified minority applicants into the employment process. Joe and Dr. Grunstein approached the top executives in the County of Muskegon and the cities of Muskegon, Muskegon Heights and Norton Shores, and all recommended adoption of the *plan* and funding for implementation to their elected officials.

Federally funded local government contracts primarily involved construction which, in Muskegon as elsewhere, was entirely managed through union apprenticeship and union hiring halls. Union membership was nearly all White and it was clear that racial integration was not their priority. And because that had been the case forever, a major component of the home town plan was to train individuals so they would be ready to move into jobs when they came open.

The national Urban League established the Labor Education and Advancement Project (LEAP) across the country and, to support the *plan* Muskegon's Urban League established a program to train minority individuals to work in the construction trades. It was hoped that unions would hire those who were trained into a kind of pre-apprenticeship role that would eventually lead to full union participation as journeymen. Additionally, Muskegon attracted an affiliate of another national training program, Opportunities Industrialization Center (OIC), whose mission in part was to prepare poor, unemployed, and underemployed individuals for work, and to connect workers to employers. The majority of those trained by OIC were people of color, primarily black.

In 1971, Muskegon's home-town plan partners formed and funded a nonprofit, the Urban Opportunity Development Team to oversee the *plan*. Jerry Lottie, a thirty-five-year-old black man, active in local politics and local issues, well-spoken and highly respected for his calm and effective approach when confronting difficult issues, especially those involving race, was hired to head the team. The Muskegon Board of Education provided office space near the corner of Irwin and Terrace Streets in a building where general education degree requirements (GEDs) were taught. The office was small and held two desks with chairs, filing cabinets, some guest chairs, and maybe a table.

The job was tough from the beginning. Muskegon did not have a robust employment market. The union attitude and, to some degree, local attitudes did not particularly favor integration. Unions were reluctant to share benefits. Integrating unions and construction companies was a complex process. Unions were accustomed to a give-and-take negotiating process, and to the minority community integration was a non-negotiable demand. The black community had been shut out for a long time. There was no evidence that they could depend on the good will of unions or construction companies. Contractors and unions had common interests; both were the agents of present and potential craft journeymen. If minority employment was to increase in the trades, goals had to be agreed to. In a tight labor market, getting agreement on goals was nearly impossible.

All of this was complicated by inconsistent federal policy and sporadic enforcement by the OFCC. Few federal construction programs were shut down for equal employment opportunity violations, so local construction companies and unions had every right to believe there would be no repercussions if they did not comply.

In spite of all the barriers, Mr. Lottie forged ahead. Since the word *team* was part of the organization's title and he was the only employee, he recruited another talented individual to support his efforts and complement his skills, one who had spent the past year getting educated on civil rights issues. I was that person. It was a life-changing experience for me.

If you want to change the world, be ready for those who don't want it changed.

It's pretty heady stuff to have an awakening about any area where you had been at best uninformed and at worst ignorant. Like many people, I have a basic sense that the world ought to be fair, that we all ought to have a level playing field if we are expected to compete, an equal opportunity to be all that we are able to be. I recognize our personal responsibility to acquire the skills we need to get wherever it is we want to go. I realize that we have different abilities and skills, and we must focus our efforts in those  areas where there is a fit between our skills and the work that is to be done. In order to get those skills there must first be an equal educational opportunity, and then once appropriately educated, a barrier-free entry into the work we want to do. The awakening for me was that there are indeed barriers for some in their ability to get an appropriate education and in the ability to use that education in work. Those barriers are often based on characteristics over which individuals have no control, specifically race and gender. There are those people who through some kind of super-human effort can buck all the odds and make it in spite of the barrier. That is darned hard work and it shouldn't be that hard, especially when it's not that hard for everyone.

So, with these new insights, I was excited and energized to have an opportunity to work for change in my own community, to play a small part in helping remove some of those barriers for people of color and women. On some level I thought it might be difficult, but was sure with right on our side we would win out in the long run. Actually, I hoped

195

for the short run. When Jerry Lottie, pictured on the previous page,, approached me to work with him as part of the Urban Opportunity Development Team (UODT), without hesitation I quit my job with the City of Muskegon and jumped on board. He explained we would work to integrate local construction companies and unions that worked on federally funded construction projects, and also help local governmental units that funded our efforts integrate their own workforces.

The first task in a team is to make sure the members are on the same page, and that they communicate well with each other, that each member understands his or her part in reaching organizational goals. It is also the responsibility of each team member to ensure that the work environment is open, friendly, and pleasant. We had a little work to do in that area: no problem with the issue of passion for the cause, just some personal issues to resolve.

One of the first issues was that I was a smoker and Jerry Lottie was not. Our small office, with one window, had no air circulation. In those days people smoked pretty much anywhere they wished. I assumed I could smoke in the office and I did. Mr. Lottie joked that he would be out in the community working, come back into the office, and have to crawl on his knees to his desk because smoke rises to the ceiling and there was only about a three-foot smoke-free space between the floor and the place where the thick cloud of smoke began. Maybe it wasn't that bad, but it was pretty bad. Other than his jokes, bless his "let's go along to get along" attitude when it came to working together, he never asked me to smoke someplace else. Amazing.

Another issue was my recently awakened feminist spirit. In my zest and passion for equality, I could be--that is, I often was--insistent that when talking about equal opportunity we needed to consider the issue of equality for women. Jerry Lottie had been hired to work toward integration of construction companies and unions, hardly a field where people of color were welcome, let alone women.

The idea of adding another layer to an already monumental task must have been less than attractive. But, again, he listened carefully to my rants and never asked me to tone them down. We did sometimes go toe to toe because he was much more traditional in his ideas about women and their place than I was. He was a thoughtful and caring person and above all, fair, so he considered what I had to say and credits me with educating him on women's issues. I know I tested him to the limit, but he always respected my opinion. He says today that I walked around the office singing, *I am woman, hear me roar, in numbers too big to ignore.* Not exactly true, but I was flexing my feminist muscles.

The third issue was determining my role in the team. I think Mr. Lottie envisioned I would be a kind of secretary/receptionist. I envisioned I would be a full partner in organizational activities, that we would discuss strategy, come to an agreement, and move forward each doing our own part. Just like at home, though, practically speaking, it doesn't take a team to do the dishes. In this case, I was the one who knew how to type. To Jerry Lottie's credit he did share strategy and included me in negotiating meetings, and I credit him with giving me an opportunity to move out of a secretarial role and to learn a great deal about the attitudes and practices of construction employers and unions.

As part of the bid process for award of a federally funded construction project, contractors were required to complete a form identifying the racial and gender makeup of their workforce. We analyzed the forms and scheduled an appointment for a meeting, hoping to negotiate a plan to improve employment opportunities for minorities in their company. Since most construction companies in Muskegon County hired their workers through a union, and as stated earlier unions weren't integrated to any degree, consequently, there were few minorities listed on the workforce makeup form. Construction companies, at least in the beginning, felt some pressure to show an effort. One of the less than subtle tactics was for companies to suddenly realize they had several American Indian employees. In fact, the sudden increase in the percentage of American Indians in the construction trades may have been larger than the population of American Indians in the entire county of Muskegon. When we called on construction companies, we had access to the workers. I clearly remember meeting with an individual who had identified on the form as an American Indian and I asked about his heritage. He told me that his boss said, *Indians were the first people to inhabit the country, so it's likely that all of us have some Indian blood.* Clever.

Often in the meetings between Mr. Lottie and the construction company representative, the refrain was *there are no qualified minorities.* Mr. Lottie talked about the work being done by the Urban League to train young men in the construction trades, and asked the company to take them on at a reduced wage and help them gain the additional skills needed to become journeymen. The response most often was *hiring is done through the unions.* When Mr. Lottie talked to the unions, often the response was, *there isn't enough work, opening slots for union membership depends on job availability, of course we're interested in integrating the union, but if there are no jobs it isn't practical.*

Sometimes, a union or construction company representative made the mistake of making a racist remark. Mr. Lottie, who never raised his voice and who always spoke in a deliberate and measured way, would change in an instant. He was never rude but his words were clipped and firm, deliberate and to the point. In far fewer words than he usually used, the offending party got a clear verbal message that what had been said was not okay and would not be tolerated. Their attitude may not have changed, but they did shut up.

I do not know where Jerry Lottie got the strength to keep pushing for change, slowly, methodically, consistently, and despite all evidence that the people with whom he negotiated had no real interest in change and, further, that the governmental units that paid our salaries and the federal government that made the laws had no intention of enforcing change. There was some progress in integrating local government but very little in integrating the construction trades.

Part of our work was to engage with other minority organizations in the community. By this time, I was no longer responsible for clerical functions and we shared a secretary. We were both members of NAACP and the Urban League. I was on the Urban League Board and the board of another newly formed organization, El Centro Latino. Mr. Lottie encouraged me, as part of my work at the UODT, to engage with the Muskegon-Ottawa chapter of the National Organization for Women, formed in 1974.

I left the Urban Opportunity Development Team in June, 1975, to form a brand- new organization, Every Woman's Place, a center for women. The UODT closed when Jerry Lottie was recruited to work as Equal Opportunity Officer for the City of Muskegon. In our new jobs we were able to make changes that we were never really able to make at the UODT but our experiences there gave both of us the credibility for the work that followed.

An activist for women NOW

In 1972, my consciousness had been raised. Former co-workers in the city's Community Development Department, personal experience limiting my advancement based solely on the fact that I was a woman, a job that involved working to advance the civil rights of people of color, college classes where equality was a frequent topic, and an emerging women's movement on the national level were the catalyst. I was ready to get involved. But how and where when almost no one in Muskegon, Michigan, where I lived was talking about women's rights?

There was one exception…Ruth Marcus. Ruth ran for Congress as a Democrat against Guy VanderJagt, the Republican candidate. She identified as a feminist, raised issues of women's equality, and organized a march on Women's Equality Day as part of her campaign. Her campaign was not universally accepted, she was ridiculed, and many portrayed her as not a serious candidate, but there were women in Muskegon who were excited about what she said. That same year, a group of women, most of them in their twenties, started a local chapter of the National Organization for Women (NOW), the largest organization fighting for women's equality in the country, then and now. They included Ottawa County and the organization was named Muskegon-Ottawa NOW. Its mission is

…to take action to bring women into full participation in the mainstream of American society now, exercising all privileges and responsibilities in truly equal partnership with men. NOW seeks to eliminate the roots of sexism in society by actions including lobbying, educating and mobilizing the community on women's rights.

Portia Morrison, the local chapter's first president, was joined in the formation by women who, like me, were just beginning to understand the differences in the way women and men were treated in the workplace and in society in general. Susan Harrison, a popular reporter for our local paper, the *Muskegon Chronicle*, began writing articles about the NOW chapter and its activities. At the time most newspapers, including ours, had women's sections filled with issues thought to be of interest to women, weddings, clothing styles, cooking, and recipes. Susan was young, right out of college where young women framed women's issues as issues of equality. Many news accounts portrayed the women's movement as a group of radical *man-haters*, Susan treated the issues seriously. Women in our community began to pay attention.

I can't imagine this now, but at age thirty-six I thought that because the women whose pictures were shown in articles about the new local NOW chapter were young, I would be uncomfortable and would not fit in. However, I gathered my courage and went to my first meeting, held in the community room of a Muskegon Heights apartment complex. I needed an outlet for the anger that had built as I increasingly recognized the injustices against women in our country based solely on their gender, and how I personally had been affected. I was greeted at the door by Virginia O'Toole Brautigam, a woman who was around my age, and my apprehension immediately eased.

On this night, the discussion topic was sexual harassment in the workplace. Two waitresses who worked in a local hotel restaurant described how they and the women they worked with were treated by some male guests. They said, "Sometimes when we deliver food to a room, the door is answered by a man who thinks it's okay to come to the door naked. They sometimes make crude comments." The women said they were uncomfortable, even fearful that one of these men would go too far. They reported this behavior to their boss and his response was, "Deal with it, I'm sure you've seen naked men before." The women also said that in most of the places they and their sister waitresses had worked, the bosses themselves made suggestive and inappropriate remarks.

They had organized a picket to protest this treatment. They asked for our help, and invited us to walk the picket line with them. NOW members joined them, and increased numbers marching brought more attention to the issue. The news coverage initiated considerable conversation in the community about sexual harassment, particularly among women.

Women began to talk to each other about their own experiences, and I remembered well the unnerving behavior of my boss at Norge. Telling our stories mattered, consciousness was raised; we knew it was wrong and we wanted others to know it was wrong. The restaurant lost business. This caused the owner to agree that he or a male staff member would contact any offending guest and express, politely, the inappropriateness of coming to the door undressed. One of our actions most appreciated by the waitresses was that we took over the picket line completely on Easter Sunday so they could be home with their families. We won their hearts; they won on the issue.

National NOW took positions on a number of issues of importance to women, and the more than one hundred members in our chapter worked locally on the national issues where a majority had the most interest. One hundred women isn't an enormous number, but we made a huge difference. We attended school board meetings demanding the board implement Title IX, equality in women's sports. We joined women who were picketing the Friend of the Court for not enforcing child support orders, carrying signs that said things like, "Children go hungry and the court doesn't care." We confronted judges, asking them to intervene and demand that the Friend of the Court enforce their orders. The judges were not happy, but newspaper and television reporters were there as we marched. We held educational forums on women's health and reproductive freedom, and supported individual women who were filing unequal pay complaints. We worked for political candidates who supported women's equality. We confronted law enforcement and court officials on the handling of domestic violence and sexual assault incidents. Members spoke at community forums. We attended marches in Washington to promote the Equal Rights Amendment (ERA) to the United States Constitution. In an effort to convince the Illinois legislature to put ERA on the ballot, busloads of Michigan NOW members, including women from our chapter, rode to Springfield to stand on street corners asking people to sign petitions.

In 1974, I was elected president of our local NOW chapter. I was on the bus to Springfield. I marched in three different national marches in Washington, D.C. I was almost always on a team of women who approached local officials on various issues of women's equality to negotiate a change in their policy. I walked the picket lines, and I spoke at community forums and college classes. The focus of the Urban Opportunity Development Team where I worked at this time was expanded to include women's equality, and these issues and actions were considered part of my job. They were far more to me, they were deeply personal, and my commitment was, and still is, to ensure that women have full and equal access, that their work, be it in or outside the home, is equally valued to the work men do. I believe women must be free to make their own decisions in every aspect of their life, equally represented in every aspect of society in which they choose to participate, equally paid, and safe both on the street and in their homes.

The women I worked with in NOW are still my closest friends. I liken our friendships to those of men who were in battle together. They call themselves brothers. We call ourselves sisters. We fought together, we were often maligned and called names, we stood up for each other, and we formed consciousness-raising groups and learned together. We shared our stories.

Our work together was fun, particularly when we engaged in what we called *zap* actions: Move in, make your

203

point, and move out. My favorite zap action was taking over the tennis courts at a public park where a men's tennis tournament with cash prizes had been scheduled as part of a community-wide celebration. A group of young women came to us and said they were not allowed to compete in the tournament, which was being held on public property. NOW members showed up and took over the courts an hour before the event. When the men who were to compete and their sponsor showed up, they asked us to leave the court. We refused, saying it was a public court, first come, first served, and we weren't leaving. They were upset. The event sponsor approached us and asked what we hoped to gain. I was spokesperson and told him that these young women wanted an opportunity to play tennis for cash prizes equal to those given to the young men. He agreed and said it was too late this year but he would do it the next year. We asked him if he would be willing to talk to a reporter (who had shown up after we notified the paper that we would be there) so that we could hold him to his promise. He was willing and he did keep his promise. One of the men who confronted us as we took over the courts was an official in the city's parks and recreation department. As we discussed our presence on the court he stood six inches from me, much taller and bigger, and he was angry, so angry that his lip quivered and he shook as he insisted we get off the court. I could see he was having difficulty controlling his anger. It was the first time I realized that standing up for what you believe in is a brave and powerful thing to do.

My place at Every Woman's Place

In early 1975, as Muskegon-Ottawa NOW chapter president, I was invited by Julia Sands, a local real estate sales person interested in women's issues, to join a women's taskforce to establish a women's center in Muskegon. Centers had recently formed in Grand Rapids, Ann Arbor, and Kalamazoo. We understood we could, perhaps, apply for start-up money from federal grant funds allocated to the County of Muskegon by the federal government under the Comprehensive Employment and Training Act (C.E.T.A.). Grant requirements were broad, and the focus was job creation.

We named our proposed women's center Every Woman's Place, chosen to reflect our desire to reach out to any woman who needed support or action. Another committee member, Sue Ashby, and I wrote the request for funding, and on the day our proposal was scheduled for action by the county commission, the taskforce packed the room with women supporters, Democrats, Republicans, black, Hispanic, white, and native. Our grant was approved, four months' funding, $13,000, to pay for five positions and facility costs. We were thrilled and a little bit overwhelmed. The group advertised for an executive director, and I wanted the job.

I had some things going for me. I had personal experience with domestic violence, I was president of a highly visible women's equality organization, and I was beginning to be known as someone who could get things done. Applying for this job may have been one of the bravest things I've done. I was a single parent with three children to support, and I had a safe job with benefits including health insurance. Four months' funding and responsibility for finding the money to keep the center going was scary, but sometimes you know that you absolutely have to do something no matter the personal risk. For me, this was one of those times.

In order to apply I was required to resign from the committee. The group set up a separate search committee and included several women of color; there were none on the original taskforce. I knew these women, and worked with them on issues of equality for people of color at my current job with the Urban Opportunity Development Team. I had proven myself a committed activist on equal rights. But, the other women on the search committee were more traditional. They supported women's issues but they were not activists. In fact, I was probably a little too activist for some of them. Complicating my chances, I did not yet have a college degree, and the woman who was my competition for the job had a master's degree in counseling. The discussion, I was told, centered on activism versus education, with the women of color supporting activism. My primary supporters were Rillastine Wilkins, mayor of Muskegon Heights, and Jane Gonzalez, a Muskegon County commissioner. They, and hopefully I, were convincing and I got the job.

I recruited four other women to work with me: Sue Ashby, Addie Randall, Nancy Thompson, and Mary Johnson. Three of the four were women of color. If we were going to serve every woman, they had to be represented on our staff. We rented offices in a building on Terrace Street directly across from City Hall, and were given free office furniture-- large, ugly green metal desks, government surplus. Telephones were installed, we had a small office supplies budget, and we were ready to open the doors. Susan Harrison interviewed us, a photographer took our picture, and an article appeared in the *Muskegon Chronicle* telling the world we were there to help women. Our first day on the job we looked at each other and one of us asked, *"What if no one shows up?"* Not to worry, in short order we were overwhelmed by women calling and walking in our door asking for help with things that were happening to them at work and at home.

By the end of the first four months, the county had funded us again and we had attracted community donations.

In the beginning we went to great lengths to deal with every issue a woman brought us, either through referral to another agency or by figuring out a way to help. We counseled women who were getting a divorce and had no idea what their family resources were. We listened to domestic violence and rape survivors, tried to find shelter for them, assured them that they were not to blame, and guided them through the criminal justice system if they wished to pursue charges. I took women home with me when we couldn't find any other shelter. We spoke out at every opportunity about the issues confronting women, particularly domestic violence and sexual assault. We helped women find employment and/or training. The variety of issues went way beyond what we imagined when we opened the doors. Each of us dealt directly with clients, there were so many. In addition, I did the executive chores, accounting and fundraising, managed staff, developed new programs, and represented the agency to the community. The stress was incredible, but the difference we were making was also incredible.

Eventually, the county, for one dollar, deeded us a house on Clinton Street and we had a shelter. There was no longer a need to take women and their children home. After we had the experience of a shelter, the volunteer board at the local teen runaway program, Webster House, asked us to take on their shelter. They were unable to sustain their greatly needed services. We now had two shelters, one for women and one for teens.

Federal funding for domestic violence and for job preparation became available, but it took some time before United Way funded us. We were considered too radical. We had wide support from women, but most community funding decisions were made by men. We continued to pack the house when we asked for funding support, and eventually they could not ignore either the need for specialized services for women or the support we enjoyed in the community. Today, with nearly forty years of helping and supporting women,

Every Woman's Place/Webster House is an accepted and respected community helping organization.

My experience in NOW taught me to look at the issues confronting women from a systems change point of view. That is, if we continued to focus only on the problems of each woman who walked in the door, we would only change the circumstances of that particular woman. We had to work to change those community systems whose practices perpetuated the inappropriate and unequal treatment of women. That meant we must educate police, prosecutors, judges, attorneys, teachers, ministers, anyone who could affect change to benefit women in our community; help them understand the dynamics of those situations that hurt women; and figure out a better way to deal with the issues that caused women harm.

I am still a NOW member, and I will be until I can no longer write a check for membership. The women in NOW, and at Every Woman's Place, were and are part of a national movement to change the world for women, to keep them safe, to ensure opportunity so they can support themselves and use their gifts as fully as they wish. I'm proud to have been part of this work, and count it as my second most important legacy, right after my children and grandchild.

Love, support, and commitment to home town

Muskegon County, Michigan, is home. I moved there after high school and my children were born and raised there. I lived in the City of Muskegon for thirty years. Even though I travel to warm places seven months of the year, like homing pigeons Jose and I return to Muskegon County every year. Two of my children still live there. It's a lovely place, located on the edge of Lake Michigan, about halfway up the western side of the Lower Peninsula. It is sprinkled with small lakes in every direction, and in the fall, when the leaves change, no place is prettier.

Muskegon is the name of the river that runs through the county; named by the Chippewa/Ojibwa Indians, it means *river of the marshes.* It was settled by French fur trappers in the 1600s, and at the turn of the twentieth century its white pine forests attracted the lumbering industry. More than forty-seven sawmills dotted Muskegon Lake, and lumber barons built large Victorian houses, some of which have been restored and are part of what is now known as the downtown historic district. Our library, art museum, and a downtown park are named for Charles Hackley, Muskegon's most prominent and philanthropic lumber baron. Without a reforestation plan, the trees disappeared and so did the lumber barons.

For much of the twentieth century, Muskegon 's industry was diverse and included paper, cement, chemical, engines, motors, bowling equipment, and auto-related manufacturing. Michigan was, and some would say still is, the automobile capital of the country. For perhaps the last forty years, the state and Muskegon have suffered difficult times as the auto industry moved its operations to other states where labor was cheaper, creating one of the highest unemployment rates in the nation. Muskegon's per capita income today is much lower than Grand Rapids, Michigan, a larger city to the southeast with more diverse economic opportunities.

Muskegon County is comprised of seven cities, four villages, sixteen townships, and four unincorporated communities. Each has its own governing body, as does the county itself. The county government oversees some joint services, particularly for the townships, villages, and unincorporated communities, but the cities, five of which are contiguous, have their own police, fire, street maintenance, and garbage pickup. Muskegon and Muskegon Heights provide water to the other governmental units, and wastewater is handled by the county, as is the emergency call system, 911. This proliferation of governmental units is costly and inefficient, but it continues because those who live in each community strongly identify with that community. The 2010 U.S Census indicates the population is just over 172,000; it is 77 percent white, 15 percent black, and 5 percent Hispanic. Eighteen percent live below the poverty line. We are a working-class community with only 18 percent holding a bachelor's degree or higher.

Community leaders have worked hard to diversify industry and to promote travel to our beautiful beaches. In spite of difficulties, those who continue to live there love Muskegon, and that includes me. We may be the first to criticize but we are also fiercely loyal. I think Muskegon is exactly the right size. It's big enough so everyone doesn't know your business, and small enough so that people can get involved and make a difference if they choose.

In my lifetime Muskegon has had two levels of leadership. In the early 1900s, when industry was locally owned and booming, those who were looked to for leadership were men with money and influence, often local business owners. In the 1960s and '70s, local industries were purchased by national companies; leaders were brought in from other places and did not have the same commitment to Muskegon. Simultaneously, because of changes throughout the country, working-class individuals, women, and people of color began to see leadership as a possibility for themselves.

Certainly when I was struggling in and out of marriage, trying to raise children mostly by myself, I had little thought of community involvement beyond being a room mother in my children's school. That changed in the mid-1970s. My work became more public, and I became a voice for women. The women's movement was in the news, and people knew my name. I had a constituency.

My first community involvement outside of work was to join the Muskegon County Child Abuse Council board. The organization was in its infancy and struggling, and two members asked if I would join the board and become its chairperson. It was not difficult to expand my passion for ending domestic violence to a passion for ending child abuse. I helped recruit an executive director and supported her until the council was on its feet and thriving.

Next, I was recruited to the board of El Centro Latino, an organization whose mission was to support and advance Hispanic people in our community. That organization was also in trouble. Most board members believed the executive director was not doing his job. Connections are close in the Hispanic community, and it's difficult to stand up without a lot of criticism. After the board established that the complaints were justified, I helped members set performance expectations which subsequently the director refused to meet; he resigned and was then replaced.

Community leaders began to see me as someone who was not afraid to take on tough issues. I was asked to join the Urban League of Greater Muskegon, a struggling organization with yet another problem executive, and a board that was afraid to confront problems. The board began to insist on appropriate structure, he left, and we recruited a new leader.

In 1977, two years after Every Woman's Place was formed, I was asked to run for the Muskegon City Commission. Those who asked said it was time for some new blood and that they would help with my campaign. I didn't have to think about it for long. I remembered well that this body, although not the people currently serving, refused to support my boss's request to promote me out of the secretarial pool because they believed no woman could aspire to any job higher than that of secretary to the city manager. I thought if I could be elected it would be the most productive kind of vindication.

It's common practice today to go door to door asking for votes if you're running for office, but it wasn't in 1977. I chose a hard-working campaign manager, Althea Stevens, and well-known campaign treasurers Jim and Jackie Fisher and formed an election committee. These were people experienced in working to get others elected. They helped me raise money and they gave me advice. They did research and told me that campaigns were won in the three districts on the west side of Muskegon and my efforts should be concentrated there.

Nearly every day for months I knocked on doors. This was an exceptional experience. Not everyone welcomes strangers at their door. A decision has to be made about how badly you want a vote when you are greeted by a very large growling dog. People, especially men, are not always careful about what they're wearing and I evidently interrupted several wrapped in a towel right after their shower. Once I broke my bra strap and needed a pin and more than once I needed a restroom. Fortunately, I was able to find people I knew on my route. Some listened attentively when I talked about why I was at their door, others cut me off quickly and said they weren't interested. Most took my brochure.

In November, another newcomer, Terry MacAllister, and I won the election. We ousted two of the three incumbents. I was the top vote-getter, a heady experience. I served four years on the City Commission. During my term much of our work was concentrated on two of the major urban renewal projects I spoke of earlier, reinventing the Froebel neighborhood and the downtown mall. While we helped set the groundwork, only now, thirty-five years later, is the neighborhood showing some promise and new housing development. Downtown enjoyed success for a while, but eventually, following the trend in most cities, a suburban mall was built and the downtown mall closed. Slowly, a new and very different downtown is emerging. It will be a combination of living, entertainment, and business spaces.

I liked serving on the City Commission even though progress takes years and in my short time there was no substantive change. There was, however, a major event that ended my political career. A city police officer shot and killed a black man. The man who was killed had been sitting with friends in a car parked outside a local store. When they pulled away, a police car followed them. The men panicked and sped away to try to elude the police. Trapped, they jumped out of the car, and the police officers jumped out and shot and killed the driver. The driver was unarmed.

City commission members and almost all of the police officers, in fact, most of the city employees, were white. The black community was understandably angry and demanded that the officer be charged. This was the second unarmed black person this officer had shot. The first was a young man who had broken into the high school. Fortunately, he lived. I worked for many years in the black community, and leaders looked to me for action. I moved the officer be suspended. My motion was supported by another member who did it just to get the motion to a vote, and it did not pass.

The meeting where this issue was confronted was frightening. Half the room was packed with policemen from all over the state, each carrying a gun and there to support their brother officer. The other half was filled with black people who lived in the community and were angry that another young black man had been shot. Tension was high. When the motion failed, I suggested that race relations training be mandated for all city police officers. I believed then, and I still do, that white officers react differently when confronting someone who is black. I believe that they were much more likely to fear violence from blacks, and that fear was the root of the overreaction. This suggestion did not pass. There was no violence at the meeting, but the black community was unsettled and unhappy. Although today police officers are more aware and work harder to gain trust in the black community, there are still issues of trust.

I paid a price. At first it was only hate calls to my home. The phone rang frequently, I picked up and heard an anonymous voice say, *"nigger lover."* I began to experience small acts of vandalism. The police and firefighters organized, recruited a candidate, backed him, and worked against me in the primary election when most voters were white. When I won four years earlier, friends held a big party to celebrate. The night I lost I sat in my home talking to a reporter from the local paper. A few close friends stopped by.

Later, a newspaper photographer snapped a picture that made the next day's front page, an image that is stuck in my memory. I wore a red, white, and blue striped dress, a victory dress. I sat on the couch alone, my shoes off, one leg tucked under me. I looked like I felt: sad, numb, abandoned. It took awhile to recover. It's painful to lose. It's a blow to your ego, and perhaps especially hard for me, a woman who still struggled with issues of abandonment. I don't mean to sound like Pollyanna, but in retrospect it was a wonderful lesson. I no longer measure myself in terms of what I do, position or rank. I have learned to measure myself by whether I am living my own values; I am happier, and my life works better that way. But that night, I was sad.

I continued to be active in the community, mostly on nonprofit and local government boards. My friend, Rillastine Wilkins, asked me to again take a leadership role in the local Urban League. A long-time director left and the organization was in debt. She had been an excellent leader, but race relations were no longer a priority for funders. There had been changes during the civil rights movement; many problems remained but less money was directed at solving them. I worked to rebuild the board by bringing in strong leaders, and we hired a young, energetic executive. We established a plan focusing mostly on training and development that would lead to jobs because that's what the funders would pay for. The programs established by the new board and executive worked for a while, but eventually with too little money flowing in, the organization became difficult to maintain. Interest waned in support and funding for the Urban League and for other organization's focused on improved opportunities for people of color. The executive director moved on, volunteers tried to continue the work, but eventually the doors closed. This has been a pattern across the country.

I served on the Muskegon City housing commission, the zoning board of appeals, and another housing committee staffed by the Muskegon Planning Department. In 1984, I left Muskegon and moved to the east side of the state. I focused on finishing college, my career, and my faith.

I remember my local political career fondly. I formed strong relationships with Marguerite Holcomb, the woman who was mayor and with Terry MacAllister, the man who ran at the same time I did. At the same time, I recognize that I do not have what it takes to be a politician. It's impossible for me to not speak out when I believe a wrong has been done. I understand the importance of building support before you speak if you expect to get reelected, but I just don't have the patience to stand by quietly while the support is building. That's okay. Politicians are not highly respected in the early twenty-first century. I am grateful for all I learned, and the lifetime experience of our annual trips to National League of Cities conferences in Washington, D.C. Each year the President of the United States attended the opening ceremony. I watched as the secret service prepared for his arrival, the band played "Hail to the Chief," and Jimmy Carter walked in.

In the third year of my service, my fellow commissioners chose me as vice-mayor, serving with Marguerite, the city's first woman mayor. I was the second woman ever elected to the city commission, and this was the first time, and so far the last, that women held both the mayor and vice-mayor positions. I participated in two mayor's exchange days where I became honorary vice-mayor of Port Huron and of Saginaw while their mayor and vice-mayor came to Muskegon. Both were a fun learning experience.

I helped shake things up a bit, which was the reason those first folks approached me to run. We fired the city manager within the first year I was elected, and three of us worked to fire the man the majority had appointed to replace him. We liked the new guy, but we believed the city needed a more aggressive leader. He was good at keeping his commission constituency close, and we were never successful in our attempts. To his credit, he never engaged in retaliatory behavior, so maybe we were wrong and he was the right guy.

I am in Muskegon for such a short time each year now that there is little time for community volunteering. I worked hard to get a friend, Marcia Hovey-Wright, elected state representative in summer of 2010. I went door to door on her behalf, did office work, and made phone calls, and she won. The time comes when there are new, younger people who take on community work. I've not been active in Muskegon for the last ten years. I'm happy to let it go, to do the grunt work, and let others take the lead. I take life more slowly. I play more.

I will always love Muskegon. I continue to vote here because I will always want Muskegon to succeed and flourish and have the best possible leadership. While I'm there I look for little ways to continue my commitment to my hometown. I subscribe to the local paper. I give to local charities. I shop at local businesses. Maybe someday I'll live there fulltime, but even if not, my heart will still belong to Muskegon, my hometown.

An empty nest and bringing more kids into my life

Julie, my youngest child, left for college in 1980. I had been a mother of my own three and five others for twenty-three years, and the mother of teenagers for the last fifteen. They were trying years, they were fun years, and they were years that gave my life structure and purpose. I was not what might be thought of as a traditional mother. I had a career, I was a community activist, I had friendships that were important to me, and I was in a relationship. With so much busyness, it never occurred to me that there would be an empty place in my life when the children left. In fact, it was pretty stressful during their teen years when they were pushing limits, and I was looking forward to living alone...something I had never done.

But, I had forgotten how much I like kids and what they add to life. The first set of *special* kids to come into my life after my own kids went off on their own were the Menning kids...Matthew, Rachel and Rebekah. They lived with their parents, Bruce and Vicky, directly behind the house where I rented an apartment in 1980. Their dad was the minister at an inner city church where Every Woman's Place opened their child care center, Every Child's Place. I became friends with their Mom at the DeColores weekend when I made my Cursillo. I don't remember how we started spending time together but it became a pattern that we would go out to eat every month or so. I let them eat the junk food their parents would have frowned at, and they made me laugh. For example, once while driving home from dinner out, the kids decided that whenever we had to stop next to another car we would make a funny face and freeze in place. We laughed uproariously at each other and were delighted that the people in cars next to us might think we were goofy. Silly stuff, but everybody needs silly stuff, even grownups.

And then I started giving other close women friends with younger children a break from motherhood and took their kids for sleepovers. Leah and Eric Ruth and Christopher and Elisabeth Altman were favorites. Leah and Eric's mom, Liz O'Hara, and Christopher and Elisabeth's mom, Jane Cirona were close friends and in my support group. I rented movies and stocked up on junk food. They stayed up as late as they wished and I got to be silly. On one weekend with Leah and Eric we must have watched the movie *Ferris Bueller's Day Off* at least three times. These kids did not have grandparents nearby so I was an honorary grandma, a great privilege.

In 1987, I became Austin Jabour's grandmother. My son, Brian, was dating and later married Austin's mother, Donna. Austin was a year old. He was an active, never-sit-still, little blond guy, as cute as he could be. I traveled to Georgia where he lived and he spent a week at a time with me in Michigan. I drove halfway to Georgia where his parents met me and handed him over. He was a joy. His visits continued until he was sixteen, and as is true of most kids, he wanted to be where his friends were. I continued to visit him in Georgia.

A special note about one of the most special of my special kids…sometime in the early 1990s, Tynesia Pittman came into my life. Ty lived with her grandmother, Jeanette, who worked with me at the Association for the Blind. All of us at work adopted Ty one Christmas and I stayed adopted. We went shopping for school clothes, and she came for weekends when I lived in Michigan and visited me when I lived in Chicago. When she took driver's training I let her use my car. She loved Red Lobster and I took her there often. At age twelve, Ty was diagnosed with lupus. The disease affected her skin, leaving dark smudges on her cheeks, and I took her for a makeup session so she could learn to cover the marks that bothered her. Eventually, her kidneys failed and she required dialysis. Even with her illness she graduated high school with honors. I visited her when she was in the hospital, so sick that we weren't sure she would make it. She was the bravest child I ever met. Once, when she was in the hospital, she asked me to advocate for her with the nurse. I explained to the nurse what Ty had said she needed. The nurse said, "Who are you?" Before I could open my mouth Ty said, "She's my white grandma, that's who she is." It made me laugh and I was honored that she thought of me as grandma. She had big dreams; she wanted to work with children, wanted to love and be loved. The dialysis three times weekly made it impossible for her to work. But, after a long time, she did find a man who loved her and she loved him back. Ty went for dialysis one day and never came home. She had lived longer than many young people with lupus, into her early thirties. Our friendship started because I wanted to make a difference in her life, but it turns out she made a difference in mine.

In 1996, my one and only biological grandchild Tessa was born. She, too, lives in Georgia, and I visited her or she visited me at least three, and sometimes four, times each year. We have been together on each of her birthdays. She was a delightful little girl, actively engaged in sports from the time she was four years old. I have been to countless soccer games, and watched her golf and play basketball, bowl and rollerblade.

After Brian's divorce, he dated Felicia Walters, who had two children, Jessica and Phillip. Like Ty, they are honorary grandchildren. Phillip and Tessa are the same age so when I visited Georgia I took them both to movies, out to eat, bowling, skating, whatever they decided they wanted to do. Phillip is nineteen now and still calls me grandma.

My daughter, Julie, married Brian Linstrom and his daughter, Melissa, began to call me grandma. Today, Julie is no longer married to Brian, Melissa is married with two children, and she still calls me grandma.

Jose's four children have been in my life since we started dating. Laura, Jose, Jr., Victor and Alicia ranged in age from five to thirteen then. I often went along when Jose picked them up on his visitation weekends. We went snowmobiling, four-wheeling, out to the movies, and just hung around the house. My children and his got along well together. Now that Jose and I are married, I get to be grandma to his grandchildren, Joe, Jade, and Jill Mainwaring; Jeffrey, Tiffiny, Troy, and Chayton Olivieri; and Shelby and Trevor Robinson. And so far, there are six great-grandchildren.

As a young girl I did very little babysitting. I wasn't particularly interested in children. It was not until I had the experience of mothering my own that I realized that while there is responsibility in caring for children, there is something else they offer, something that was especially important to me given my childhood: unconditional acceptance. As long as kids know that you genuinely like and appreciate them, they like and appreciate you back. They accept you for who you are, something they don't do as easily with their parents. If you are silly, they will be silly with you. If you want to play, they will play with you. You never appear foolish to little kids.

I am proud to say that all of those kids, sadly except for Jose, Jr. who died in his forties, and Ty, are still part of my life. They live in various places around the country, and whenever I am geographically close to one of them I visit. I am included in weddings and baby showers; I keep track of events in their life. Most of them are Facebook friends, so I keep up with what they do. They are an important part of my life and I know, because they all have told me, that our time together in their childhood was special to them. Whatever I was able to give to them came back to me many times over.

A perfect grandchild

On Friday, March 25, 1994, I witnessed a miracle, firsthand, up close, and very, very personal. My granddaughter, Tessa Brianna Geyer, came into the world at 9:30 a.m. Other than that of my own children, I had never before witnessed a birth and this wasn't just any birth. This was the birth of the only biological grandchild I would have.

I went into the delivery room, invited by Tessa's mother, Donna, and her father, my son Brian, with a camera determined to capture this incredible moment. It was just the three of us, the doctor, and the nurses. Brian stood by Donna, holding her hand and talking her through her labor; she had an epidural so her pain was reduced and she was awake and aware. This was her second child, so she knew what to expect and was as relaxed as one can be while in labor. Her son, Austin, had been born eight years earlier and a neighbor was caring for him while we awaited his sister's birth.

I stood off to the side until the doctor said he could see the baby's head. I was so excited. I wanted to meet this new little person. I loved her already and I didn't even know she was a her. At the doctor's words I moved to the foot of the birthing table where I could actually see the baby leave the womb and come into the world. I was snapping pictures every minute or so, probably with flash. After a few snaps, Donna politely asked me if I would mind moving up to her other side and stop taking pictures until the baby was born. She was far more polite than I would have been. I had totally forgotten there was a person birthing this baby. I was all about the baby — rude, to say the least.

Finally, with some guidance from the doctor, there she was with a head of dark hair and a healthy cry. It's not easy to come out of the warmth into the chill of a hospital delivery room. The doctor announced it was a girl. Daddy and Mommy had big smiles. Perfect. Now they had one of each kind. The doctor placed the baby, soon to be named Tessa, onto her mommy's tummy. He handed daddy the scissors and he cut the umbilical cord. She was a separate person, connected to her parents only by love. It was written all over their faces. Dad had that kind of goofy smile he still gets in those special moments in Tessa's life. Mom checked to make sure she had all her toes and fingers and she looked a little goofy over this baby, too.

The nurses took Tessa and put her on the scale. She weighed seven pounds, nine ounces. They cleaned her up, wrapped her in a blanket, and handed her back to her mother. We all stood over her and stared and cooed. I could hardly wait to hold her and I finally got my turn. After awhile, Tessa was taken off to the nursery, and her mother was taken to a room and freshened up. Then Tessa was brought back and we all gathered round. By that time, Tessa's other grandma, Janet, had arrived. She too fell in love.

Someone went home to get Austin and bring him in to meet his sister; maybe it was me, I don't remember, but it seems likely. The hospital gave him a button to pin on his chest that said *I'm the big brother.* He wanted to hold Tessa and he did. I think Donna and Tessa stayed in the hospital two nights, and then came home to their house on Park Chase in the Jones Creek subdivision of Augusta, Georgia. Austin and Brian had installed a wooden stork on the lawn announcing her arrival to the neighbors.

Tessa's room was ready for her. Her crib, made up with decorated sheets, was along one wall. Next to the crib was a white rocking chair, a gift from me, and maybe more for me than for her. I could hardly wait to hold and rock her. On the other side of the room were a changing table and a basket for dirty diapers. The shelf below the changing table had baby powder, diaper salve, clean diapers, changing pads, and all the other supplies. Her closet would soon be filled with cute little girl outfits, and a chest of drawers held sleepers, blankets, little undershirts, and more. This was a fully stocked baby's room. All of the bedrooms were on the second floor.

Mom and dad's room was right next door and brother was across the hall in a room with bunk beds. I slept in the bottom one during the week I stayed to help out.

My favorite time was the middle of the night when I got up and had a chance to rock Tessa back to sleep. I loved the feeling of her warm little body, held in the crook of my arm while she drank from her bottle. I looked into her face and quietly sang to her as I rocked, the same songs I sang to her daddy and that millions of parents have sung to their children and grandchildren: "Rock-a-bye Baby," and "Lullaby and Goodnight." I stopped the feeding every few minutes to burp her. She was warm and moist, making little snuffling noises and smelling of baby powder, and I loved snuggling her up to my shoulder, patting and rubbing her back. After she fell asleep I put her back into her bed, on her side with a kind of brace behind her especially made to keep her in that position. I gently pushed the mattress up and down to continue the rocking motion because she woke up slightly when I put her in the bed. She quickly settled in. She was not a baby who cried a lot.

The first several years of her life I visited her three or four times a year. Donna was attending college and I got Tessa all to myself while she was gone. She was very generous about letting me take care of Tessa while I was there. Her dad always got her up in the morning so he could have

some time with her before work. Never did a little girl have a dad who loved her more than Brian loved Tessa. When I was there, I took over when he left. I got Austin up for school and then Tessa and I played. Donna got a rare chance to sleep in.

I bought Tessa's first stroller. Unfortunately, I also ran over it when it was left behind the car in the garage. I bought her a plastic garden toy that she could crawl in and out of, a turtle sandbox, a Barbie car she could drive, and a walker that she could hang onto before she could walk on her own. I was there when she took her first steps. Her brother loved to roller blade and she was very excited when she got her first pair. I bought her a baby doll and Barbie dolls; feminist that I am, I don't approve of Barbies, but I wanted her to decide whether she liked them. She really never played much with dolls. She liked the roller blades more.

Austin loved Tessa from the beginning. He was eight when she was born, and when she got old enough to respond, he loved to tickle her and make her giggle. Sometimes he was rough with her but Tessa never seemed to mind. She may have had every toy available, I'm not sure. Her mother, who liked clothes and could make inexpensive clothes look expensive in the way she accessorized, made sure her little girl was a well-dressed baby. That good taste eventually was passed to Tessa. Her closet is packed with clothes and she has too many shoes to count. There is little she likes better than shopping.

One of the highlights of Tessa's day when she was a toddler was when it was time for her daddy to come home. She stood on her tiptoes by the windows of the front room closest to the driveway and peeked out. She fairly danced when she spotted his car. He said hi to Donna and whoever else was home, and immediately came to Tessa, picked her up, and started talking to her.

Sadly, Tessa's parents divorced when she was five. Donna moved just a few blocks away, and whatever the problems between them, it never affected their parenting of Tessa. Tessa had a room and clothes and toys at both houses. She decided where she would stay and when. Brian saw her nearly every day.

Because Tessa's parents put her first, they always lived close to each other, and Tessa has been able to attend daycare, elementary, middle, and high schools all in the Evans school district. Brian started teaching math to Tessa when she was three or four. She could add and subtract by the time she went to school. Math was easy for her, but it never became her favorite subject. She was good at sports, beginning with T-Ball before she started school. She played soccer on a traveling team from the age of five or six and continued to play on her school team through high school. Later, she played on the high school basketball and golf teams. She was the only girl on the golf team. Her favorite always was soccer. She liked being part of a team. In high school, even though she was better than many of her teammates and a good scorer, she frequently passed the ball to give others a chance to score. She went in to recover if they failed. She was a natural at golf and her dad, who also plays golf, really hoped she would continue. Girls who are good at golf get great scholarship opportunities for college, but her heart was not in it. Golf is a sport where you basically perform alone. She wanted to play with a team.

At maybe age eleven or twelve, Tessa decided to move in with her dad. He was living on Hammond's Ferry Road in the Bobby Jones subdivision, about six blocks from the house they lived in when Tessa was born. His house had seven bedrooms and five and a half baths, lots of space for two people. Tessa's room was on the first floor. As a teenager, she loved to sleep in. Getting her up for school was more than difficult. She's definitely a night person and would stay up playing with her computer or texting on her phone until midnight or later. Once, when I was visiting, I went to her room to wake her and started singing, "Rise and shine and give God the glory, glory." She covered her head and moaned. I went in every few minutes to try to get her up. She asked me to let her stay home because she was so tired. I said I couldn't do that but she could call her dad. She got up, threw her phone across the room, stomped into the bathroom, and got ready for school. That is the only time I have seen this dear girl angry. I was shocked, but night people do not like mornings.

In 1997, when Tessa was three, Jose and I bought a house in Florida. Instead of traveling to her on Thanksgiving, the family came to us. After I retired and we started traveling, and Tessa was into her teens, my time with Tessa and her dad changed to twice a year. Like most teens, hanging out with her friends was important to her. I spent every birthday with her, and she and her dad came to Muskegon for a week in the summer. Sometimes she stayed longer and Brian and I met halfway so he could take her home.

Tessa's family liked to go out to eat. She was comfortable in restaurants from a very young age, but she also  loved it when her grandma cooked. When I visited for her birthday I stayed a week and cooked for her every night except on her birthday. She especially loved my sausage fajitas, lasagna, and any dessert I felt like making. On her birthday, I treat Tessa, her mom and dad, brother Austin, and often her Grandma Janet to dinner. Tessa chooses the restaurant. Her dad carefully selects a sentimental, to my daughter, birthday card, and both of them tear up when she reads it. She adores her dad, picks out the same kind of card on his birthday, and they get teary again.

I've watched her grow in size and in every other way, and I have loved her in every phase. She was an outgoing, happy toddler. She went through a pre- and early- teen period where she was very social with friends and responded with one word answers to adults, always pleasantly, but not in a forthcoming way. Then, at about age seventeen, she opened up and started sharing again about what she likes and who she is and some of her hopes for her life.

She is funny, much like her dad, and her classmates voted her the senior with the best sense of humor. For her senior project she went to Atlanta to a stand-up comedy school and performed in front of a few hundred people. She did the same performance for the senior project committee and wrote a paper on the value of humor. She said she was scared, but the DVD presents a young woman who is not only funny, but completely at ease.

She graduated from high school in 2012. I came for the ceremony as did her Aunt Julie. The look on my son's face as Tessa walked across the stage to get her diploma was priceless, and his pride and joy in her apparent. Tessa left that fall for Kennesaw State College in Kennesaw, Georgia. She's on her way. She has become a thoughtful and caring young woman, beautiful inside and out, and I adore her.

Done with marriage but not with men

In many ways, Jose and I could not have been more different. He was a traditional Latin man. I had changed a lot after two difficult marriages, and I was anything but traditional. Jose came from a family where the women asked permission for anything they did before they did it; their focus was on family. I was she who did *not* obey. When we started dating I was unsure of myself and what I wanted in life. During our time together, I had become someone different. My children were grown and on their own, either in school or working. I was pursuing a college degree and focused on my career. I truly loved Jose, but our relationship was not my life, it was a part of my life.

Jose was diagnosed with a treatable cancer. He was approaching fifty and began to ask himself those things many ask when they reach middle age, *Is there more to life? What am I missing?* I was wrapped up in my own life and failed to notice his restlessness. We grew apart and, in 1983, he ended the relationship and we went our separate ways. I write this without emotion, but there was a lot of emotion. The end of our relationship broke my heart. I cried until there were no more tears to cry, and still I cried more? I felt again like that little girl in the Whaley home, abandoned, unloved. It took a long time to recover. He was the only man I had truly loved. I needed and wanted a life of my own, but I wanted him in my life too.

It was time to look at my life, the failures in relationship. After marrying two alcoholics, and upon divorcing the second, I was smacked right in the head with a profound truth. I could find plenty of negative things to say about both of my ex's, but that doesn't negate the fact that I married them. Alcohol may have been a common denominator, both were alcoholics, but alcohol doesn't make decisions. I was truly the common denominator.

Sure, I could and did find a multitude of explanations for why I chose alcoholics. There is a strong history of alcoholism in my ancestry. I felt abandoned as a child when, for all practical purposes, my mother disappeared. My father was critical and my grandparents, while providing what I needed, were not affectionate. Farmed out to foster homes and institutions, I sought acceptance and approval. I learned co-dependency, and given the era in which I was raised, I wanted to rescue these guys who undoubtedly drank because they weren't understood. I thought each of those things at some point. On a less than conscious level it may be there is some truth to each of these excuses, but they were excuses.

The fact remains, I married two men who were hell-bent on destroying themselves and who did not have the capacity to love and care for anyone, including themselves. Me, I did it. At my most honest, I knew both marriages were a mistake beforehand, but I ignored that inner voice and leapt into marriage anyway.

Here's the truth. When I was dating my first husband he didn't go anywhere without having beer in the car; he drank while he was driving, and sometimes I was in the car. After I became pregnant with his child and we decided we had to get married, he flirted with other women in my presence, including once making out with one of them. It's hard to tell what he might have been doing when I wasn't present. I also knew he was controlling around issues of money. He rarely spent any: There were no dinners out or movies; our dates were visiting others and making sure there was alcohol. Because I was pregnant, it made a decision not to marry difficult, but the fact is I married him. I married him knowing he was an alcoholic, he was controlling, and he was more than frugal when it came to money.

When I was dating my second husband he had a wife in a mental institution. She had been sick for a long time and I convinced myself that it would cause her no harm if we dated. Since he was married, we couldn't marry and that was okay.

It was having my cake and eating it too. He took away that rationalization fairly soon and filed for divorce. It unsettled me, but I still told myself that nothing would convince me to marry him. After we dated for a while, I started to get calls from bill collectors, calls about bills he owed. This was before laws regulated what bill collectors could do. They called him at my house, and, get this, I defended him. It didn't occur to me that this was a good indicator that he couldn't manage money. But, he was taking me out to dinner and the movies, which meant he wasn't tight with money. He did not try to control me, and I thought both of these things were an improvement. In terms of his drinking, he never drank without getting drunk. He didn't drink every day like my first husband, but he did get drunk whenever he drank. I didn't like him when he was drunk, but I didn't stop dating him. And, with all this information right in front of me, I married him.

I was thirty-five years old the day my second divorce was final. I felt old, but the reality is that I was not. It was unrealistic to think I would spend the rest of my life alone and celibate. I had no desire to give up men; there were still too many I found attractive. I didn't think I could change that, nor did I want to. I had a truckload of responsibility--three children ages fifteen, twelve, and ten, and too little money-- but, fortunately, I had a job. I had no idea what I wanted to do with my life, and not yet any sense that I had any control over it.

What should you do after two unsuccessful marriages? I can tell you the answer now, but I'm not at all sure it was clear then. *Do nothing.* That's right, and it's a thought that was then totally foreign to me. Do nothing? How does that help? But here's the thing. Doing nothing doesn't mean doing nothing about everything. It means doing nothing that would cause me to repeat the same mistake I had already made twice, getting into a marriage which, if I'd taken ten seconds to think about, I would have known wasn't going to work. It means under no circumstances should I marry until I was sure that both the man I would marry and I were emotionally and spiritually healthy, that we could commit ourselves to marriage, caring for and wanting the best for each other. How long does that take? For me it was more than twenty-five years. But let me assure you, I didn't give up on men.

I entered into a twelve-year relationship with Jose, my first longer-term relationship after my second divorce. Confusing, isn't it? Jose was a major improvement. To start with, he was not an alcoholic, and he was not controlling with money. He paid his bills and his child support and was a present father even though he did not have custody. And the physical attraction between us, well, since my kids and grandkids, and maybe even future generations might read this, let me just say this, I came to life at age thirty-five. I never reached a point of commitment to marriage, even with all we had going for us. I was growing, becoming someone new. I started college, I became an activist in the women's movement, a recognizable person in my community; I found my voice, and my faith in God had become more and more important to me. Jose was not growing in the same way or at the same pace. He was raised in a culture where men are in charge and women were expected to follow their lead. I was learning to be a leader in my own right. Eventually, our differences separated us. The last three years together were very rocky, but the physical attraction kept us trying. Finally, he found someone else, and our relationship ended. Heartbroken though I was, I was still not ready to be without a man in my life.

I was forty-eight, and I had been successful in many ways. My kids were grown and I wasn't poor anymore, but there was one area where I had not grown as much as I needed to. I felt incomplete without a relationship. This is something many women deal with, and maybe we're even programmed at some level to want to couple. Who knows, and maybe it's okay. What isn't okay is to be in relationship with someone who is not able to fully commit to you, or to be in a relationship with someone to whom you cannot fully commit. What does that mean? I now believe it means you have to have a good relationship with yourself before you can have one with someone else. You have to look at all the garbage you have stored, day after day, year after year, which tells you, deep in your bones, that you are not good enough. And you have to deal with it.

After the breakup with Jose, I had not reached that place, the place where it was okay to be in a relationship but not okay to be in one because I was afraid to be alone, afraid I  wasn't good enough or attractive enough. So, two months after Jose's final conversation in which he told me it was over, I had a date with Jim, a man I had gone out with for a short time when I first started dating Jose. I had worked with Jim. He was single, college-educated smart, a recent veteran who had long hair and a beard and very liberal ideas. He understood feminism and called himself a feminist. He was eight years younger than I was, temporarily living with his parents, and looking for a teaching job. He couldn't find one, so he took a job in the Community Development Department at city hall where I also worked. He was fun and we shared many interests, but when Jose asked that we date exclusively, I quit spending time with Jim other than at work. Soon after Jim and I stopped dating, he left Muskegon, moved to Chicago where he worked in a law firm, and added his second master's degree to his resume.

Jim called me out of the blue. He had been in a relationship with a woman who had died of cancer only a couple of months earlier. He asked if I was single, and I said yes. He invited me to come to Chicago for the weekend, followed up with a plane ticket, and I went. Chicago was exciting. We talked non-stop about ideas, not so much about ourselves. The talk was exciting. He followed with phone calls and a trip to Muskegon, and he followed that with a week's vacation in the Bahamas at his expense. He got a teaching job, finally, at a community college near Bay City. I drove across the state to see him and he drove to Muskegon to see me. The following year I took a job with the State of Michigan and traveled throughout the state. My children were on their own, all working and supporting themselves. I was free to live anywhere within Michigan. Driving back and forth was a strain for both of us, especially in winter, so I moved to Bay City to live with Jim. There was no talk of marriage, and I was happy with that. I wanted a relationship, but I did not want marriage.

Jim and I lived together for ten years, first in Bay City, then in Ludington, and then in Greenville as he moved up the ladder in teaching positions. In Greenville we bought a house. Jim drank socially, we had an equal relationship relative to money, he valued and shared my feminist perspective, and he encouraged me to dig deeper especially as it relates to books and music. We shared political values. I finished both my bachelor's and master's degrees while we were together. It all sounds almost perfect, but it wasn't. There was no electricity between us, my faith was getting deeper, and Jim identified as an atheist. In the beginning he tolerated my faith. Later he mocked it, arguing with me about the ridiculousness of faith. He sometimes had problems with co-workers, but he was respected and revered by his students, and, by all accounts, he is an outstanding teacher. I was used to the fact that Jim was different, meaning he didn't fit into any traditional mode. There was the problem of not much passion, but that seemed minor. What was making it more difficult for me to accept Jim was his position on faith and his denigration of my faith. As I

233

began to isolate and pull back from him, he began to move away from me and eventually started seeing other women— not openly, but at the end he stepped over the line and invited one to our house and bed when I wasn't home.

The relationship ended and I moved to Chicago. Finally, I was tired of relationships. I was numb. Relationships with men in the way that I had engaged in them were not the answer. For nearly two years I dated no one and had no interest in doing so. I sought counseling, joined a twelve-step program, and focused on my faith. I worked on liking myself, exactly as I was, no relationship required. I was not happy with my job, the one I took to move away from Jim, but I was happier with myself. I learned that *I* was responsible for the character of my relationships, not Bart, not Clint, not Jose, not Jim, not anyone I might meet in the future. For the first time I understood that I must value myself in order to make good relationship choices.

MID-LIFE: TIME TO LEARN, GROW AND HEAL

"For grace to be grace it must give us things we didn't know we needed and take us places where we didn't know we didn't want to go. As we stumble through the crazily altered landscape of our lives, we find that God is enjoying our attention as never before. "

Kathleen Norris from Acedia and Me:
A Marriage, Monks and a Writer's Life

My thoughts: Surviving mid-life is the only way to get to old age

There was a time, not so long ago, when people didn't live to old age as we think of it now. Our life expectancy continues to lengthen, and more people are living to one hundred than ever before. My generation likely will live well into our seventies, and a good many of us will reach our eighties. More of us are better off economically than our ancestors; life has been easier for us. Our ancestors worked hard and were likely to die in those years we call middle age, the late forties to mid- fifties. They didn't have the luxury of pondering their future as we do.

For many today, mid-life is a time of reevaluation, contemplation, perhaps a time for change, or at least a time to learn acceptance. The young years are behind us; we can't get them back, although many will try. When we are young, most of us have a vague idea that when we reach mid-life we will be successful in whatever way we define success, we will be satisfied with our lives, and we will have accomplished enough. We have dreams and hopes, and we live day to day doing what we have to or want to do, not thinking much about what comes next. Life happens.

And then we're fifty. We realize that our marriage may not be as exciting as our courtship was. Our children are no more perfect than we were at their age. Our job is not as fulfilling as we imagined it would be. We look in the mirror and see that wrinkles are forming and our skin is not as firm. There is a niggling question on our minds...*Is this it? Is this all there is?*

Fifty might not be everyone's age of reconciliation. For some it happens in their forties and some barely notice. Not many, but some. We question ourselves. Am I still attractive? Am I as successful as I once thought I would be? Could life be more exciting than it is? This is a time when people may think about leaving their once-settled marriage, dumping their job to start something new, or, a less expensive option, buying a red sports car.

We are a youth-oriented culture. Old has less value. Women may notice that when they were younger they attracted attention and now they are nearly invisible. Men their age are looking at women twenty years their junior, women their daughter's age. Men may look at where they are in their career and see that young people are moving up the ladder faster; their own salary is stagnant, there is no upward momentum, and no one is seeking their advice. Maybe they are bored with what once excited them. Our image of ourselves is shaken, perhaps not in an earthquake kind of way, maybe only a noticeable tremor, but shaken nevertheless. Do we act? Do we sink into despair? Do we accept that we are on the edge of old, or do we deny it? We know we have lived more years than we are likely to have left. We fear old age and we're not ready to think about death. One thing is for sure, though, we can't control our aging, we can't stop it, and we can't even slow it down. In fact, it feels as though time has sped up.

The majority of people will get through it. We are knocked about emotionally. We make decisions we regret and other decisions that we know are right for us. We leave relationships; we form new ones. We start running marathons, or at least working out on the treadmill. We have a religious conversion and increase our faith, or we decide that God is a human-made illusion and Heaven was created to make dying less frightening. We leave our job and start a small business. We buy organic foods and become vegetarians. A few of us sink into despair and don't come out.

The only way to avoid mid-life is to die before you get there. That won't happen for most of us. The most we can hope for is that either our lives will be happily settled by then, or we will develop the resources to get through it. And, when we do we just might find that old age is the very best time of all.

I'm old enough now to look back more than three-quarters of a century and this is what I see. For a long time, I put on a tote board the things I had done, accomplished, overcome, in order to maintain a belief that I mattered, that I was lovable, that I was successful. I had it together because I had done this, and that, and the other thing.

In 1986, I turned fifty. I had been married and divorced twice. My relationship with Jose had ended, and he was in a relationship with someone much younger than I was. I jumped into a relationship with someone I had known earlier just to be in relationship, and undoubtedly to prove to myself that I was still attractive and lovable. I had been through more than I expected, and I had accomplished more than I had dreamed. I had only an inkling that I needed to heal some long-standing hurts. I had made changes, but there were many more to make. Replacing one man for another, as I regularly had, would not be enough to bring the peace and assurance I was just beginning to realize I wanted.

I loved Jose. Losing the relationship was painful. I had accomplished a lot but it didn't matter much in the heartache of that loss. The illusion that what I had accomplished defined who I am, and would get me what I wanted from life, was ripped apart. I looked inside myself and realized that all the doing in the world was not enough to fix what was broken in me. And, what was broken was that I did not believe that I was good enough and lovable enough simply because I am who I am, simply because I exist. The abandonment I experienced as a young child and all the fears it created were still there, now uncovered. I literally was knocked to my knees, empty of answers.

It was from that place that I began to build my life on a stronger foundation. I found a faith that humbled me. I learned that God does not value me for my accomplishments. I began to understand that God created me to be exactly who I am. I don't have to be perfect; God loves me unconditionally, and because he does, I could learn to love myself in the same way. It took time. Change did not happen overnight, and it did not happen without action on my part. *Doing* was still important to me, but how I rated it and my reasons for doing changed. I worked to measure the doing by the difference it made rather than how it reflected on me.

I learned to acknowledge my strengths and confront unhealthy behaviors. I surrounded myself with positive people. I studied and learned what it takes to live a healthy, joyful life. I sought counseling and developed skills to intervene when I began to think negatively. I learned to change my thoughts from the old familiar *you're not good enough or lovable enough,* to a positive statement of *yes, you* are *good enough.* I learned to change the way I talked to myself. I told myself I was lovable; I don't do everything perfectly and not everyone will love me, but I do some things well enough, and God and the people who matter in my life love me.

Damage was done when I was a child and scars were formed, but I came to see myself as a survivor. I would like to say that I never feel insecure or diminished, that I never revert back to the emotions of that little girl who didn't feel good enough, but it wouldn't be true. What is true is that I get better and better at intervening and figuring out what I can change and what I can't. I cannot change what others do or say, although sometimes I wish mightily that I could. I can only change how I choose to react. I can and do stop and think and ask myself what is true, what is right, and what I want to do about it. It sometimes takes a day of stewing before I get to a peaceful place, a place where my mind is not churning. But I do get there.

Cancer: One way to learn you're not invincible.

I started having annual physicals in 1986 when I turned fifty. In the summer of 1988, when I was fifty-two years old, just before I moved from Ludington to Greenville, Michigan, I had my annual physical. As part of the physical my doctor's office person scheduled a mammogram, which was done early one morning at the local hospital. I remember every detail.

I found my way to the breast imaging department, where the receptionist invited me to sit in the chair across from her desk, just inside the door. I provided insurance information and signed releases. She then walked with me to a small cubicle at the back of the office. She asked if I had used deodorant that day. I said no, which was the right answer. She handed me a waist-length cotton gown and told me to remove all my clothes from the waist up including any jewelry, put them in the locker provided in the cubicle, lock it with the key, and come back into the waiting room when I was ready. I undressed, removed my jewelry, put on the half-gown and tied it, hoping there were no gaps, and locked the locker. The key had a coiled band that I slipped around my wrist. I walked into the waiting room holding the gown closed even though it was tied, picked up a magazine from a small table, and sat in the middle chair of five or six with wooden arms and cushioned seats.

The woman who would take pictures of my breasts called my name and I followed her to the imaging room. This was my third time for a mammogram so I knew what to expect. When she finished she asked me to go back to the waiting room while they determined the images were clear and didn't have to be redone. I covered myself, went back, sat down, and a few minutes later she came and said I could go; the results would be sent to my doctor within the next couple of days.

I didn't think about the mammogram again until I got a call from my doctor's office a few days later asking me to come in the next day to discuss the results. I did what I usually do when I anticipate bad news. My mind detached from my body. I don't know how else to describe it. When I am worried or scared I somehow am able to detach and keep myself busy doing whatever it is I think I have to do. My mind doesn't race. It's almost like I'm watching myself.

I kept my appointment. I met the doctor in her office and not the examining room. She was at her desk and I sat across from her as she looked at the images of my left breast. She said, "You have a small abnormal mass here." She pointed to a spot that looked like a white dot and said, "I would like to set an appointment with a surgeon for you to have a biopsy to see what it is." She explained that a needle would be put into the mass to draw out some tissue, which would be examined locally and also sent to Mayo clinic for an independent diagnosis. We set up an appointment for that week. The procedure was done at the hospital and I was anesthetized during the process. My significant other, Jim, went with me. I made him promise not to tell anyone. I wanted to know what I was dealing with and how I would deal with it before anyone else was told.

The results of the biopsy came back. It was cancer and it was microscopically invasive. That meant that it had spread slightly. I asked what the options were. The doctor said surgery was recommended and that she would set up an appointment with a surgeon who would talk with me about my choices. She said that hearing the word cancer was scary, but because the cancer had been caught early, the prognosis was excellent, and she assured me the surgeon was someone I would like. There were no female surgeons in Ludington, or anywhere else nearby for that matter, and she knew my preference for women doctors. For many years there were none, and doctor visits were more comfortable for me when I had a woman doctor.

I met the surgeon. He was business-like, but very open to questions. "Your choices are one, we take the entire breast; two, we remove the lump, a small amount of surrounding tissue and do radiation; or, three, we remove the lump, surrounding tissue, all of the lymph nodes on the left side, and do radiation." He said, "If you choose a lumpectomy with removal of the nodes, your chances of no recurrence are about 95 percent." Removal of the entire breast was a radical choice, and removing the lump and lymph nodes seemed much less invasive. The odds were pretty good at 95 percent, and I preferred the less invasive action. There was time for more later if it came to that. We scheduled the surgery.

On the way home I told Jim what the surgeon said and the choice I had made. He was very quiet. When we got home I told him I had noticed his lack of response. Ten years previously, Jim had spent two years taking care of his sister, Paula, before she died from lung cancer. During that time he met and fell in love with his sister's therapist, Virginia, who facilitated a cancer support group Jim attended with Paula. Six months after Paula's death, Virginia was diagnosed with lung cancer, and Jim moved in and cared for her until she died. He and I had reconnected just a couple of months after Virginia's death.

Jim said, "I don't know if I can handle taking care of someone with cancer again." This response was understandable, but not comforting. I responded, "I understand how you feel, but I haven't asked you to take care of me. You don't have cancer. I have cancer. You don't have to handle anything. If you need to talk to somebody about how hard it is for you to deal with me having cancer, I support your seeing someone, but I need to use my energy to deal with how I feel about having cancer."

The only other conversation we had about my cancer related to telling my children. I didn't want to tell them. I didn't know why. I thought maybe it was my belief that it is the mom's job to worry about the children, not the other way around. Jim said, "It isn't fair not to tell them, they deserve a chance to step up to the plate." I knew he was right and reluctantly called each of them, told them I had cancer, that it was found very early, the outlook was good and that I was scheduled for surgery. Each of them asked if I was okay, when the surgery would be, and promised to be there.

The day of the surgery I felt like I was holding my breath. I wasn't really afraid of the surgery. My head was still separated from my body and I was in a *let's get this done* mode. I realized I was holding my breath because I was afraid that my children wouldn't show up. This wasn't about them. They were not the kind of people who broke promises. It was old baggage carried from a childhood with a mother who more often than not didn't show up. They did show up, of course.

The surgery went fine. I had a tidy scar about three inches long and I couldn't lift my left arm for a while. About six weeks later, after I healed a bit, I met with Dr. Jacquelyn Watson, a radiation oncologist at Butterworth Hospital in Grand Rapids. The nurse put me in an examining room, handed me another half-gown, told me to undress from the waist up, and said the doctor would be in. Dr. Watson was young, probably in her early thirties. She was about my height, with curly ash blonde hair and a big smile. She said she had the report from the surgeon and that today she would place marks on my breast to indicate where the radiation would be directed. She had a permanent black marker with ink that would not come off in the shower. She marked circles in several places on the left side of my breast and under my arm. When that was finished, she told me to get dressed and we would talk again.

I got dressed. Dr. Watson took me to the radiation room. It was maybe the size of a high school gym, with high ceilings. There was a table under a large piece of equipment in the center of the room. In the corner, steps led up to a small room with glass windows. Pointing at the equipment, she said, "The radiation technicians will arrange the equipment, aiming it on the marks I've made, and then they will go into the small glass room where they will operate the equipment. You won't feel anything. There is a microphone so the technicians can talk to you, and they will hear anything you might say." She asked if I had any questions and walked with me to the receptionist, who gave me the schedule of appointments. I was to be at the hospital at eight in the morning, Monday through Friday, for the next six weeks. Once a week I would meet with Dr. Watson after the radiation treatment.

The following Monday I showed up in the radiation department and was directed to a small cubicle where I put on another half-gown. Then I went to the cancer patients' waiting room until my time for treatment. That was the tough part. I will never forget walking in that small room each morning where five or six patients waited for chemo or radiation. Many had no hair. Some were so thin they looked as though they might fall over. The conversation was mostly between patients who had gotten to know each other there, each asking the other about his or her progress. It was clear some of them would not make it. For the next six weeks, I never said anything except hello when I walked into that room. The reality of cancer finally hit me.

The radiation tech came to take me to the room I'd been shown earlier. I hopped up on the table and lay under the equipment as still as I could while the tech arranged my body so the equipment was focused on one of the circles. It was cold and he gave me a blanket. He asked if I was okay, I said yes, and he walked up the stairs to the little glassed-in room. When he got there, his disembodied voice came over the microphone, "Are you okay?" I said yes. He said to stay very still. I lay on the table looking up at the equipment, and I cried for the first time since I heard the words *it's cancer*. The tears slid down my cheeks and I couldn't move to wipe them off. The tech came down and rearranged the equipment several times. I cried through the whole process. I felt very alone, sad, and at the same time relieved that it was unlikely I would die from cancer. My cancer was totally curable.

I showed up five days a week at eight in the morning for the next six weeks and during that time Dr. Watson and I became friends. It happened because one day I walked in and said hello and asked her how she was, and she burst into tears. She was very embarrassed. I immediately walked over and hugged her and asked what was wrong. She said, "My dad is dying of cancer. I had a call this morning that he is near the end. I know pretty much all you can know about cancer, and I can't do a thing to help him. I'm so sad." She pulled herself together and apologized again. After that, at each of my appointments she and I talked. I asked after her father and she asked me about the work I did. Her father died, and I sent a note of condolence. The last time I met with her she asked if I'd like to have lunch one day and I said yes.

Today every person who does not die from cancer is called a survivor. I suppose we are but I am embarrassed to claim the title because there are so many who aren't as fortunate, who don't find their cancer at such an early stage, and who undergo excruciating treatment. If they live, they really are survivors. I'm grateful for sure and having cancer is a sobering thing. It does make you think about what matters and what doesn't. When I lay in that big room with the radiation equipment and the voice echoing out of the little glass enclosure, I knew for sure that I wasn't invincible, a thought that had not occurred to me before.

I'm not sure that cancer runs in our family. My paternal grandmother had uterine cancer that spread to her liver. She lived in a time when people didn't go to the doctor for an annual physical. She waited too long for a diagnosis and she might have been saved. To my knowledge, no one else has had breast cancer. But my granddaughter will need the information when she is fully grown, visits the doctor, and has to fill out those family history forms.

Smoking: From glamorous habit to disgusting addiction

In the dead of summer in 1945, when I was nine years old, my cousin Patty and I were playing *olly, olly over, not quite over*, on the roof of my grandparents' detached garage. She was on the backside of the garage and I was between the house and the garage. I threw the ball over the garage to her on the other side and out of my sight hollering, *olly, olly, o-o-over.* She was waiting to catch. When I didn't throw hard enough, and the ball didn't make it over, I hollered, *not quite o-o-over!* After awhile, we tired of the game and I joined Patty behind the garage.

It had been a hot summer. Grandpa watered the grass in the side and back yard but behind the garage the weeds were allowed to grow and they were dry. Pat snapped off an eight- or ten-inch weed, which was rigid and hollow. I think it was ragweed. The opening was about one-fourth the size of a straw. Patty, always the daring one, asked me if I would like to learn to smoke.

She was only a year older so you might wonder that she knew how to smoke. She was pretty precocious and a daredevil. For quite some time, she had been stealing cigarettes from her stepfather when he came to visit, and I was her accomplice. He always took off his jacket and put it on the arm of his chair. He kept his cigarettes in an inside pocket. Patty sat on his lap and chattered at him while I sneaked a cigarette out of his jacket. She had invited me to smoke before but I didn't like the way cigarettes smelled.

On this day of my first smoking lesson, Patty said, "Run into the house and get some matches." They were the wooden kind, kitchen matches we called them, that Grandma used to light the stove. I got the matches and headed back out. Patty lit the weed, held it between her index and middle fingers, lifted it to her mouth, sucked in, took the cigarette out, threw her head back much like the movie stars who smoked in many of the movies we saw, and blew out. "Here, your turn," she said. I followed her movements exactly. It smelled like a burning weed, which of course it was, and the smoke left a slightly bitter taste in my mouth. I don't believe either of us inhaled. I'm not sure there was enough smoke to do so. I felt very grown up and glamorous.

We continued to smoke our weeds that summer until Grandma caught us. There was never any doubt what was going to happen when Grandma caught you doing something she thought was nasty, and smoking surely fit that description for her. She ordered us, "Go get a switch." It never crossed our minds to not get a switch when we were told to. Patty and I got a knife from the house and, filled with dread thinking of the punishment ahead, we went to a tree in the yard with low-hanging branches and cut a thin switch. We handed it to Grandma, who took the knife and shaved the leaves off the switch, narrowing it so that it snapped when she swatted. It was summer and our legs were bare. Grandma took Patty by the arm and swatted her across her legs three or four times. My anxiety increased as I waited for my turn. Being switched stung more than iodine on an open cut and I cried immediately. Patty didn't cry, even though I knew it hurt her too. Grandma warned, "You'll get worse if you ever do that again." My stinging legs convinced me that was true.

I moved to Detroit near the end of that summer and didn't try smoking again until I was thirteen and starting seventh grade. My dad, brother, and I moved back to Flint and rented the apartment upstairs from Grandma, and I quickly and eagerly fell under Patty's spell. She certainly made my life much more interesting.

One Saturday afternoon shortly after our return, Patty and I went to the neighborhood movie theater. After the movie we went into the ladies restroom and Patty pulled a cigarette from her purse. She lit it, inhaled, and blew out. She had become lots more practiced since I saw her last. She said she would teach me how to inhale. Ever the eager learner, I took the cigarette, grasped it between my index finger and middle finger just below my knuckles, as I had seen her do, and brought it to my lips. She told me to suck in and swallow the smoke really fast and she demonstrated how. I was looking in the mirror over the sink and watched myself do exactly that. I immediately felt light headed and dizzy, and I fell to the floor. I was only out a minute. Patty told me I would get used to it and that wouldn't happen next time. She was right. I tried again and it didn't happen. At first, I only smoked with Patty. She carried a supply of Sen-Sen, little licorice candy bits that we sucked after smoking so Grandma didn't smell cigarettes on our breath.

By eighth grade in 1950, at age fourteen, I was an addicted smoker, sneaking of course. I smoked Pall Malls and was loyal to that brand ever after. I thought the name and bright red package looked sophisticated. Most of my friends smoked also. Dad caught me once when I was in tenth grade. I was standing on the corner after school waiting for the bus, chatting with my friends, and puffing away. He got out of work early, drove by and saw me. My back was turned and I didn't see him. He tapped me on the shoulder. I turned around and was struck with fear. I didn't know what was coming, but I knew it would be embarrassing. With his teeth clamped shut, and in a voice loud enough for my friends to hear, he said, "What in the hell do you think you're doing?" I didn't open my mouth. "You look like a prostitute standing on the corner with a cigarette hanging out of your mouth. Get in the car right now." My friends were dead quiet and I wanted to disappear and never be seen again. I got in the car and we drove home with Dad not saying a word. The punishment was grounding for what seemed an interminable time. He had given up spankings, always with a belt, when I turned thirteen. That may have been one of the better rewards in becoming a teenager. On the other hand, a spanking would be over with quickly and I could be back hanging with my friends. I continued to sneak and smoke. The addiction was stronger than any punishment.

I started smoking openly when I moved to my mother's house at age sixteen. It seemed to me that a majority of people smoked. My parents both smoked. Movie actors and actresses smoked. When we got our first television set in 1950 many of the news reporters, actors, and actresses smoked. People smoked anywhere they felt like smoking, in restaurants, on the street, in movie theater lobbies.

Frankly, for a long time I loved smoking. Cigarettes were the first thing I reached for in the morning. A feeling of well-being and pleasure washed over me when I took that first drag on a cigarette after a meal. In the early years after I had children I didn't have much money. A pack of cigarettes cost twenty-two to twenty-five cents. I never threw away a smokable cigarette butt. One morning I remember running out of cigarettes, going through the ashtrays to find one I could get a couple of puffs on, and digging through my purse and looking under the couch and chair cushions, places where I might find loose change. This was true addict behavior.

By 1981, at age forty-five, I had developed an annoying cough. At night when I lay in bed and in the morning when I woke up, I coughed, cleared my throat, and coughed again. I never blamed it on cigarettes. I always said I thought I was having a problem with my throat. I decided in early summer that year that I had put on some weight and started jogging. I read someplace that after awhile you would get this runner's high and learn to love jogging. The first day of jogging I covered a mile and came into my apartment wheezing loudly. My chest felt like it would split open. It hurt. I knew it was smoking. Dramatically I threw my cigarette pack into the garbage and said *that's it!*

That evening after work, my then sweetheart and later husband, Jose, picked me up for a weekend in Traverse City. Jose had quit smoking before we started dating in 1971. When he came to the door I announced that I had given up cigarettes. Then, he was by my side all weekend and I was too embarrassed to renege. I got through the weekend without a cigarette. It wasn't easy. It was almost all I thought about.

But when I got up Monday morning back home I was feeling pretty good about myself. I still wanted a cigarette but it wasn't quite as pressing. I went to work and called the Lakeshore Lung Association. They conducted stop-smoking classes. I said to the man who answered the phone, "I've smoked for more than thirty years and I haven't smoked for the last three days. Can you tell me what I should do to stay off cigarettes?" The thing I remember most is that he said, "Take a lot of showers." "Why," I said. "Have you ever smoked in the shower," he asked. I hadn't. He also said, "It will be soothing to your skin as you go through the physical withdrawal, which will take a week to ten days. The psychological addiction will last longer. Call me when you feel like you want to smoke." Sometimes I wanted to smoke, but I never called. I was determined to quit by myself.

After I had been off cigarettes for a while, I found that I truly disliked the smell of tobacco smoke. When someone who smoked stood near me, I realized they reeked of tobacco. Not an attractive smell. I wondered how in the world Jose managed to kiss me given what my breath must have smelled like. I'm happy to say I've never smoked again, and I've been a non-smoker for as long as I was a smoker. The man I called when I first quit was right, however. The psychological addiction did last a long time. I sometimes still dream about smoking. Even now, every once in awhile, I see someone smoking and I recall the pleasure of that first drag in the morning or right after a cup of coffee. I can see in my mind the relaxed letting go that I felt back then. I have convinced myself, though, that I was such a hopeless addict that if I took one drag now I'd be right back to that annoying cough, smelly breath, and difficult breathing. Quitting that disgusting habit was one of the best things I ever did for myself and those who care about me. And, oh, by the way, I never did get that runner's high my runner friends said I would get.

Other addictions: Food and Relationships

I can't remember exactly when food became a problem for me. I remember the first time I ate a candy bar and realized that it altered my mood. I was a teenager, lying on a blanket, reading a magazine, and sunning myself with a Milky Way bar next to me, also in the sun. I picked up the candy bar, peeled the wrapper down from the bar, lifted both to my mouth, licked the melted chocolate from the wrapper, and took my first bite. The chocolate on the outside was almost liquid; the caramel was soft and creamy but didn't overwhelm the chocolate. I rolled that bite around in my mouth. I didn't chew it so much as run my tongue around it until it melted even more. Today I would describe the feeling as sensuous, but then I didn't know the word. I just know that I felt happy, relaxed, and wanting another candy bar.

Here are some statistics about addiction taken from the website, Addictions and Recovery.org.

- Addiction is due 50 percent to genetic predisposition and 50 percent to poor coping skills.
- The children of addicts are eight times more likely to develop an addiction.
- We all have a predisposition for addiction because there are evolutionary advantages. It is hardwired into our brains.
- Repeatedly abusing your drug(s) of choice permanently rewires your brain; you'll chase the buzz even more.
- Your genes are not your destiny. The 50 percent of addiction that is caused by poor coping skills is where you can make a difference.

I've already noted that addiction runs in my family and talked about what a great cook my grandmother was, that food was a central part of my experience in living with her, and that I lived with her right after my parents divorced and my mother was unavailable on a regular basis. I was seven and few seven-year-olds have good coping skills. I overate, we all did, but I was physically active enough so that weight wasn't a problem. I was chubby in my pre-teen and early teen years when I spent more time reading and daydreaming than I did being physically active.

I became unhappy with my body before I noticed that food gave me pleasure and soothed me. Lots of teenagers, especially girls, are unhappy with their bodies. My father did not hesitate to tell me when something I wore made me look fat. I saw kids make fun of other kids who were fat. I was never fat enough so that anyone except my father called me fat, but in those years I saw myself that way.

Around age fourteen, I developed an interest in boys, enough of an interest to want to attract them, and without consciously dieting, I ate less and developed an acceptable shape. I was not skinny, but I was curvy. I recognized that certain foods, particularly sugary foods, soothed me.

My relationship with food changed in my first marriage, after my first child was born. I didn't gain a lot of weight with any of my pregnancies, but I certainly lost firmness. My husband regularly called me fat. He was quite thin, his upper body was muscular, but he had very thin legs. He frequently said it embarrassed him to be on the beach with me because my legs were fat. I've already said that his abuse went beyond verbal, that he was physically and emotionally abusive. I began using food to relieve the emotional pain and stress. An unhealthy cycle began: I overate, I beat myself up emotionally because I overate, and then I overate because I hated myself for my lack of self-control.

This pattern continued for years. Weight gradually stayed on my body, and each decade I weighed a little more. However, whenever I was single and seeking a relationship, I lost weight. I was constantly on a diet. I tried many fad diets from the grapefruit diet to SlimFast, but I didn't stick to any of them. I joined a weight loss clinic program where they provided the food. I lost weight and money; the weight came back and the money didn't. I joined Take Off Pounds Sensibly (TOPS), and as I look back, I laugh because the group's mascot was a stuffed pig. If you gain the most weight among those at a meeting, you take the pig home--not exactly a positive motivator. Once while I was a TOPS member, I got down to one hundred seventeen pounds. I ate four days a week, and starved myself for three days before weigh-in. I got sick, went into the hospital for gall bladder surgery, my thyroid whacked out, and I lost seventeen pounds in three days. TOPS meetings were held at the hospital. I got out of my bed when I could hardly walk, and went to the hospital basement where the TOPS group met. I wanted validation that I had reached and exceeded my weight-loss goal.

My weight gain accelerated when I became an activist in the women's movement. Activism required me to step out of my people-pleasing comfort zone and speak out against those practices I began to realize were harmful to me and women in general. I ate to cope with the stress, I was ashamed of my eating and weight gain, and I ate to cope with the shame. I lost a lot of weight when Jose and I broke up and I was confronting that mid-life milestone, turning fifty. I was in so much emotional pain that I couldn't eat. There wasn't any coping mechanism that would have eased the pain, including food. Or so I thought.

What made it possible for me to eat again was to get into another relationship. Having someone, a man, find me desirable was a comfort in the same way that food was a comfort. I did not love Jim, and sometimes I didn't respect him. Unlike my first husband, he didn't attack my weight; instead, he attacked my intellect. If I expressed an opinion that he didn't agree with, he made it clear that he was smarter. If I read something that he considered beneath him, he showed his disapproval. Same with what I watched on television. I put up with this because I didn't value myself, and I ate too much for the same reason. Food was no longer much of a comfort. The positive sensation of eating to cope began to last a shorter time before I got to the part of the addiction that led to shame. There were two parts of my life where I felt adequate: work and school. I spent as much time as I could at work and studying, both to avoid dealing with the relationship and my addiction.

I still hadn't really labeled overeating or relationships an addiction, but neither was bringing much pleasure. The beginning of recognition came one afternoon when I received a call from someone I love who gave me news that I did not know how to deal with. I'm not revealing the person or information because it's not my story to tell. I was overwhelmed with emotional pain and a sense of helplessness, and I reacted by eating a whole pizza. When I finished the pizza, I was still in pain, so I went to the refrigerator, took out an unopened half-gallon of ice cream, got a tablespoon from the silverware drawer, and ate the whole thing standing up. I could hardly get the last bites down but I kept shoveling it in. The pain did not go away. The next day I called a therapist to ask what I might do to help the other person and he said, in these circumstances the only person you can help is yourself.

I had been reading about addictions. My reading was to understand others in my life. I never labeled myself. In fact, I thought I had escaped the family addictions because I didn't drink to excess, I had quit smoking, and the only other drug I had ever used, marijuana, did not create an addiction. I went through a brief phase of dope smoking because it was a cool thing to do, and although I liked the high, I also experienced a couple of episodes of paranoia while using it and that was a deterrent with more strength than the high. When the therapist suggested I needed to help myself, and after ingesting a sixteen-inch pizza and a half-gallon of ice cream in one sitting, it dawned on me that I was using food to cope with life and not coping with life itself. That is the definition of an addiction.

I joined a twelve-step program, Overeaters Anonymous, to learn about food addiction. I followed the steps religiously. It wasn't about losing weight. It was about dealing with those issues that made me want to eat. Overeaters Anonymous gave me a road map to teach me how to cope with life, how to get through uncomfortable emotions without using food. After a couple of years of attending meetings, reading, and listening to others in the program, I understood that I used relationships in the same way I used food; the relationship addiction had progressed in the same way and served the same purpose as the food addiction. I got into a relationship to cope with emotional issues, and when the relationship didn't work, I didn't deal with the issues. I ate too much, I worked too much, I withdrew emotionally. I chose men who would affirm what I already believed about myself.

Finally, and gradually, and with the help of my faith, I began to genuinely accept myself, to like myself in spite of my imperfections, to loosen my need to control. I began to talk to myself when my emotions got the best of me, to forgive myself when I made mistakes, to find other ways to cope when I was stressed. I stayed away from relationships for two years, and sought counseling to help me learn how to cope with feeling inadequate, not good enough.

I do believe that when you are born into a family with generations of addiction, the chances are greater that you will slide into addiction. I do believe your brain gets wired when you practice that addiction. That is what happened to me when I got less and less relief from eating, and slid into shame which took me back to eating in a never-ending cycle. Overeating became a habit. Seeking unhealthy relationships became a habit.

The only solution was to learn new ways to cope. Now when I am feeling uncomfortable emotions and want to eat, I ask myself if I'm really hungry for food or if there is something else going on. Am I angry, lonely, tired, or bored?

255

Am I feeling bad about myself because I have said or done something which puts me at odds with my values? Am I doing those healthy things I need to do? In other words, I have learned to recognize the symptoms of addiction before I attempt a cure that I already know will not work. Once I recognize a symptom I can ask myself *why, what can be done?* I can intervene and slow down that immediate uneasy discomfort that drives me to food.

Am I cured? I don't think there is a cure. If I stop practicing the coping mechanisms I've learned I will be back where I started. Unlike alcohol addiction, one cannot stop eating. One can, however, stop overeating. Do I sometimes fail and resort back to food? Yes, sometimes I do. But the cycle is over. I do not overeat, and then hate myself and feel shame for overeating. I forgive myself. If I mess up again, I forgive myself again. With the help of my faith, a twelve-step program, and counseling, I don't spiral out of control. I am coping with life and life is a lot more fun than it used to be. In fact, it's more than fun, it's glorious.

From couch potato to healthy and fit

In 1996, I was obese. It's difficult to say but it's true. In the picture on the left, I weighed sixty-five more pounds than Weight Watchers recommends for a person my height. It is difficult to be obese and consider yourself healthy. For years any exercise I got was purely by accident. The things I liked to do mostly entailed sitting, working at my desk to earn a living, reading, writing, and going to the movies as social activities. I was the epitome of couch potato.

A year earlier I had recognized that I was unable to control my eating, sought help, and lost thirty pounds. I did this by doing lots of walking. I lived in Chicago where you can walk to everything, and in my case, I could even walk to work. I was pleased at the improvement in my health, but now my life was about to change and I was worried.

I was leaving Chicago and would have to drive forty-five miles one way to my new job. I was turning sixty and realized that I was no longer young and, therefore, closer to dying. Everything I read said that life is extended if you eat healthier and exercise regularly. I was on the path to good health, but I was not there yet. I needed to figure out how to keep exercise in my life. I bought a treadmill.

I know lots of people who have treadmills and after the first week they use them to hang their clothes on. I did not want that to happen. I committed to walking two miles every weekday morning. This was a huge change for me. It's very different to build walking into your life because you need to get to work or you need to go to the store, and building it into your life by getting on a machine in your basement. Walking the streets of Chicago is interesting. Walking in your basement is not.

But I did it. How? By asking myself every time I did not want to get on the treadmill whether I'd rather go on a boring walk which took me nowhere, or whether I'd rather die ten years before my time. It's no contest--living longer wins. I walked, and if I missed a weekday, I walked a weekend day. It was difficult to do more. I was up at six in the morning to walk, and the commute to work got me home close to six-thirty in the evening. By the time supper was prepared and eaten, I was ready to get back on the couch.

In 2002, at age sixty-six, I retired from full-time work and Jose and I moved into our motor home. You cannot carry a treadmill in a motor home. Our plan was to spend summers in Michigan and travel in the winter. We found an RV park north of Muskegon in a small town, Montague, that was located on a twenty-five-mile bike path. By this time I had gotten used to and even liked using a treadmill. It was boring to others, but turning off my mind and just walking without distraction worked for me. It wasn't that I loved the treadmill, but I loved how I felt after using it. I checked into gyms and found there was a small one less than a mile from our park.

I made an appointment with Nick, a personal trainer at the gym, who designed a program that included exercises to improve cardio and strength. Every weekday I got out of bed, which was the hard part, and went to the gym, barely awake and before breakfast. Nick encouraged me to increase my time and speed on the treadmill and to gradually increase the number of repetitions and sets of my work with weights. For a brief time in the early 1970s, I joined a gym and liked the way my body had been firmed and shaped by using weights. I set up a program that eventually had me on the treadmill for three miles, one-half mile warming up, one mile walking briskly, one running, and one-half cooling down. I worked with a combination of free weights and weight machines, two sets of twenty to twenty-five repetitions of each of fourteen exercises. By the end of the summer I had lost another ten pounds and I looked and felt better than I had in years.

Before leaving Michigan at the beginning of October, I asked Nick to design a strengthening program I could do with free weights while traveling. My cardio exercise would be hiking with Jose, who loves to hike. For the next six years, I continued my gym program in the summer and hiked and used free weights in the winter. There were many mornings I struggled to make myself get up and work out, but what kept me going was the knowledge that I always felt better after exercise. As I aged, like many people, my body ached more and I was less flexible. Exercise lessened the pain and allowed me more flexibility. I got lots of positive feedback from people in the gym, most of whom were much younger and capable of doing less. That felt good, too.

In 2009, we began to spend more time at an RV park in Arizona that had a well- equipped exercise room, so now there were nine months of the year when gym exercise, my preference, was readily available. I also joined Weight Watchers, attending in Michigan and Arizona, to begin to learn healthier eating habits. By 2010, I had lost every one of the sixty-five pounds and I was no longer obese. Today, I continue to exercise every weekday and eat in a much healthier way. I've relaxed some because life without ice cream is no life at all, but I will never be obese again.

In 1936, the year I was born, life expectancy for women in the United States was

sixty-five years. In 1954, when I graduated from high school, it was seventy-two years, and in 2002, the year I retired, it was slightly over eighty years. Unlike many my age, I am using only one prescription drug, a statin that my doctor says helps prevent heart disease that

259

runs in my family. My hearing has diminished somewhat but digital hearing aids have made a huge difference. I go to the doctor for an annual physical and leave with an A plus for good health and a good attitude. I have given up my couch potato life, and I am indeed fit and healthy. I don't know really how much life I have left, who does? But I do know the quality is better because I committed to seeking good health.

Finding my power by making a difference for others

Women's centers opened in many Michigan communities through the 1970s and into the early 1980s. Most were started after October, 1978, when the legislature created the Domestic Violence Prevention and Treatment Board to lead statewide efforts to eliminate domestic violence in Michigan. The legislation specified that the governor would appoint board members to recommend policy, allocate funding, provide technical assistance and training, develop operating standards for funded programs, and monitor programs based on those standards. Most members over the years have been individuals who worked directly with domestic violence survivors, such as police, prosecutors, judges, attorneys, hospital and school personnel, and counselors.

The board hired consultants Connie Jones, Molly Resnick, and Kate Ross to help board-funded programs get established. All three had been associated with Safe House in Ann Arbor, the first shelter program in the state. Many of the women who started domestic violence programs had plenty of passion, but little administrative experience. The consultants reported that board-funded programs were all over the map in terms of quality and recommended hiring a person to help the board develop quality assurance standards, monitor each program's progress in complying with the standards, and provide technical assistance when needed. The position title would be Domestic Violence Quality Assurance Monitor.

Jones, Resnick, and Ross had visited Every Woman's Place several times; we were one of the first programs funded by the board. They encouraged me to apply for the monitor position. The timing was excellent. Julie, my youngest child, would graduate from college that year. My sons, Brad and Brian, were on their own and supporting themselves. My long-term relationship with Jose had ended. I had a long-distance relationship with Jim who was teaching and living in the Bay City area. I was free to travel and to live anywhere I chose. I believed I had done everything I could in the nine years I had been executive director of Every Woman's Place. I did then, and I do today, believe I was the right person to start that organization. As a survivor with a passion for women's issues I had been able to authentically articulate the need and seek support. I had been a fearless advocate and gained sufficient respect and resources to assure the organization would survive and thrive. From the beginning, the focus was to educate the community to recognize the need for specialized services for women, and to believe that this particular organization was the right one to deliver those services, to sell a new way of thinking about women and their place in the community. We preached the gospel that survivors of violence must be protected and not blamed as had been the norm, that those who abuse others must be held accountable, that historical inequities have negatively affected both women and men, and that community laws and practices perpetuated those inequities and must be changed. The message was not always welcome but we worked so hard that even those who didn't like the message respected our commitment.

We helped women believe they could control their own lives and choose what they wanted, who they wanted to be. The community did provide a safe place; police, prosecutors, and judges changed the way they approached violence and held perpetrators accountable; and women learned that much more was possible than they had been raised to believe. Every Woman's Place was a valued community resource. The next executive would strengthen administration, streamline programs, increase financial support, and, I hoped, continue to embrace the founding philosophy. I was over the moon excited at the opportunity to not only leave the legacy of Every Woman's Place in my home community, but for a new opportunity to strengthen and expand services to women throughout the state.

I got the job. It was a humbling moment when the consultants called. I thanked them, hung up the phone, and cried. Nineteen years earlier I had survived a marriage where I had been battered and threatened with a gun. I had no control in the relationship, no access to money. I was beaten physically and emotionally. It was only when I felt my children threatened that I had the courage to leave. Since then, I had worked to ensure that women in my own community had help and a place to go. I learned and grew and gained strength through that work, and now I had an opportunity to shape services in communities across the state. I was overwhelmed and grateful.

So it was that I wrote the first quality assurance standards that would guide the operations of domestic violence programs throughout Michigan--today more than sixty. Those standards were based on the Domestic Violence Board's stated philosophy, which I quote below. It too was revolutionary, used feminist language, and has been copied across the country.

"Domestic Violence is rooted in an antiquated, sexist social structure that produces profound inequities in the distribution of power and resources, in the roles and relationships between men, women, and children in families, and has devastating effects on victims, their children and the entire society. It is criminal conduct that cannot be tolerated. A comprehensive community response to domestic violence through education, advocacy and appropriate intervention is necessary to bring about change and end the violence. Battering stops only when assailants are held accountable for their abuse. The MDVPTB shall promote the empowerment of survivors and seek social change to redress the existing power imbalance within violent relationships. To make informed decisions for themselves and their children, survivors need access to safety and information about domestic violence, available options and community resources. The MDVPTB is committed to treating survivors with dignity and respect and to providing them the

support and advocacy necessary to realize their right to self-determination."

I spent the next six years visiting every program in the state, fifty-five at that time, seven in the Upper Peninsula and forty-eight in the Lower. The goal was to have services available in every county, which meant some programs in less populated parts of the state covered more than one county. I reported directly to the board, working alone under contract and in cooperation with the board's staff in Lansing. The program was housed in what was then the Department of Social Services and is now the Department of Human Services. In the beginning the board did not have the power to hire its own staff. Sometimes the lead staff person was a career state employee with bureaucratic leanings and, threatened by my independence, wanted the board to put me under her supervision. The board chose not to do so believing it would inhibit the work I was doing. I was grateful for that, too, and I understand that I am not easy to supervise. I had been a supervisor of others for quite some time.

After six years, most Michigan domestic violence programs met the established standards. There were a few that were consistently troubled and required special attention. I was beginning to tire of traveling to fifty-five programs throughout Michigan every year, more than one a week. I was then settled in Greenville, Michigan, sharing a home with Jim, and I was offered a job in nearby Grand Rapids. I gave my notice, but I continued my involvement in the field of domestic violence. A seat opened on the Domestic Violence Board, and at the urging of board members and staff, I submitted my resume to the governor. Those appointed to state boards must be credentialed, which means you have done work on behalf of the governor's party. Jim Blanchard, a Democrat, was governor, and although I had not been affiliated with a party, I had plenty of Democratic contacts. I was appointed.

As a board member, I worked with the staff to pioneer a peer-monitoring program. We gathered leaders from programs across the state to update the standards and to develop a new process. Instead of one person working from a state-level monitoring community programs as I had, a team of people who worked in those programs did the monitoring. The standards and the peer monitoring process is active today, and nearly every year I serve on at least one peer monitoring team. I have worked in the field of domestic violence continuously for the past almost forty years. In the early 1990s, the Michigan Coalition Against Domestic Violence and Sexual Assault, an advocacy organization whose members work in domestic violence programs around the state, honored women who were pioneers in the domestic violence movement. Governor John Engler presented the awards, and I am proud to say I was a recipient.

My last full-time job, maybe

Networking is magical. I don't mean the calculated effort to get out and make as many contacts as you can with the goal of moving your career forward, although there is nothing wrong with doing that. I mean the everyday interactions one has with people that end up bringing good fortune your way.

I met Vicki Weaver in a class at Grand Valley where we both were working toward a degree in public administration. I'm sure we talked about the work I was doing for the Michigan Domestic Violence Prevention and Treatment Board, so she knew something about me besides the fact that we were in class together. Later, Vicki founded Direction Center, a nonprofit management support organization in Grand Rapids. She asked me to lead a workshop on working with a nonprofit board of directors. I did. She called again and asked if I would work with a board of directors of a small nonprofit struggling with the performance of their executive director. The staff had come to the board expressing their concerns. That is how I came to know Vision Enrichment Services (VES), whose mission was to teach people with visual impairments daily living skills to help compensate for their vision loss.

I met with the board of directors, the executive director, and the staff. The situation was particularly sensitive because the executive director had been a board member and also because he was blind and a role model for the organization's clients. He had never been employed by a nonprofit. He had owned a small business and had a staff person who helped with paperwork. There is no doubt everything becomes a bigger challenge with serious vision loss. The VES board members were concerned that maybe he just couldn't handle this job.

After talking with everyone I determined the problem was not his vision loss, it was that he did not understand the value systems in a nonprofit organization. For example, he raised the salary of a male employee with less seniority than a female employee doing the same job. He also told the male employee that he was in charge of other employees but not to tell the woman because she would be upset. This organization had only twelve employees. It took perhaps a day for all of them to know what had happened, and it created chaos. Employees also complained that he hung out in their offices and talked for long periods of time when they had work to do. He seemed not to have work of his own. He had never prepared a nonprofit budget or raised money by asking for it from others--so he just didn't do it. His executive assistant put the budget together and she had never done so before. It rattled her and she feared it wasn't adequate.

I spoke with the executive director about my findings. He agreed that they were true. I explained how he might do it differently, and he became defensive. I reported my findings to the board with recommendations for what would be required to continue with this executive director. I had little faith that the director could do the job, but I was not hired to tell the board whether they should keep him or not. That was their job. They chose to let him go.

The board conducted a search but found no one they thought was the right fit. The board president called and asked if I would apply. I told him that I was concerned about making recommendations that may have led to the firing of the previous director and then applying for the job. His response was to ask me to come and talk to the board and the staff and pose that question to them. I told him I needed to think about it.

The idea of a job in Grand Rapids, about a half-hour from where I lived in Greenville, was tempting. After six years of constant travel I was getting tired. I knew I could do a good job and, in fact, it would be a lot less stressful than working for equality for people of color and women as I had been doing for the previous eighteen years. And, as a plus, I

267

would still be working for a cause where advocacy was required. People with vision loss, actually people with any disability, have plenty of issues related to equal treatment. As I said, though, I was seriously concerned about the way in which I'd been introduced to VES. Before I made a decision I needed to talk to the board and staff.

The board urged me to talk to the staff first. I shared my work experience and my belief systems around advocacy and said I was open to any question they had. One of the first came from the woman and man who had been pitted against each other relative to salary and responsibility. Neither was happy with the situation and how it came about. They asked me what I would have done. I told them there were two issues from my perspective. First, I said that it was inappropriate and damaging to the work environment to put them in that position. Second, the director's actions could have brought a lawsuit to the organization and it was to the two employees' credit that they had chosen not to take that route. There were other questions that I don't remember. The staff member who was interim manager reported the staff's recommendation to the board.

When I met with the board they said that they were impressed with my resume, but they were more impressed with my professional assessment of their situation with the previous director, my hesitation to take the job based on an ethical concern, and the response from staff about my meeting with them. They had no questions. They said the job was mine if I was interested, and they hoped that I was.

I had only one other person to talk with, Vicki Weaver, who had hired me to work with the organization in the first place. I trusted her judgment and she could help me walk through the ethical issue. She said that it was clear to her that I had no idea the job would be offered when I did the consulting work and no intention of going after the job. She further said that if the issue were ever raised, she would respond on my behalf. So, it was entirely up to me. I decided

268

to take the job and my ethical concern was never raised by anyone else.

VES was struggling with a variety of issues. The agency occupied a building that was much too large, on the edge of a downtown area dotted with homeless shelters, people begging, and prostitutes plying their trade. The Catholic high school and the diocesan offices where the bishop lived and worked were next door on one side. On the other side, mental health day program patients gathered outdoors to smoke, talk to each other, and pace back and forth, occasionally stopping to peer in or tap on the windows at VES. VES was an anchor in a sea of difficulty, The board put the building up for sale but there were no offers.

VES had recently lost a tenant who rented the entire second floor of the building to the mental health program before it was consolidated in the building next door. The rental income had paid occupancy expense for the entire building. This loss created a budget deficit of $50,000 a year, and VES was using its savings to compensate.

VES did not have a fund development program. It had been a community agency for nearly a hundred years, one of the first to be funded by the Red Feather, then Community Chest and now United Way. The number of nonprofits had proliferated in recent years. It seemed as though many people with a good idea started a new agency to address the issues they cared about, much as I did with Every Woman's Place. All were interested in United Way funding. United Way was losing market share because its model, the only organization raising funds in the workplace, had been challenged. Some communities were allowing other organizations to solicit in the workplace. United Way's response was to make the hoops for funding harder to jump through and to try to make less money go to more organizations. Twenty-some years later, it is struggling with the same issues.

VES had changed its name from the Association for the Blind and lost some of its identity. The people now served,

269

compared to those served at the organization's beginning, are more likely to be older and to have a vision loss related to age. There was a concern, some of it real, that this population wished to avoid the word *blind*. The new name, however, was not one that donors particularly identified with.

I had lots to tackle. We knew we had to stay in the building we were in. There was no market and the second-floor maze of small offices made the building particularly unattractive. It was a lot of space in a not-so-good neighborhood. But we needed to make it more efficient and, perhaps, create an opportunity for rental. That set the next priority. We needed to attract more funding, both operating and capital. Was that possible?

I wrote a successful grant to conduct a feasibility study. The findings indicated we could raise enough to remodel the building if we clarified for potential funders who and what Vision Enrichment Services was. When the person doing the study told potential funders that VES was formerly the Association for the Blind, recognition was much higher. I wrote another successful grant to hire a marketing consultant to help us come up with a new name, develop a marketing plan to expand our donor base, and manage the name change. We decided to go back to our old name and add a description to cover those who did not see themselves as blind. We became the Association for the Blind and Visually Impaired (ABVI), and that name exists today.

Long story short, between 1990 and 1994 we conducted a successful capital campaign that allowed us to remodel our building and engage board members in a solid fund development program to increase our annual operating budget. Our intense efforts increased the value of the building; raised awareness of the organization in the community; gave us more attractive, accessible, functional, and easily rented space; and provided an attractive, light-filled board room to replace a dark, narrow room in the basement. Capital campaigns are exhausting. I worked long hours, and I was ready to relax and enjoy a lull.

The lull didn't last long. Work was calm, but my personal life was disrupted once again. In 1994, Jim told me he was seeing someone else and he wanted our relationship to end. One of us had to move out of the house we shared, and I suggested he leave because he initiated the change, not me. I had been perfectly content (well, maybe not perfectly) to have things remain as they were. I loved the house on a nice little lake, I had friends nearby, I was close enough to work; finding a new place was up to him.

But then, my dear friend Susan Back came to me with an offer. Her husband, Harold, owned Erie Development Company, a real estate development business in Chicago, and he was looking for someone to manage it while he concentrated on expanding the company's ownership of shopping malls. Wow! I considered my choices: on one hand, stay in a job I liked and knew I could do well, but live in a house with unhappy memories, or on the other hand, live in a fun and exciting city and work in an industry I knew nothing about. Pros and cons to both. I chose Chicago.

A Move to Chicago

One wonderful thing about Chicago is that you can live close to where you work. Erie Development Company's offices were on Erie Street, a block off Michigan Avenue. I was looking for a condo within a mile. Harold and Susan Back had lived in a condo at 1150 Lakeshore Drive on the corner of Division. I liked the location and there was a vacancy. Susan made an appointment for me to see it and a couple of other nearby condos. I drove down, stayed with her, and looked. It was not a difficult decision. The condo at 1150 was on the third floor in the treetops, overlooking Lake Michigan. I offered $95,000 and it was accepted.

After the mortgage was negotiated and a move-in date set, my friends Shelly and Rick Whallon traveled with me to Chicago on a Saturday and Rick, who is an interior designer, measured the space. The small kitchen was on the right as we entered the condo, and a large pass-through opened to the living/dining area. A short hallway to the left, just past the kitchen, led to a small coat closet, a bathroom on the left, and a very large bedroom on the right. Storage closets were located at the end of the hall. Each condo was assigned extra storage space in the basement near the laundry.

Rick laid out a furniture design and we went shopping. But first, he asked me to go through magazines and pull out things that I liked so he could narrow the search. I chose furniture with clean lines; I liked neutral backgrounds with splashes of color. The only furniture that I kept was an antique oak desk, two dressers, and a television. Everything else was new, right down to the dishes and silverware. This was the first time I had ever had an opportunity to create my own space, exactly as I wished. My friend Liz O'Hara and her kids, Leah and Eric Ruth, gave me a kitten, my moving present. I named her Eleanor Roosevelt. She would be my companion, there to greet me when I came home.

I moved in a few days before I would report to work. I quickly learned that I lived in a neighborhood, not just a big city. I walked to the grocery store and had my groceries delivered to my door for three dollars. Nearby were two major drugstores, a drycleaners which did alterations, beauty salons, restaurants, several movie theaters and, of course, world-class shopping on the Magnificent Mile. I attended Fourth Presbyterian Church five blocks from my condo. It was a mile to work, and if the weather was particularly bad, I could catch a bus right in front of my building or the doorman would hail a cab. I parked my car in our building's underground garage, but I used it only when I visited Michigan. On the corner across Division Street, a tunnel under Lakeshore Drive led to Oak Street Beach. What I liked especially about my neighborhood was the incredible human diversity. I could hear any number of languages as I walked.

My title at the company was president. Harold explained that my job was to manage the business while he developed new business and financing. Erie Development had a small staff, a bookkeeper, a leasing person, and a secretary/receptionist. Susan had been Harold's human resource person, recruiting staff and developing policy, and would continue in that role part-time while studying for her master's degree in social work. At the time that I went to work, they had just sold the Muskegon Mall, owned a mall in Park Forest, Illinois, and were negotiating for a mall in Kalamazoo, Michigan. The former Muskegon mall manager, Faye Hoffman, was brought in temporarily to manage Park Forest. She would move to the Kalamazoo mall after the deal was finalized.

All of the employees reported to me including the mall managers. It didn't take long for me to realize Harold was unable to turn things over to me. He required approval of every decision down to the smallest action, every hire, every expenditure; I could do nothing on my own. I sometimes sat for hours in his office waiting to run decisions by him while he

273

talked on the phone. He chastised employees if they did something which was not done as he wanted it done. It was clear that I had no authority; I was their supervisor on paper, but Harold was their boss. Our values differed. I was used to the nonprofit world where moving forward required relationship building. If I said I would do something, you could depend on it being done or on having an explanation for why it could not be done. In this business, we told people what they could expect us to deliver; however, we did not always deliver what we told them if to do so conflicted with making a profit, the bigger goal.

I was increasingly frustrated and unhappy; I felt stuck, powerless. I had left everything that was familiar. I lived alone, away from my entire support system. I had no one to talk to except for Susan, who was in the difficult position of having her best friend and her husband engaged in a dysfunctional work relationship. When sides had to be taken, she needed to be on his side. She did defend me privately, but I didn't know it at the time. I had a couple of conversations with people who did some contract work with us, men Harold knew. I was seeking support. That was a mistake, inappropriate and hurtful to Susan, and under normal circumstances this is not something I would do.

I started counseling twice weekly with a therapist. For nearly six months I cried for most of the time I spent with her. Eventually, I began to see that the situation was impossible and I would need to take action. It took some time after that before I did. I loved living in Chicago and I loved my living space. Except for work, I was happy there. I went to Overeaters Anonymous twelve-step meetings and met a couple of women that I could do things with socially. I joined a women's group at church. Still, I was not successful in work, something I was not at all used to. I made no decisions, something else I was not used to. For many years I had been self-directed and worked with a team that tried to head in the same direction. It affected my self-confidence when I was not trusted to make decisions.

I kept plugging along hoping something magic would happen. And, I was scared. I was fifty-nine years old. Who would hire me? I had some money saved but not enough and I wasn't old enough for social security. I was stuck, unable to make a decision. I prayed, I talked to the counselor, and I talked to friends from Muskegon and Grand Rapids.

And then, Jose came back into my life. He visited me in Chicago. I visited him in Muskegon. I took scuba diving lessons and we vacationed together. I reestablished Michigan contacts. I was regaining some strength. I went to Harold and told him that something needed to change, that the arrangement wasn't working for either of us, and I needed to leave. I asked for six months' severance. He took a couple of days, and offered me one year's salary. I was surprised by his generosity and thanked him.

I put my condo on the market and moved in with Jose in Muskegon. Before the condo sold, I had another surprise. The Association for the Blind's board president called and asked me to meet for lunch. The board had fired the man they had hired when I left for Chicago. We met to brainstorm, and at the end of lunch he asked if I would consider coming back either as interim or permanently. I said I wanted to talk to staff and see what they were thinking. I did and they urged me to come back. The decision was made. I moved to Muskegon and later the condo sold.

There had been no strings attached to the year's salary Harold offered. My position was that I had taken a risk moving away from my life and support system to take the job with Erie Development Company, and that the job never became what had been described. Harold may have had second thoughts but he continued to fulfill his agreement, and the checks came twice monthly for the year he promised. For ten months I had two salaries and I banked one. It has made all the difference in retirement, so while there was considerable personal loss, there was financial gain.

   With emotional distance my understanding of my time in Chicago is clearer. I came to Chicago at a very vulnerable time after the loss of a relationship and I left behind those things that were familiar and comfortable, my established support system. Harold was born in South Africa and his parents died when he was young. He was left to support his younger siblings in any way that he could. Relatives abandoned the family and did not help this young boy. He scrambled to survive and to make sure his family survived. When his siblings grew up, he gathered enough money to come to America. When he got here he had little money in his pocket. I understand why control, particularly of anything having to do with his money, was so important to him. He would always be that young boy saddled with so much responsibility, scared every single day that there would not be enough. No one could have worked harder than Harold. He was smart in business and he was street smart. We both had strengths that should have made it possible to work together, but our vulnerabilities made it impossible.

   It would take ten years before Susan and I could become friends again. I kept in touch with notes and cards on her birthday and holidays, and I apologized and took responsibility for failing to make the job work and for not handling the separation appropriately. I knew that the loss of our friendship was as hard on Susan as it was on me. We react differently to loss; Susan forgives but draws away to heal, and I reach out to heal. Eventually we set a date for lunch and we began to talk and share as we had before. We visit every year when I am in Arizona. Last year, Harold and Susan visited Jose and me together. Harold treated me as he used to when we first met, warmly, because I am Susan's friend. It is a joy that Susan is still in my life and a pleasure to again know Harold as he was when I first met him, smart, warm, friendly and a good husband to my friend Susan.

Starting my own business

In a way, starting a for-profit business was an accident. I had accumulated a lot of experience in both the public and nonprofit sector and had a smattering of experience in the for-profit world. I augmented my work experience as a volunteer on several community nonprofit boards, and I have been an elected member on a local government board. I strengthened my work experience with bachelor's and master's degrees in public administration. Those are all hard qualifications.

But there are also soft qualifications and in some ways they are more important. I genuinely like most people and I take the time to stay in touch. I don't make this effort with any thought of future benefit. I just enjoy staying in touch with people I like. I also have some gifts, as we all do. I love to problem solve and I don't mind confronting difficult situations in a straightforward way. I notice the gifts of others and acknowledge them. I am organized, thorough, and have good communication skills, both verbally and in writing. And, I know what I'm not good at: routine and suffering fools gladly.

In 1990, friends who were leaders in nonprofit organizations began to ask me to consult with and/or train their constituency organizations. Vicky Weaver, a friend from college, and executive director of Direction Center, a Grand Rapids nonprofit management support organization, was the first to hire me. I was going to do it as a favor, but she encouraged me to charge a fee.

Next, Mary Kieft, executive director of the Michigan Coalition for Domestic Violence and Sexual Assault, an advocacy and training organization whose members work in domestic violence programs, and also a friend, asked me to provide nonprofit board training at a member conference. That exposure led to calls from domestic violence program executives who hired me to train their board of directors. Another friend, Liz O'Hara, executive director of the Michigan

Association of Centers for Independent Living, hired me to facilitate strategic planning for her board. That job led to other jobs with her member agencies. LeAnne Moss, a young woman I had mentored, invited me to work with her board. All three suggested I charge for my work. I did, but I didn't think of it as a business. I was earning extra money and learning.

In 1994, the friend who invited me to Chicago, Susan Back, had also been doing some consulting and suggested we form a partnership. Her expertise was in human resources. We incorporated as Management Innovations and developed marketing brochures. We worked together on a couple of jobs but, sadly, my departure from her husband's business left us at odds. We had invested an equal amount in startup which paid for legal and marketing costs, so there were no assets to complicate the process. In fact, since the marketing materials referred to us both, they were not usable. She signed the business over to me.

I continued to consult occasionally while working full-time. In 2000, I got a call from Cathy Lucas, executive director of the Nonprofit Alliance, a nonprofit management support organization in Battle Creek, Michigan. Cathy had formerly been the executive at the domestic violence program in that city, and knew I had designed quality assurance standards for the operation of domestic violence programs in Michigan. The Alliance is funded by the Kellogg, Battle Creek Community, and Miller Foundations to help local nonprofits build capacity. She started the conversation with, "Come have lunch with me, I want to pick your brain."

Cathy hired a University of Michigan professor, Dr. John Tropman, to design a model identifying the characteristics of a successful nonprofit. Now she needed practical tools, based on Tropman's model, to assess an organization's current level of capacity. After explaining the project, she asked, "Would you consider designing the tools and field testing the process with five local agencies?" It was a great opportunity, and I quickly said yes. The Alliance's funders were pleased with the outcome, so pleased that they agreed to encourage other nonprofits in Battle Creek to engage in an assessment process.

I was still working at the Association for the Blind and could not possibly conduct all of the assessments that might be done, so Cathy hired me to create a trained pool of consultants. In addition to conducting some of the assessments, I reviewed the assessment reports and problem solved with each of the consultants I had trained. I became a consultant to the consultants, work I continued to do for Cathy's successor when she moved into other work. Meanwhile, I was also doing occasional consulting work in Muskegon and Grand Rapids. All of this came without marketing, unless intentional relationship building without any purpose other than to believe that it is the right and professional thing to do, can be called marketing.

I retired from full-time work in 2002, we traveled in our recreational vehicle during the winters, and for the next ten years I continued consulting when I was in Michigan each summer. I used the internet and my phone to work with the consultants I had trained. In 2012, at age seventy-six, I could see that I had to work harder to do things that I had done easily in the past. I wrote more notes to myself because I could not depend on my memory for the detail that I used to remember easily. I had no difficulty problem solving, and I was still quick at coming up with solutions, thinking on my feet. I decided to narrow my consulting work to participating on team assessments for the Michigan Domestic Violence Board, which I had been doing long before I had a consulting business.

There have been wonderful, unplanned benefits from having my own business. The income has provided a better retirement than I might have otherwise had. I have not had to withdraw investment income which ensured that the rest of my life is financially secure. I have continued to use my skills and kept my brain active, which has added to the quality of my life. I have always been clear with myself that I wanted to be the one to decide when it was time to quit, when I'm not feeling quite as sharp as I once was, and before anyone else says I'm not. The day has come. I'm grateful to have had the opportunity. I'm ready for full-time play and hoping for another ten years to do so.

From this day forward

In October, 1995, Jose's youngest daughter, Alicia, called me. We caught up on each other's lives, and then she asked, "Are you seeing anyone?" I told her no, and she said, "Neither is my dad." I asked, "What happened to his girlfriend?" She laughed, "Ding, Dong, the witch is dead, and we think Dad made a mistake and I wonder if you have any interest in getting back with him." I laughed, both at the witch comment and her straightforward question. "I don't know, Alicia. I haven't seen your dad in twelve years. "Well, you know," she said, "he'll never make the first move, but I think he'd be happy to hear from you. Think about it. I'll give you his phone number and address." I told her I'd think about it, we chatted about her life, husband, and kids, and she gave me the address.

Part of me wanted to make the contact, but the other part was afraid. Rejection is not fun. I talked to my friends. Some felt he hadn't treated me well in our breakup and I should leave well enough alone; others told me to listen to my heart. I had loved Jose and done enough soul searching to know that I had some responsibility for our breakup; the blame could not all be laid on him. I was busy with work, growing and changing, and I paid only as much attention to the relationship as was required to keep it going.

Finally, I decided to send a note. I couldn't get up the courage to call. Three weeks later Jose called. I invited him to come to Chicago to visit and he did. I was nervous that morning before he came, and when he arrived, it was a little awkward. Both of us chattered, and I could tell he was nervous too. I showed him my apartment and took him up to the rooftop to see the view of the city and Lake Michigan. I suggested he might want to move his car to the garage in my building, but when we walked to the place he had left the car, it wasn't there. I realized, because I lived in Chicago, that he had parked in a tow-away zone where cars were required to have a parking permit.

We spent half the day trying to find out where it had been towed. I called every place I could think of to find out where his car had been taken. Finally, someone suggested a garage where we might find it. We took a cab to rescue the car and the cab got in an accident. The driver told us we had to stay until the police came, but we said *"No thank you."* We got to the garage and an attendant said the car was there but couldn't tell us exactly where it was parked. Jose walked up and down rows of cars and finally found it. He brought the ticket back to the clerk as instructed, paid the $115 fine, and retrieved his keys. While all of this was going on, I found myself feeling uneasy. In this kind of situation in the past, Jose would have been upset with himself, withdrawn and been miserable, not at all open to any friendly response, and when he withdrew, I always felt rejected. I said, tentatively, "You must be upset by all this." He looked surprised, "No," he said. "I'm just glad I brought enough money to pay for it." I thought to myself, *maybe there has been a change since I saw him last.*

The rest of the weekend was fun. I invited him back to Chicago, he invited me to his home in Muskegon, and in between we talked on the phone. He talked a lot about his latest passion, scuba diving, and asked if I might like to take a dive trip with him. I remembered his previous passions for snowmobiles and four-wheeling, which were not all that exciting to me, but, what the heck, I said I'd give scuba a try. I learned there was a dive training school near my apartment, signed up for lessons, and earned my certification.

Over time, we each remembered and owned mistakes we had made in our past relationship, and we were able to let go and focus on the many positive things we liked about being together. It turned out that the thought I had in the parking garage about a changed Jose was accurate. He was more comfortable with himself, more confident, and there was far less withdrawal.

We dated long distance for a while, and when I left my job in Chicago in the summer of 1996 and returned to Michigan to work, we decided to live together in his house in Muskegon. In early 1997, with Jose looking toward retirement, we bought a house in Florida, and signed legal documents so that we jointly owned both homes. He adopted my cat, Eleanor Roosevelt, not legally of course, but in all other ways. Neither of us seemed to be concerned about merging our lives.

Had I waited for a marriage proposal, marriage might never have happened. Jose did not get up the courage to actually ask me for a date in our first round of relationship, although it was clear we were mutually attracted. I made the move that led to twelve years of dating. I knew we loved each other, and so did he, but he's a little slow on taking the next step. He tells me he never asked his children's mother to marry him, either. So, we sat in a restaurant one evening and I said something like, "Now that we have two houses and a checkbook in both our names, have you considered the possibility of marriage?" Looking only slightly pale, he responded, "I've thought about it." "So, what have you thought?" I asked. Sometimes pulling sensitive information out of Jose feels like I'm working for the FBI and interrogating a terrorist who knows he has something to lose if he says too much. He finally responded, "I'm thinking all good things. Let's get married." We made a plan and on September 13, 1997, we were married in the little church I attended while living in Greenville, Michigan. Pastor Lynne Kronewetter officiated, my daughter Julie was my attendant, and Jose's son Victor was his.

I was sixty-one and Jose was sixty-five. I had been unmarried for twenty-six years and Jose for twenty-seven. In our first meeting, he was a skinny guy who couldn't speak English, and I was a young girl having a great time playing

 the field. In our second incarnation, he was my brother-in-law and the best man at my wedding. We were both struggling with difficult marriages. In the third incarnation we ignored our differences, and went with the terrific chemistry between us until the chemistry could not outweigh the differences. In our final incarnation, I realized he really was the best man, and he figured he was strong enough to deal with a woman who would never obey.

Jose is the love of my life. I had finally reached a time when I was able to make a healthy relationship choice. From the day of our marriage, until death we do part, we will be together. Every year has been better than the last and all of them were good. He is still leading me into adventures, and I remind him often that the chemistry is still working.

Peace and beauty and underwater adventure

When Jose and I reconnected in October, 1995, after a twelve-year gap, he said in one of our conversations that he had gotten his scuba diving certification three years earlier. He had been on several dive trips to the Caribbean and excitedly described the experience. I particularly remember hearing the words *when I opened my eyes I was surrounded by sharks.* Immediately after he asked, "Would you have any

interest in learning to scuba dive?" Well, this wasn't a marriage proposal, but it meant he saw a future to our relationship. Laughingly I said, "I'll get back to you on that." I found it hard to think simultaneously about diving with sharks and a future. I thought about it the next week. I wasn't at all sure I would ever have the courage to dive with sharks, but I learned to swim at a very young age and loved being in the water, so I was interested.

Jose arranged for me to take a pre-diving class at the Young Family Christian Association (YFCA) pool in Muskegon with an instructor from the local dive center. Everyone has to go through specific training for scuba diving certification. Here is what it was like for me. The first thing you learn to do is breathe underwater using a second stage regulator, a device with a mouthpiece and a hose that connects to an air tank. When swimming underwater you hold your breath and come up when you need air. With an air tank you breathe underwater through the mouthpiece which you clamp in your mouth with your teeth. It's not as easy as it sounds.

At first I felt claustrophobic and had some difficulty trusting the breathing apparatus. My instructor was great.

He recognized the panicky look, pulled me up so my head was out of the water, and said, "I'll hold your shoulders like this," and he gently put his hands on my upper arms. "Now, look me in the eye the whole time, I won't take my eyes off you, and we'll go under together. If you need to come up, just nod your head." He paused briefly and said, "Ready?" I nodded, he again took me by the shoulders, and we moved down into the water. I found that when I looked him in the eyes, the claustrophobia disappeared and I relaxed.

The next thing I learned to do was to become buoyant in the water, which requires staying level underwater without bobbing to the top or touching the bottom. This is done by regulating your breathing. As instructed, I breathed in, filled my lungs with air, and began to rise to the surface; then I breathed out to sink further into the water. The idea is to breathe in a relaxed way, taking in just enough air and letting out just enough air to keep level. The instructor declared after we worked for an hour that I would do just fine.

When I got back to Chicago I checked the phone directory for dive schools and learned there was one within a couple of miles of my condo. I signed up for a two-weekend class. In early January, with below-zero temperatures and the wind howling off Lake Michigan, I drove to the dive school, parked the car, and went in. There were about fifteen students, all ages from twelve to fifty-nine. I was the fifty-nine-year-old. The first day was book instruction. There is a lot to learn about the mechanics and the rules involved in diving. The next day more book instruction, and we learned how to put on our buoyancy vests and hook the second stage regulator to the air tank. Then we got into the pool and practiced our breathing.

The following Saturday I continued dive instruction, more book work, more breathing and buoyancy practice, and learning to use the dive computer, which tells your depth, how much time has elapsed, temperature of the water, rate of ascent and descent, and time to come up before you go into decompression. On Sunday we did our last confined water dive and took a written test. I passed, the paperwork was completed, and I was ready for the final certification stage, an open-water dive.

Jose had booked a one-week February dive trip to the Turks and Caicos, a chain of forty islands and cays, only eight of which are inhabited. They are located five hundred fifty miles southeast of Miami, east of Cuba, and just below the Bahamas chain. Our base would be Providenciales on Grand Turk, the largest island in the chain. I would do my open-water dive there.

We arrived on February 24, and after settling into our room, Jose and I gathered our diving gear and met Dale Woodhams, the dive master who would test me in open water. He watched me hook up the air tank and put on my fins, and told me to walk backward, sliding my feet on the sand instead of lifting them out of the water. He asked me one-by-one to demonstrate the hand signals used to give and get instruction from your dive partner and to signal if you're in trouble: yes, no, surface now, turn around, ascend, descend, I'm okay, I'm in trouble. Finally, we dove, he watched my buoyancy, we surfaced, and he was ready to sign the certificate that said, "*This diver has satisfactorily met the standards for open water diver as set forth by PADI (Professional Association of Diving Instructors).*" I was certified to dive in open water and restricted to diving no deeper than 100 feet. In order to dive deeper, I would have to take more instruction and be certified as an advanced open-water diver.

My first dive in the open ocean was the next day. We took a boat ride to the dive site. The captain sat at the helm in the bow of the boat. There are benches on either side with a tank rack about eighteen inches above the benches; the rack has round openings that the air tanks fit into. I wore my brand-new dive suit, black and purple, and bright pink fins, dive mask, and snorkel. I had ordered the glass in my dive mask fitted with my eyeglass prescription. My weight belt was at my feet. I was nervous. Would I remember everything I'd learned?

When we got to the dive site the captain shut off the engine and the crew dropped the anchor. Everyone started dressing for the dive. I pulled up the top of my suit, zipped it to my neck, and put my weight belt around my waist, which allowed me to descend into the water without having to swim down. Then I attached the air tank to my buoyancy control vest (BC). The back of the vest has straps with Velcro to hold the tank. I then attached my regulator to the tank. I sat down, put my fins on my feet, positioned my mask above my eyes, and slid my arms into my vest.

When it was my turn, with butterflies in my stomach, I walked carefully to the platform at the back of the boat and pulled my mask down over my eyes, making sure it was tight so water wouldn't leak in. The crew checked my air tank and turned on the air. I pushed the valve on my hose to add air to keep me buoyant when I first hit the water. I put my mouthpiece between my teeth, took one giant step making sure to avoid the ladder to the platform, and I was in the water. I lifted the hose with the valve to release air from my BC and began my descent. Once my head was underwater I pinched my nostrils and blew to equalize pressure. Jose never has to do this, because his ears adjust by themselves.

A master diver guides the dive and you always dive with a partner. Of course, Jose was my partner. When we got down about eighty feet we leveled off and I looked around for the first time. The water is crystal clear in the Caribbean Sea and you can see for a long distance. There are walls of coral in a myriad of shapes and colors, tubes, fans, cones, vase-like forms in red, green, yellow, orange, shades of brown. I was surrounded by fish of every shape and size, multi-colored angel fish, yellow, blue, red, fish that look like rocks, fish that look like sand. They travel in schools and the schools ebb and flow with the movement of the ocean. I swam with them. They don't swim away unless you do something to startle them. It is very quiet and all I could hear was my own breath, in and out, in and out. It's mesmerizing. Jose tapped me from time to time to show me things: a huge green lamprey eel hiding in the coral, a nurse shark swimming below us, a barracuda hanging still in the water just a few feet away, a tiny almost invisible sea horse sitting on coral, lobsters hiding behind a rock, a sea snake. We stayed down an hour on that first dive. I was so relaxed in the water that I was able to conserve air better than most first-timers.

When it was time to ascend, we were back under the boat. We ascended very slowly and when we were between twenty-five and fifteen feet from the surface we made our ten-minute safety stop. This is done because when you're underwater your blood absorbs nitrogen with the pressure. The safety stop closer to the surface allows you to equalize your system with atmospheric pressure above water and rid yourself of the nitrogen, preventing you from getting the "bends", a decompression sickness that can cause severe joint pain, paralysis, and even death.

When I got to the surface I was behind the boat. When it was my turn to board, I waited for a wave to push me to the ladder, grabbed hold, slipped off my fins one at a time, and handed them to a crew member on board. I then undid my BC with the air tank attached and, still holding the ladder, guided it to a position where the crew could grab it and pull it up on the deck. I took off my mask and walked to my place on the bench, exhilarated about completing my first open-water dive. We headed for our next dive site and the second dive was just as amazing as the first. We did two dives each day for the next four days, ten dives total for the trip.

The following summer on August 16, I completed my certification for advanced open-water diving. I trained in a water-filled, very deep gravel pit in Gilboa, Ohio. Visibility was less than one foot, and I learned to navigate with no visibility. Training also required descending more than one hundred feet and staying there for a period of time. It was cold. Advanced certification allows me to regularly dive beyond one hundred feet, night dive, and dive wrecks if I choose.

Jose and I took many dive trips between 1995, when I was certified, and 2002, the year of our last dive. We dove in Costa Rica, Honduras, Cozumel, the Greek Isles, Bonaire, Grand Cayman, Turneffe Island off Belize, and several times in Puerto Rico.

Any description of scuba diving that I give cannot begin to capture the beauty and peace under the sea. Every above-water thought goes away and you glide side by side with the fish as if you were one of them. It energizes and relaxes simultaneously. I don't know if we'll dive again. Jose does his adventures in phases, and we've been busy seeing the country with our feet planted on the surface. He wholeheartedly jumps into one activity, and when he tires of it moves on to the next: snowmobiling, four-wheeling, scuba diving. I don't know what's next, but as much fun as the adventures have been, if it's sky diving I'm not going. Once you leave that plane, if it doesn't go as planned, you are likely to die. I'm not ready for that yet.

Making it through mid-life strong in mind and spirit

It seems as though I have always known that I was strong, a survivor. My earliest memories are that grownups believed I could take care of myself. When I was seven years old, shortly after my parents divorced, my mother came to my grandparents' house for one of her infrequent visits. I cried and told her I wanted her to live with us. She told me she missed us too, but that I would be okay. She said that I was smarter than she was when she was young, and I would always be able to take care of myself. I don't know if at that time she believed those words, but I think now that she needed to believe them.

When I lived with her my last two years of high school, she often told me she had never felt able to take care of herself, that she got into relationships because she believed she needed to be taken care of. She said she didn't want that for me. She said I was smart and would always be able to take care of myself, and she hoped I would never be in a relationship because I had to, but only because I wanted to.

My dad also said I was strong and that my mother and my brother were not. Each time we were moved from place to place, he told me to take care of my little brother, who wasn't as strong as I was. He told me often that my mom was weak, had a drinking problem, and did not live up to her responsibilities, but that I would not turn out like her. Sometimes, when he was angry about something I did, he told me that if I didn't straighten up I would end up like my mother. It was confusing

My grandmother told me she would never have to worry about me; she said I needed to look out for my brother, and that sometimes I was too independent for my own good. When I lived with her and was sent to the Whaley Home, what I took from the experience was that somehow I was the one that could handle it. Why else would I have to leave while my brother and cousin continued to live with Grandma?

Frankly, inside I did not always feel strong and smart. I felt scared and often unloved. In spite of that, over time I did come to believe that I was strong and smart, that many people sometimes feel scared and unloved, no big deal. I developed a warrior spirit. If you have a warrior spirit you speak up for what is right and you stand up for yourself and for others who cannot. You learn that if you get knocked down, literally or figuratively, you get back up. You believe that you are an individual with your own gifts, and that it's not a good idea to live your life based on what others think you should be. You get to decide who you are, what you need, how to live life. You share your life with others, and because you care about them you do what you can to be a positive presence, but you do not let others define you.

Why state this so strongly? In my first marriage, as a young twenty-one-year-old woman, I nearly lost that warrior spirit; I nearly lost myself. Today I guard it and I know without a doubt that I will never come that close again. My mother never fully gained a warrior spirit. Thank God, I did, and I believe I've passed it on. My daughter has a warrior spirit and things are looking pretty good that my granddaughter does also.

RETIREMENT: THE YOUNG OLD YEARS

*"To be what we are, and to become what we are
capable of becoming, is the only end of life."*

Robert Louis Stevenson

What does it mean to be old today?

If we retire at sixty-five, the age when individuals can receive full social security payments, many of us can expect to have fifteen years to do whatever we wish providing we are healthy and have enough to live on. What a marvelous gift.

People define old differently. When you're young, fifty is old. I define old as having three stages. These descriptions are generalizations, not absolutes, based on what I have noticed about people my own age and older. I call the first stage the young-old years. If you are blessed with good health as many are, these are active years. Our grandmothers, and even our mothers, could not have imagined living life as many young-old people live today. People work, they exercise rigorously, travel, volunteer, run for political office, go back to school, take up a hobby, or fulfill a dream abandoned when young and they were limited by day-to-day responsibilities. Many focus on time with their grandchildren if they have them. They continue to look toward the future, thinking about what they would like to do next.

The second stage is the old years. Most people, not all, slow down. Health problems may begin. Minds are sharp, but the information retrieval system is often not as quick. Aches and pains settle in. Exercise helps, but it's evident many don't feel as spry as they once did. Vision and hearing loss are common. People who matter to them die, maybe even their spouse. They live in the present--sometimes reflecting on their past, reliving the good times but sometimes reviewing regrets. If they're healthy enough, they're hoping for more time, yet aware that they must make the most of the present. Most don't dwell on those thoughts, but they are there.

Finally, if they live long enough, they become one of the old-old. Some are healthy enough to continue living alone; others will need assistance. Life narrows. There may be less travel. If they've moved to warm places in the winter and back to their home base in the summer, as I have, they may now settle on one or the other. They continue to lose people they care about to death. They spend more mental time in the past. There are more years there than in the future. They may have lots more prescription containers lined up in their medicine cabinet, or maybe they have one of those little boxes where their daily medication is organized by days of the week and times of the day. If they haven't had a face lift, they're likely to see a lot of wrinkles on that face in the mirror but they're looking less often so it doesn't matter so much. Their biggest hope for themselves is for good health and an easy death. They may wish they could go on forever or, if they are ill, they may be ready to join those who went before them.

There are attitudes about age in our culture, ways in which those who are younger view old age in a different way from the person who is aging. In our culture we don't have a history of valuing and honoring old age. We don't seek out the wisdom that many older people have gained through years of living and learning. In fact, old people are often trivialized, neutered, and patronized by the young, not intentionally but in ways that are clear to the elder. Some people, total strangers, call old people *honey* and *dear*, and look at them with the same smile they give to precocious children. Sometimes they will pat or rub the elder person's shoulder as they do with children. The old-old person knows he or she is not viewed as an equal. It is the rare person who looks an old person directly in the eye and offers a handshake as they once did. I have been the recipient of this negative attention, mostly by people in service jobs. It annoys me no end; I am the same person I always was and while the day may come, I have not yet drifted into senility. I have never suffered fools gladly, so when someone calls me *honey* and *dear*, I just smile nicely and say, "I'm not your honey, my name is Beverly."

Here's something you don't know until you are old. Old age is the most wonderful time in life for those who are healthy as I am lucky enough to be. Youth spend considerable time worrying about whether they measure up. Middle-aged people spend considerable time worrying about getting old and not being as vital as they once were. Most old people know they don't have enough time left to worry about the things they cannot change. They live more in the moment. They are comfortable in their own skin, and they don't worry about sags and bulges. They are who they are and most of them like who they are. When they gather with others their age, hilarity ensues. They laugh at their frailties and brag about their grandchildren. They like feeling useful and will jump in to help. They are not afraid to be silly. Their greatest wish is that they remain connected to their family.

So, for all of you who are reading my story and have not reached old age, I give you hope that it is way better, way, way better than you can possibly imagine.

A part-time marriage in a retirement home I never lived in

Jose could hardly wait for retirement. In October, 1997, at age sixty-five, one month after we married, he resigned from his job as a mechanic for the City of Muskegon's Public Works Department. Happily he was eligible for full social security benefits and vested in the city's pension fund. In the 1970s, he had started his own business, Jose's Boat Service, which meant he worked two jobs for more than twenty-five years. It was time to play.

In the spring, just before his retirement, we visited my friend and former mother-in-law, Elinor Geyer. She lived in the River Ridge housing development in New Port Richey, Florida. We took a walk one day, stopped at the clubhouse, read postings on a bulletin board, and found an advertisement for a two-bedroom house on Baltusrol Street, fully furnished, $75,000. In this development, you owned the house, but the development company owned the land, which was perfect for us because all of the yard work was handled by the developers. On a whim, we called the number and were immediately invited to view the house.

We loved it. There were two bedrooms and two full baths, one on each side of the house allowing for considerable privacy. The large living room, which ran the full length of the house, had a dining area on one end. The kitchen was fully equipped right down to the silverware, a family/television room was off the kitchen, and a screened-in porch faced the backyard. The laundry room opened to the oversized car garage. The subdivision amenities included a golf course and a swimming pool next to the clubhouse. The pool was never heated, so we wouldn't use it, and we don't play golf.

We returned to Mrs. Geyer's house, talked it over, and made an offer that very day. A local attorney prepared the closing paperwork for us while we went back to Muskegon.

We made one more trip and took some furniture, most importantly a bed for the second bedroom. The following fall, shortly after his retirement, Jose drove down, moved in for the winter, and began updating the house. He ripped down the ceilings, which were made of a popcorn-like material, and put in flat ceilings. He replaced the screening on the back porch with a heavy plastic type of material that allowed us to use the room in cooler weather. I bought a desk for that room, and we moved the second bedroom's sleeping couch out there so kids could sleep on it. He worked hard on the lawn, including planting trees and flowers. Everything was painted fresh. He also spent time helping Mrs. Geyer and her daughter, Gloria, fix things that needed fixing. He played cribbage with them, and they often shared meals that the two women prepared.

I negotiated with the Association for the Blind and Visually Impaired board of directors so that I could work from home in Florida for periods of time during the winter. I spent two weeks at Thanksgiving, returned just before Christmas and stayed through January, and spent two weeks around Easter. I added a computer, a copier/fax machine, and a phone, and worked at my desk in the Florida room.

My children, Brad, Brian, and Julie, and Jose's daughter Alicia and her family, either some of them or all, visited at Thanksgiving, Christmas, and Easter. I loved the Florida house, the only house Jose and I had bought together. I loved spending time with him in that house. I loved getting away from Michigan's cold and I loved being with family on holidays. But there were some tensions.

When I visited Florida I flew into St. Petersburg and took a shuttle directly to our door. When I walked in, Jose was delighted to see me and I was delighted to see him. There was always a momentary period of adjustment, a re-entry issue. I walked through the house reacquainting myself. Jose is a person who likes to have a project going, so there was always something changed. When we moved in, I was the one who arranged things in the cupboards and closets in a way that was comfortable for me. When I visited, Jose had rearranged some things, putting them in places that seemed logical to him. In the beginning I would ask, perhaps territorially, "Why did you move that there?" He responded, "Because I wanted it there." I was trying to reclaim some of *my* territory, and he was letting me know it was *his* territory. After a couple of these power struggles, I recognized that it was my problem, that I was moving from complete independence to interdependence, from answering only to myself to sharing my life with someone I loved; he was not an enemy who was trying to usurp my independence. I realized how silly it was to care which cupboard the glasses were in.

I also loved living by myself in Michigan when I wasn't in Florida. Prior to our marriage, I had been living in Chicago alone. I was used to planning my own time and doing whatever seemed like a good thing to do in the moment. I have a lifetime of friends in Muskegon with whom I like to spend time, or I can spend hours reading. I love to go to the movies alone. I could have meals when I was hungry without concern for feeding anyone else. I always gave a lot to my job and I often stayed late to finish something or came in early to get a head start on a project. It seemed like a perfect situation. I was content. But, after four years or so, Jose was restless. He hated the Florida traffic, and had run out of projects to occupy his time. He had attended some meetings of a social group for men who lived in the subdivision, and also the homeowners' association meetings. People were not welcoming, so he didn't go back. Jose is a friendly guy and will chat with anyone, so they must have been quite standoffish. He was ready to move on.

When I came to visit in spring 2001, he wanted to look at motor homes. We ended up buying a Safari. Jose drove it home, and that summer we parked it at Crystal Lake Campground between Ludington and Scottville, Michigan. We went there weekends and back to our house in Muskegon during the week. He winterized it and left it in Muskegon when he returned to Florida. I turned sixty-five in August, 2001, but unlike Jose, I was not eager to retire. I couldn't imagine what I would do and I loved working. I didn't have any hobbies other than reading. At the end of October, Jose went back to Florida. I knew a decision had to be made, and it meant that our half-married, half-not, life would end. For five years, we owned a lovely two-bedroom home in Florida that I had been looking forward to living in when I retired. My dream for retirement was to spend summers in our Muskegon home and winters in our Florida home. During those five years, Jose had lived more or less patiently alone for half the year while I continued to work. He was bored and he had a different dream. I was beginning to think I would never really live in this house I loved. We had two houses and a motor home, too much real estate for two people who lived by themselves for six months each year. Something had to change. But what? And how would I adjust?

In January, 2002, on my visit to Jose and our Florida house, we talked and I understood that he was unhappy and wanted to leave Florida. We planted a for-sale sign in the front yard. A couple visiting their friends across the street came over to look and made an offer. We sold the house. Jose flew to Muskegon, picked up the Safari and moved into the nearby Suncoast RV Park. When I came to Florida in the spring it was to the Safari.

Although the Safari was forty feet long, it had no slideouts and felt confining. Jose wanted to again look at motor homes. Let's face it, he likes all things mechanical. We did and he fell in love with a 1997 Fleetwood American Dream with a long slideout that expanded the living room and kitchen and provided much more space than the Safari. It was his favorite color, blue, two shades, accented with white. We negotiated with the salesman and the lowest he would go was $91,000 plus the Safari, for a total of $139,000. I was not keen on spending that much on a vehicle that would depreciate in value. We kept looking while I was there but nothing appealed to Jose. When my visit ended, he took me to the airport to catch a plane back to Michigan. He was very quiet. We bought a Starbucks latte and sat down. I said, "You really love that American Dream, don't you?" He said, "I do." I said, "Go buy it," and I got on the plane leaving behind a happy husband.

Jose and I had both been single for a long time and we were used to making our own plans and managing our time in whatever way suited us. We saw ourselves as independent, accustomed to and liking to make decisions without consulting anyone else. This lifestyle allowed us to continue to do that for half the year. When I went to Florida I was visiting. It was a little like a series of honeymoons. We were always excited to see each other. During the other half of the year when Jose moved back to Muskegon, I was still working; we had time apart, but we were together every day. We began to learn how to negotiate the private space we both needed, how we would spend our money, and what was and wasn't important to us. This separateness wasn't part of a well thought out plan. It started because we had made individual decisions that suited each of us, Jose to quit work and me to continue to work. Were we ready for a full-time marriage? It would come, ready or not.

Ten years in our American Dream

When I was young I had a young woman's dreams...college, marriage, babies, happily ever after. College didn't happen, marriage and babies did, happily ever after would remain a dream. When I had children my dreams became dreams for them. They would have what they needed and some of what they wanted. They would attend college if they wished. They would be prepared for life, able to take care of themselves. And I would do all I could to make that possible. In what seemed like only a moment, my children were grown, prepared for life, and on their own. I was no longer a young woman. It was time for a dream of my own, an older woman's dream. I could think of nothing. I had been getting up and doing what had to be done every day for so long that I had forgotten how to dream. I was not married and I didn't want to be. I was not healthy and I sort of wanted to be. I had been taking college classes for years and I assumed that someday they would all add up to a degree. I already had a career that mattered to me. A degree would satisfy my original dream. I couldn't imagine retirement. So, I just kept on doing what I had been doing, living one day at a time.

And then, in 1997, I married, happily. Somehow in the years before Jose came along I had made exercise a part of my everyday life and earned two college degrees. I had managed to save some money for the time when I would no longer choose to work, but I was not ready to retire. I loved my work and the feeling of competency I got from working. My husband was ready to retire and he did. He waited five years for me to be ready. He's great at keeping himself busy, but five years was long enough. He had a dream. I still didn't, so, I decided, why not try his. His dream, and now mine, would be lived in our 1997 Fleetwood American Dream, a forty-foot motor home.

We established four basic rules. We would travel anywhere we could get to in the Dream with as little planning as was practical. We would avoid traveling anywhere cold. We would come back to Michigan for an extended time in the summer. We would go out of our way to make visitations to friends and family who lived in various places around the country. This would include stopping every two years or so for air travel to Puerto Rico to visit Jose's original family. That answered my only concern. I would miss my friends, children, and grandchild. I needed to maintain those connections. My emotional well-being depended on it.

We set off that first year, 2002, by deciding we would head south. The direction was established because Jose  wanted an expert to thoroughly inspect the rig before we set out. We traveled to the Fleetwood headquarters in Decatur, Indiana. This would be the first of many trips to have something changed or fixed. Anything you want or need for a recreational vehicle can be found in Decatur, Indiana.

This first trip was a shakedown trip. We thought we had prepared for anything, but now we would find out. We had no sooner set out than I heard a bang behind me. I turned around to look and uttered my favorite profanity, one I learned from my mother. I had left a gallon jug of water on the kitchen counter and now we had a lake on the kitchen floor. I got up, grabbed some towels, and started sopping up the mess. It is a strange feeling to be on your knees in the kitchen in a motor home traveling seventy miles an hour on the expressway. I learned to make sure everything was off the counters, put away or tied down.

There were other lessons I would learn on other trips. Probably the most important was that I should not get up and walk around the motor home when we were in traffic and Jose might have to use the brakes. I made that mistake and learned the basics of the theory of momentum. There is no way you can stop your body in motion if the brakes are applied suddenly. There is nothing to hang onto. Believe me, I tried to find something. I went from standing up in the kitchen to falling and sliding and rolling to the front, hitting my head on the wood frame around the television, on my back looking up at Jose, hurting and shocked. He asked me what I was doing on the floor. A dumb question, I thought, but I responded, even with the pain, that I was worshipping at his feet as he'd always hoped I would do. This saved me from a lecture, although I'm really not quick enough to have thought of that ahead of time.

That first year we lived our four rules. Campground reservations were made when we got within an hour of where we thought we might stay that night. Somewhere along the line we decided we wanted to fly to Puerto Rico for Jose's sister's fiftieth wedding anniversary celebration, which required planning the location we would fly from so we could make plane reservations. This created a new rule which is, there are exceptions to every rule. We visited my son and grandchild in Augusta, Georgia, and Jose's daughter and family in Hollywood, California, and we stayed in the southern part of the country where it was warm: Georgia, Florida, Alabama, Louisiana, Texas, Arizona, and California.

We have lived full-time in our American Dream for more than ten years now. We have traveled to nearly every state including Alaska, three times to Mexico, and twice to Canada. We have thoroughly covered the south, the northeast, the northwest, and the entire west coast. Jose doesn't like busy places, so we have not traveled the east coast south of the New England states. We have visited with family and friends around the country every year and traveled to

Puerto Rico every other year. After our sixth year, and seeing most of the south, we now spend four months in Arizona every winter where we have formed new friendships; we travel back to Michigan for at least three months every summer. I write letters to friends and family describing our travels with words and photos, and I put together an album every year with pictures of where we've been. After eleven years I'm on album twenty-one. Our memories are captured.

I wonder sometimes, but not often, when and how this wonderful dream will change and what the next one will be. Jose is still excited each fall to be on the move and swears he won't stay in one place any longer than four months. We're both in good health, so why not. Recently, after I got rid of the last of the furniture I stored at the beginning of our adventure, thinking that someday we would settle in one place, I asked Jose before I made the decision when he thought we might do that, stay in one place. His response was, "We won't need furniture because the next stop will be the nursing home and their rooms are furnished." Now that's funny.

Even though I started out without a particular dream, the travel bug is contagious and I am dreaming of going beyond our current limits. You can't cross the ocean in a motor home. I'm working on Jose. We traveled to Paris to celebrate my seventy-fifth year. He was reluctant but once we were there he loved it. I'm thinking Italy, maybe Ireland, maybe Scandinavia. We do not have a plan, but our American Dream could easily become Americans with a European plan. Why not?

Marriage as a full-time job

We had researched full-time living in a recreational vehicle. My daughter agreed to let us use her address as our permanent address. We moved our income sources to direct deposit, and our few regular payments--insurance, telephone, satellite television, and internet--to automatic deduction from our checking account. We found an RV park we liked in Montague, twenty miles north of Muskegon, and made a deposit for the next summer when we would return to Michigan. On the first of October we headed out. Our only plan was the direction we would travel, and our goals were to stop wherever there was a place we wanted to explore, providing it wasn't too cold.

The one thing the research did not talk about was what it's like for two first-born children, now very independent adults, to live together in a forty-foot-long by eight-and-one-half-foot-wide living space and continue to like each other. We learned through trial and error. Actually, in the first year we only had one argument. It was, "I'm right!" "No, I'm right!" But, we had that one argument many, many times. We were like boxers who go to their separate corners when they've had enough. In this case, one stayed in the front of the RV where there was a television and the other went to the back of the RV where there was another television.

There were usually two things that created friction. What ticked me off most stemmed from Jose's well-intentioned attempts to be helpful. For example, I would be cooking a pot of something on the stove and Jose would turn down the flame and say it was up too high. I would react by saying, "I wonder how I managed to cook all these years before you were around to regulate the way I do it." The thing that ticked Jose off most was that he thought he had clearly explained something, I thought I understood what he said, I took action based on what I believed we agreed on, and then he became frustrated because the direction I took was not what he thought we had agreed on. When Jose is frustrated, he speaks in *you's.* "You never listen." You don't pay attention to what you're doing." I feel criticized and off we go.

I'm always aware that I'm more verbal than Jose. Words go from the brain to the mouth much faster for me than for him. I also know that if I don't guard what I say and how I say it the results are not worth it. He shuts down and withdraws, and when he withdraws I feel abandoned, and it's just not a good thing. I learned to go to the back of our bus before I opened my mouth. By the end of the first year in confined space we had experienced more arguments than we were comfortable with, so when we weren't in an aggravated state, we talked about our issues and the way we each deal with frustration. We agreed that it wasn't working very well, that the important thing was that we love each other and want the best for each other, and that we needed to figure out how to get beyond our bickering. Ninety percent of the time we loved our new life on the road, but the 10 percent left us feeling not so good about ourselves. We agreed that our marriage, our relationship, was our full-time job. The marriage came first. If we unintentionally hurt each other, and it was unintentional, the fun we intended to have, the joy we wanted in our life, would be tarnished.

So, we changed our ways, at least most of the time. I quit reacting when Jose gave me instructions in how to correctly (in his view) do the housework I'd been managing my whole life. It wasn't easy, but I said to myself that he means well and he wants to be helpful. I also recognized that Jose comes from a background where men make the decisions, or at least their wives let them think they do, and he had married an independent woman who was highly resistant to following orders. That wouldn't change, but I don't react when he is trying to be helpful and discord has lessened. When we have a communication issue, and he thinks I didn't pay attention and got the information wrong, we have learned to say, "Well, I must have been speaking Spanish and you were listening in English, or the other way around." Then we laugh.

It's not that we don't occasionally get frustrated with each other. We do. But we don't hurt each other. Recently, we realized that whenever one of us suggested a path to follow, before a sentence is completed, the other one says, "I know." There it is again. We both hate to be told what to do and must quickly assert our independence. We both love to be in charge in true oldest child fashion. I vow to bite my tongue before I say *I know*. Let's see how well I do. I know that I have a great marriage with a pretty amazing man who loves me and has made my life far more interesting than it would have been without him. He and marriage are my full-time job, and the paycheck is increased joy, a payoff worth much more than getting the last word.

Summers in Michigan, winters in warm places

Michigan and Muskegon County have been home for nearly sixty years; my roots go deep. I know how to get to almost any place without a global positioning system. Two of my children, two of Jose's children, two of his grandchildren, and one of his great-grandchildren live there, as do many of my closest friends. My favorite pizza place and my favorite coffee shop are there. The grocery store I've shopped in for so long is still there. I'm comfortable there.

When we first began to travel both Jose and I worked in our respective businesses part-time, his a boat service and mine a consulting firm. He sold his service truck after our tenth year of motor home living, and I told my customers I was cutting back and might do one consultation in a summer, maybe not.

Nearly every summer, at the beginning of May, we arrive at Trailway RV Park, our summer home in Montague. It's not especially warm in Michigan in May, but the snow is gone and people are thinking summer. There are just over fifty rental spaces in the park, about half rented to seasonals like us. There are only a few who have been there as long as we have. Jose knows almost everyone and I know almost no one. I prefer to spend my time with friends and family.

Recently the small local gym, where we have gotten to know the regulars, has gone out of business. We joined the only other gym in town, and fortunately most of those we knew have done the same. We discovered a nice restaurant on a small nearby lake where we meet friends for lunch or dinner. We ride our bikes on the bike path. Jose and his son Victor, who has his own automotive repair business, often meet for lunch in Muskegon or just hang out in Victor's garage. Jose fixes things for others in the park, and someone is always knocking on the door asking for his help. I spend time with my daughter, Julie, who has just bought and decorated a house near Lake Michigan. I have lunch or coffee with friends, or we have couple friends over for dinner. I occasionally sunbathe at Pere Marquette beach in Muskegon, or walk from our RV to the small bookstore in downtown Montague. All of this has been squeezed in between our jobs. It will be interesting to see how time flows now that we are not working at all.

We usually leave Michigan when the park closes in mid-October. A few times we left earlier for planned trips to New England, the northwest, and to Alaska. In my opinion, mid-October is the most beautiful time in Michigan. It is Indian Summer; the trees are a riot of color, red, yellow, orange, and brown; it's sunny with just a touch of cool. I never like missing it, a part of me always hates to go, but after a lifetime of leaving places I cared about I get over it. We're off for the next travel adventure.

For the first six years of travel, we moved from place to place, never staying more than two or three weeks. Then in our seventh year, we began to spend more time at Canyon Vistas RV Resort in Gold Canyon, Arizona, east of Phoenix and within an hour drive of Jose's youngest grandchild. We have made couple friends there, and collectively we are the Tenth Street Circle, for the obvious reason that we all live on Tenth Street. The difference between an RV park and a resort is the abundance of activities and amenities. Canyon Vistas has a great exercise room, two large pools, and a community room where dances and potlucks are held and entertainers perform. The activities schedule includes exercise and writing classes, card games, hiking clubs, sewing and carving classes, and all kinds of crafts and computer classes. If you have an interest and others are also interested, there will be an effort to start a class.

The weather in Arizona is the reason we're there, and I have learned to love the desert. It has a beauty all its own. It took awhile, because people from Michigan like lots of green trees. We're close to Phoenix, a large city with cultural opportunities including two great independent film theaters, yet far enough away so Jose can climb mountains.

Membership in a Write Your Life class, taught by Coleen Ehresmann, a former teacher, sparked considerable joy and led to this book. I like it here, but as I've said before, our stay is limited because my adventurer husband likes being on the move, and I'm always going to move with him.

The Road to Enduring Friendship

In early January, 2004, Jose and I were two of forty-six strangers in twenty-three RVs gathered in El Paso, Texas, to travel with Tracks to Adventure Tours through Mexico's Copper Canyon. We were all over fifty, most over sixty, and we all love RV travel, some full-time and others part-time. Twenty-seven days later, with 1,796 Mexico driving miles, 900 miles of canyons on a train, and an overnight ferry ride on the Sea of Cortez, we landed in San Diego. Ten of us had become friends forever. We have much in common, we love to travel, and we're retired and free to do so.

Bob and Sue Derber are difficult to ignore. Bob is six feet, five or six inches tall, and Sue is around six feet. They literally stand out in a crowd. Bob loves a discussion and will argue either side. He is an engineer and likes to figure out why things are the way they are. Sue is a teacher, a soft-spoken, pleasant person who has strong beliefs but would prefer to just get along. She enjoys crafts and makes beautiful things. On this first trip Bob was appointed sheriff, and his job was to find *infractions* for which we might be fined when we had our morning meeting. The money collected was donated to a charity for children in Mexico. Each day started with laughter because of Bob's sense of humor and clever, original reasons for fining people. They are from Springfield, Illinois, and travel with their dog, Trapper.

Bill Ferguson and Susan Hansen both worked for the Riverside, California, sheriff's department. We first noticed them when their truck nearly fell off the railroad flatbed car as it was being loaded. Their efficiency was impressive. Bill immediately gathered others to get the truck back on the flatbed, and Susan documented the accident with her camera. They were calm and polite, not once losing their cool. They travel with two dogs, Domino and Sarah. Bill is quiet, but when he says something people listen. He loves motorcycles, boats, and action. Susan is meticulous in everything she does.

She is particular about doing things right, a committed protector of animals; their dog Sarah is a rescued stray. Little will upset Susan more than mistreatment of an animal.

Nick and Trish Nichols have homes in Marshfield, Missouri, and Las Vegas, Nevada. Nick is a large man and sports a gray beard. He has more hair on his face than on his head. His smile lights up a room. Trish is interested in others, articulate and smart, and immediately you know she is wise and capable. Nick was our weather forecaster, announcing every day what we could expect by the clothing he wore. If it was going to be sunny, he wore shorts and a colorful Hawaiian shirt. He makes people laugh and is a gifted writer. At community dinners he often shared what he had written about our travel experience. He found out that I like wine with dinner, and made sure I had a glass at each meal. Trish was a fundraiser for United Way, and we immediately connected over our experience working in the nonprofit sector. Nick was a cabinet maker.

David and Rosalee Castell are from Edmonton, Alberta, Canada. David was a banker and owns a chain of battery stores. He would be described as thoughtful and dignified, and curious about and interested in knowing people. Rosalee is pretty, friendly, and outgoing, a homemaker whose passion is her grandchildren. David and Nick connected when Nick's side mirror was knocked off by a truck on one of the harrowingly narrow roads in the Baja peninsula. David helped remount the mirror, and as a joke marked the one on the driver's side with bright orange tape.

Jose was the only traveler in the group who is bilingual in English and in Spanish and he was often asked to interpret, especially at gas stations where an attendant pumped and took your cash, not always giving the right change. He also was helpful with menus. In addition, Jose was recognized for having the cleanest RV. He took every opportunity to wash the outside of our rig. There were many comments from other travelers who teased him about making them look bad.

As often happens when you spend a month with strangers with whom you bond, there is an exchange of contact information and promises to stay in touch. "Call us when you're in our neighborhood," we all said. Intentions are good, but most often there is no follow through. This group is different because we are all travelers, and there is a greater likelihood that we will find ourselves near where the others live. It is also true that when you travel a lot you learn to connect quickly with others, perhaps not at depth, but to make a connection nonetheless.

Over the next couple of years, we contacted each of the other four couples when we traveled near them. When we stayed in Desert Springs, California, we called Bill and Susan. They invited us to theater and dinner in nearby Palm Springs. We called Nick and Trish when we were near Las Vegas, and they hosted us for dinner at their condo. Bob and Sue travel in their RV almost as much as we do. They stopped to see us in Texas and Arizona, and made a visit to our summer park in Montague, Michigan. We called David and Rosalee on our way home from Alaska. David came to the RV park where we stayed, and drove us to their house for dinner.

In 2005, Trish Nichols contacted all of us asking if we would like to travel to central Mexico for six weeks in February and March, 2006, and offered to plan the trip. David and Rosalee, who are world travelers and almost never home, couldn't make it, but the rest of us gathered in Del Rio, Texas, and spent almost two months traveling in our rigs through Mexico. On this trip we started a new tradition, naming our group *The Adventurers*. Nick designed a logo with our name and a pair of crossed maracas, printed it on paper, and we each attached it to the upper left corner of our windshields. We learned on our first trip into Mexico that if you are traveling with a tour group, and tour groups always have logos, you are less likely to spend as much time at the border and checkpoints. On subsequent trips, our logo has changed depending upon where we are traveling, but our name, *The Adventurers,* has stuck.

We quickly learned that Trish is a premier trip planner. She designed the route noting the attractions in each location, checking with us frequently to see what kinds of things we might wish to do. She also created a signature drink for each trip, another tradition formed. We learned that Bob Derber is a wonderful caravan leader, and Susan Ferguson, with her experience on police radio, is a great tail gunner. She kept track of the caravan and radioed information on our CBs. Nick as our banker puts all group expenses on his credit card, and prepares an accounting on Excel for us at the end of the trip. Jose is a master mechanic who has every tool available and knows how to fix most any problem. All of us are reasonably good cooks, and if we don't eat out we share a communal meal.

On this, our first trip after the Copper Canyon Tour where we met, Trish made sure we had plenty of social time. Nearly every day we went sightseeing, we chatted in pairs, groups of four, sometimes just the men, and sometimes just women. Each evening started when Trish delivered our first signature drink to our door, a Golden Margarita, while we prepared for our evening out or at home. After dinner we planned our route and what we would see the next day. We laughed a lot and there was no conflict. Another tradition began when we had a final dinner and Nick read from his journal the funny and helpful things others had done, and all of us talked about what we liked best on the trip.

Our next trip was hatched in late 2007, in a meeting between the Derbers and the Nichols. Trish emailed each couple and suggested we travel to the Canadian Maritime provinces in summer, 2008, and again offered to plan the trip. Rosalee and David couldn't make it, but the rest of the Adventurers were ready to go. Emails zipped back and forth, a route was chosen, RV park reservations were made, and Nick designed our logo, a Maple Leaf.

315

This trip was planned for almost three months, nearly double the time of our last trip, a long time to travel together for any group of people, but rarely was there tension. We all are seasoned travelers, and we all have done a lot of living, so if one of us became irritated with another, it never erupted into an argument. Each time someone voiced a concern it was always met with an effort to accommodate. We all know that when traveling in a group, you have to be willing to go with the flow. It helped that our signature drink on this trip was another Trish creation, the Peach Bellini, proseco and peach nectar, which is mellow, sweet, and delicious. An evening with a couple of those helped ease any strains of the day. Another tradition began on this trip. We noticed that anytime we got near some object where the purpose wasn't entirely clear, all the men gathered, stared at the object, and took turns commenting on what its purpose might be. We women, having realized that the guys were lagging behind, turned to see where they were and invariably one of us would say, "Speculating, always speculating." No one else might find this funny, but it happens so often that we have labeled the behavior a male idiosyncrasy and find it amusing. After reaching a conclusion they can agree on, the men tell us what they think the gadget is--not that we are terribly interested.

On this trip, it is my hope that another tradition began. We ate at a restaurant that served the best coconut cream pie I have ever eaten. From that point on, at every place we ate, we looked for coconut cream pie. We asked people if they knew where we could duplicate our pie experience. The worst one was when a woman sent us to a gas station that she said had delicious coconut cream pie. We really should have known better, but when an addiction takes hold you're likely to go to any lengths. Finally, one evening after dinner, Bob Derber surprised us with a homemade coconut cream pie. He got the recipe online at an Emeril website and it was fantastic.

In early 2010, I contacted the Adventurers to tell them I was planning a six- or seven-week trip to New England. Only

Bob and Sue Derber could make it. This might not have been a true Adventurers trip, because without Nick there was no logo and without Trish, there was no signature drink. We did discover Stella Artois beer, which has become a favorite, and Bob made another coconut cream pie.

In winter, 2011, the Adventurers gathered in Lake Havasu, Arizona, where Bill Ferguson and Susan Hansen have a vacation home. We had not all been together for about three years. This time Rosalee and David were able to join us. We decided that all five couples would travel to Puerto Rico, Jose's homeland, in January of 2012, this time without our RVs. Trish and Jose planned the trip. No RVs meant no need for a logo, but our signature drink was coquito, a Puerto Rican favorite made with pitorro, basically moonshine. We spent our last evening sharing our favorite thing about the trip. Every person said it was the kindness and generosity of Jose's family. Rosalee and David suggested we all travel in Banff, the Canadian Glacier National Park, Jasper, and Vancouver Island in summer 2014. I hope we can make it happen.

The Adventurers have become close. We email, we visit, and we know what is going on in each other's lives. Every trip each couple downloads all their photos onto the computer of every other couple, and Nick and I each prepare a travel journal that we forward to others. We're making memories. We share the big and important stuff--Bill is living with cancer; Sue and Bob's dog, Trapper, died as did Bill and Susan's dog, Domino--and sometimes the mundane: Sue Derber is taking Zumba, I'm taking a writing class, and Rosalee and David's grandkids are learning to ski. We remember birthdays, and we know that Nick and Trish have sold their home in Nevada. We don't know exactly what drew us together when we met by chance as we did on our first Mexico trip, but we do know why we continue to be drawn to each other, why we go out of our way to connect. We love travel, we love new places, and we love each other. We are *The Adventurers*.

More about Evelyn Stiver, best friend for a lifetime

It has been said that there are three kinds of friends: friends for a reason, friends for a season, or friends for a lifetime. When you make a friend, you never know which it will be. I always hope, when someone becomes a close friend, that the friendship will last a lifetime. Sometimes it hasn't worked out that way, but when it does there are incredible rewards. In a way it is like a marriage. There is a time when you understand that if the relationship is going to last forever, you will not only overlook the other's idiosyncrasies, you will see them as endearing. You might even recognize that you too have some idiosyncrasies. It's unconditional love and that's what my friend Evelyn and I share.

Evelyn (left) and I met in 1954, not long after I moved to Muskegon. She was with two friends we both met while attending Muskegon School of Business. We stood on the sidewalk talking, and I remember that she said something that made me laugh. Early the next year, and coincidentally, she moved into an apartment on the second floor of the converted Victorian apartment house where I lived. That's when we became best friends. I was nineteen and Evelyn was twenty.

Evelyn is taller than I am, perhaps, five feet seven compared to my five feet four. She has baby-fine brown hair that she bemoans won't hold a curl. Her eyes are the first thing you notice, large and brown under perfect eyebrows. She would say her nose is the thing you notice first. We all have a feature we aren't fond of, hers was her nose. She is long-waisted and well-endowed bosom wise, has nice legs, and is curvy. I don't think she ever really appreciated her attractiveness. But the guys did.

318

Evelyn was born on a farm in Copemish, Michigan. Like me, she had one younger brother and no sisters. When she was very young, her father was sent to a tuberculosis sanatorium and her brother had a congenital bone condition that had him hospitalized at a very young age. This put a huge burden on her mother. At some point they had to leave the farm and live with relatives. Evelyn remembers that she didn't feel welcome and says this was when she became a dreamer. She spent hours imagining a life that had no troubles and she could accomplish amazing things, mostly the ability to make life better for someone else. She tells me she can and does easily do that same day-dreaming today.

Evelyn was always up for a lark. She reminded me of my cousin Patty, except there was a naiveté to Evelyn, an innocence. I loved to get her to say off-color things that she had no idea were off-color. She did silly things that made me laugh. Sometimes the soldiers we dated sneaked us onto the army base, which was conveniently located on a secluded Lake Michigan beach. One Sunday afternoon, I remember Evelyn and her date, Mac, acting out the beach love scene from the movie, *From Here to Eternity*, the one where the couple embraces on the shore while the waves wash over them. While it looked romantic in the movie, we were all laughing so hard that it was anything but. Neither of us was a heavy drinker, but there was usually beer available. The drinking showcased another gift Evelyn had that I didn't. She could spend the whole evening drinking beer without making a pit stop. Oh, to be that lucky.

The pattern of our friendship changed when we both met the men we were to marry. We had our first children nine months apart. Her daughter, Cheryl, came first, before my son, Brad. Evelyn often said I was busy having fun making a baby while she was having no fun at all in labor. Three years later I had another son, Brian, and the year after she had a daughter, Linda. A year later I had my daughter, Julie. Evelyn and I didn't see each other on a daily basis. We both were in difficult marriages, worked outside the home, and were focused on our children. We were in touch regularly by phone, and we got our kids together when we could. They have grown up together. Cheryl and Linda call me Aunt Bev, and I truly feel like their aunt.

Evelyn and I both divorced in 1964, and we were back on the dating scene together. We were a lot wiser than our first time around, a lot more wounded, and a lot less innocent. But still we had fun. She arranged the blind date that introduced me to my second husband. I was her bridesmaid at her second marriage, and she was bridesmaid at my second marriage. We had something else in common: We were bad judges of character when it came to men. We saw less of each other during this period. My marriage brought me five additional children, and hers brought heartbreak that no one should have to bear. We still spent time with each other and talked often on the phone, but we weren't having much fun. Both of our marriages ended in 1971. I was thirty-five and Evelyn was thirty-six. Having figured out that we were the common denominator in two failed marriages, I stayed single for the next twenty-six years and Evelyn is still single.

Evelyn's greatest quality as a friend is loyalty and the ability to see me as smarter and wiser than I actually am. One time we were at an event where Betty Freidan, world-famous author of *The Feminine Mystique* and other books, was the speaker. There was a reception for her after her speech and Evelyn actually bragged to Betty Friedan about my work on behalf of women. It was sort of like, *I know you're a big deal, Betty Freidan, but I have a friend who is also a big deal.* It was embarrassing, but heartwarming nevertheless. Her most annoying friend quality is that she is always fair. You don't always want your best friend to be fair. Once, when I was angry at my boyfriend, now husband, Jose, I said, "Jose says some really hurtful things sometimes." Her response was, "Well, but basically he's really a nice guy." In the middle of anger at your boyfriend, you do not want your best friend to take his side. You want her to say he's a jerk for treating you that way and that's what I told her. She said, "Okay, then, he's a jerk."

She has a quirky sense of humor. Once when we were in our mid-thirties, and both single, we went out to a bar where there was dancing. I was on the dance floor and she was talking to a couple of men who stopped at our table. She found one attractive, so she asked the other one, "See my girlfriend over there?" pointing to me on the dance floor. "She spotted you awhile ago and said she thought you were attractive." Well, when I came back to the table, she said, pointing at this fellow, "See that guy over there? He told me he thought you were attractive." I looked over and caught his eye, and we spent the evening dancing, him thinking I thought he was attractive, and me thinking he thought I was. She told me this on our way home. She thought it was funny.

Since we have both retired, we lead very different lives. I am married and for the past ten years, for seven months of the year, my husband and I have traveled the country. I'm in the Muskegon area near Evelyn in the summer, usually for five months. Evelyn's first and most important activity is being grandmother to her five grandchildren. One of her granddaughters attended college on a volleyball scholarship, and Evelyn traveled all over the country to attend her games. Her grandchildren love being with her, and even her grandkids in college seek her out and stay at her house often. They fight over who gets to spend alone time with her. She rides roller coasters with them. She has a heart condition and still got on a zip line when the grandchildren did and rode to the end. This required a walk up a hill after the ride which she couldn't do, and knew she couldn't, but she wants to do what the kids do. So, she just walked up to a worker and told him she wasn't in good enough health to walk the hill and he got her a ride.

Evelyn is not just my best friend, she is my sister. Like sisters she is sometimes irritating. She is smart but she doesn't think she is. When you're out with her she talks to perfect strangers while you stand there waiting to move on. She sees her world as a cup half-empty, and dwells more often on what has been difficult in her life, and there has been plenty. I asked her once if she really thought she had things worse than most other people, and she very thoughtfully said that, yes, she did think that. I pointed out that while life was tough for her, it was sometimes much worse for many others. And that is undoubtedly *my* most annoying friend quality.

Our friendship has lasted going on sixty years. When she had a house fire a few years ago, I was there to help her sort everything out. When I asked her to volunteer for a

 friend who was running for office, she was quick to sign up. Our families get together when all of our kids are in Muskegon. When I'm traveling we talk by phone, and when I'm in Muskegon we go to movies, something we both love, and we catch up on grandkid activities. She celebrated her seventy-fifth birthday a year before I celebrated mine and I drove across the country to attend her party. She was first in line to celebrate my seventy-fifth birthday. We have been through the fun times and the tough times together. As we age there may be more tough times. As long as we are able, I have no doubt we will continue to be there for each other. Evelyn may be a friend for a reason, someone who thinks I am swell and is proud of everything I have accomplished, a substitute for a birth family that wasn't able to give me that. She is definitely not a friend for just a season. She is a friend for a lifetime, a friend no matter what, a friend who loves and is loved unconditionally.

Friends are chosen family

I've always envied people who had great big close families where generations of parents, grandparents, brothers and sisters, aunts, uncles, cousins, nieces, nephews, and siblings gathered to celebrate family. That was not my family. We were a unit of mother, father, brother, and sister in the beginning. That unit fell apart when my parents divorced and we moved away from my mother. My brother and I were shifted from place to place, which brought us closer but made it difficult to form lasting friendships with others. As it turned out, over time, I created a family of friends, some of whom have been part of my life for more than fifty years.

There are different kinds of friends. Some friends came into my life because for a time we had common interests, we worked together, took a class together, or our children were friends. Others came into my life, we were close for a while, and then for whatever reason we drifted apart. With still others, I formed a bond that has lasted. We developed trust, we share secrets, we celebrate good times, and we are present for each other when there is trouble and hurt. I was in a seminar once led by a very wise woman psychologist. She said, "You're lucky if you have five real friends, friends who put aside their own interests, and are quick to ask how they can help if you are hurting or sick or in trouble, and you would do the same for them." A woman in the audience said, "I have many more than five friends." The psychologist responded, "Tell your family not to hold your funeral on Super Bowl Sunday. They might be surprised how few show up."

I, too, have more than five *real* friends but I would define *real* differently. I believe my responsibility in a friendship is to listen, encourage, support, confront if it's important to do so, share in joy, and comfort in sadness. I describe my most important friendship requirement in one word...loyalty. I may not always think what a friend does is appropriate, but abandonment of the friendship is an option only under extreme circumstances. A friend and I may drift apart, but we do not rip each other apart.

I understand that people have different capacities when it comes to friendship. Friendship needs to be a two-way street, but a *real* friend doesn't keep track of who does what for whom. Some of my friends are quite self-sufficient, others need more support, and some have more demanding lives. My friends and I have values in common. We can have a difference of opinion about some things, but there are belief systems that would be a deal-breaker for me. I could not be close to someone who is racist, sexist, or homophobic, or someone who is violent in thought, word, or deed. I dislike lies that serve no purpose, and I believe that something told in confidence should be kept in confidence, for a lifetime if necessary. Trust is an absolute.

In the small high school I attended we were all friends. There were four girls who were my closest friends: Doris and Shirley Coon, DeDe Ardrey, and Linda Blamer. Shirley was the closest; we were neighbors and schoolmates, and we moved to Muskegon together right after high school and shared an apartment. We are still in contact although our paths don't cross regularly. We have been friends for sixty years and share memories of an important time in our lives.

Evelyn Stiver was my first new friend when I moved to Muskegon after high school, and I wrote about her earlier. We went through marriage and divorce together, we raised our children together, and we have never been out of touch. She is my best friend; we consider ourselves sisters. She is loyal to the max. I am honorary aunt to her two daughters, Cheryl Gillespie and Linda Parker, two dear young women that anyone would be proud to have call them aunt.

When I married into the Geyer family, my mother-in-law, Elinor, invited me to join her card circle. We met monthly to play pinochle. I was twenty years younger than the other members but they welcomed me and the age difference never mattered. In that difficult marriage these women provided acceptance, friendship and laughter. Three years ago, the five of us who were still living gathered to reminisce.

Many friendships that are important to me were formed with women who were active in the women's movement in the mid-1970s and early 1980s. Fighting the worthy battle for women's equality together formed bonds that have continued. There are too many to name, and I know as I name some I will miss naming others who were also dear to me. Those who are the closest were part of a consciousness-raising (CR) group I belonged to in the 1970s, and a support group formed in the 1980s. We don't meet regularly anymore because our lives have greatly changed, and many of us do not live near each other, but we are never out of touch.

Consciousness-raising groups were established for women to educate themselves and each other about the unique issues that women confront, to define which of those issues exist because of cultural expectations, and to determine what we could do together and in our own lives to change the culture for women and for ourselves. The phrase of the time was *the personal is political*. We met monthly and we shared very personal things; we trusted each other implicitly. We still do.

CR group members I am closest to are Anne Beyers, Susan Harrison, Judy Fleener, Pam Breakey (pictured with me below) and Sue Ashby. Susan is a writer and was a reporter for the local paper; Pam was a social worker and became an

Episcopal priest; Judy was a teacher, homemaker, and wife of a priest; Sue was a co-founder of Every Woman's Place; and Anne was an early childhood expert and

started the children's center at Every Woman's Place. Later she founded a women's center in Waukesha, Wisconsin, where she now lives. Susan and Judy still live near Muskegon, and Sue Mills has moved back after living in California for several years. Pamela is in southwest Michigan. There were other members but the six of us were especially close. Over time, lives got busy, people moved, and the group disbanded, but the five of us have continued our friendship for more than thirty-five years. We gather in twos and threes and keep track of what is happening in each other's lives. I organized a reunion in my seventy-fifth year. Only Anne could not make it. A year later, everyone except Sue Mills traveled to Wisconsin to spend a weekend with Anne. Today, Anne and Pam are living with cancer. Their illness has drawn us closer. Lately, we have initiated round-robin emails and our words are as deeply personal and as honest as they were in the beginning, probably more so because we have years of earned trust. No one feels a need to dress things up. Whatever we are feeling in the moment gets said, from *I don't like my husband much this week*, to *I've learned a lot from cancer and here's what I've learned.*

The women's support group formed because I thought that five of my friends who didn't know each other well had a lot in common and would like each other, and because my own life was so busy and gathering monthly ensured that I would have time with each. Susan Harrison, a member of the CR group, was also part of the support group, which included (pictured below) Liz O'Hara, mother of two, an activist in the

 field of disabilities; Jane Cirona, stockbroker and mother of two; Susan Back, mother of two, a city manager and later a therapist; me, and Theresa Siuda, social worker and mother of twelve.

For probably ten years, we gathered at one of our houses or another, even after Liz, Susan Back, and I had moved from Muskegon. Jane eventually drifted away from the group, and Susan Back lives in Arizona and we visit when I am there. I frequently spend time with Susan Harrison, and visit Liz almost every year. Teresa died a few years ago but I am in touch with some of her children.

Perhaps, this group is more typical of friendships and how they change than the CR group. People divorced and married, changed careers, moved away, had disagreements. We may have had an idealized view of each other in the beginning, and it was the ideal that changed rather than the caring for each other. I seldom see Jane unless we have both been invited to the same event. We are cordial but not close. Liz lives in Iowa and Susan B. in Arizona, and I see both of them every year. Susan Harrison and I spend time together in the summer when I'm in Muskegon. Each time Liz, Susan B., or Susan H and I meet, our conversation begins where we left off the last time we met. Our history and affection for each other will keep us connecting as long as we are able.

I have made two other very close friendships. Maureen Burns and I became prayer partners when I lived in Greenville, Michigan, in the late 1980s. We spontaneously spend time together, but meet formally every month to share the things in our life that need prayer. That kind of sharing requires deep trust and brings us very close. When I am away we continue our prayer meeting by phone, and when in Michigan we meet for prayer over coffee. We have been friends for nearly twenty-five years. Early on she gathered

seven women (left, back row: Mary Johnson, Marty Schoolcraft, Sally Morais and Maureen Wolverton; front row, Connie Borton, Maureen Burns and me) who have been meeting monthly for several years to play Scrabble. I join them for the five months I am in Michigan. We share more than Scrabble talk and have become close.

Jeanette James (below) and I have been friends for twenty years. We met when we worked at the Association for the Blind and Visually Impaired in Grand Rapids. We immediately liked each other, but because I was her boss, we couldn't really be friends. Our friendship began when she left to work someplace else. She has lived a very different life than I have, but to know Jeanette is to love her. She is impulsive, which has sometimes created problems for her, but the openness and caring we share transcends our differences.

 She knows and trusts my love for her is unconditional, even though I have sometimes been critical of the scrapes she has gotten herself into. She loves me back, and I can depend on hearing truth from her. Her cup is always more than half full, and she's fun to hang out with. She lives in Georgia now, but I see her almost every year, and we are in touch nearly every day by email or Facebook.

There are many others I count as close friends, women and men. My children's grandmother, Elinor Geyer, and her daughter, Gloria, are especially close. Elinor died last year and I miss her. I have women and men friends I have worked with, either in paid work or community activism. Peggy Jensen and I shared a wonderful beach house for two years. Gail Trill and her beautiful daughters always welcomed my dropping in when I need a comfy place to roost, and I visit her and her partner, Linda, in Traverse City nearly every year. MaryAnne Maycroft was a NOW friend, I worked with her at the Association for the Blind, and she and her husband, Tom, are couple friends. Terry MacAllister, Bob VanLente, Roger DeMeyere, John Hills, Bill Fleener, and Jerry Lottie are all men whose values I admire. Several years ago I lost a friend I loved dearly, Steven Gregory. He died of AIDS as did many young men before treatment was found that has enabled those who have the disease to live a normal lifetime. I have lost other friends too, and expect I will lose more.

There are many women I worked with in the domestic violence movement that I still see when I am near where they live. Jose and I travel with four other couples who are friends. We also have a circle of friends who gather in the same RV park where we stay for a time in the winter.

I work to stay in touch with all of my friends. Technology makes it easy, and many live in Muskegon so I see them in the summer. I know what's new in their lives, what's new with their children if they have children, how their work is going if they work, what they're doing in the community, their joys, their losses, and, because we're getting older, their health issues. We are always glad to hear from each other; it matters that we care. We are family of a sort with the very special bond of a lifetime of shared experience. I don't know how many of them will be at my funeral, but I believe each of them will be in my life until one of us leaves the Earth. Who knows after that?

What reading has meant to me

When I was about seven years old and living with my grandparents, I made my first trip to the library. I don't remember who took me, maybe my cousin Patty, who was a year older. The library was in Berston Field House, a kind of community center on North Saginaw Street, although they didn't call them community centers then. The field house also had a public swimming pool and outdoor space for games, maybe baseball. We often walked there to swim, but on this day, we went to the library.

I remember walking through the library door and into a big room with shelves on every wall and some standing in orderly rows throughout the room. There was a woman sitting at a desk just as we walked in. She raised her index finger perpendicular to her lips, the universal sign for *shhh, be still*. I could not have moved or spoken anyway. I must have been about four feet tall and the shelves, filled with books, towered over me. At least that's how it seems now. I remember thinking, *I'm going to read every book in this room.*

The woman at the desk pointed me to the children's books section. The shelves were lower here. I sat on the floor, pulled out a book, and started to read Dr. Seuss's book, *The Things That I Saw on Mulberry Street.* I was hooked. I loved the rhythm as I said the words to myself. I loved the brightly colored pictures of all of the amazing things that a little boy named Marco had seen on Mulberry Street. I read the last page,

"And that is the story that no one can beat,
When I say that I saw it on Mulberry Street."

I was in love with books. Other loves would come and go. This love would last a lifetime.

I checked out the book and took it home. Perhaps I checked out more books; I don't remember. After that, there were many more visits to the library. I read at every opportunity. In the summertime I sat in the swing on my grandparents' porch, swinging slowly and reading. Grandma would often come out and tell me to put the book down, get out and play, and *"blow the stink off of yourself."* My parents were not readers. Reading seemed like a waste of time to them, but it transported me to another place and another time. I was introduced to new people and new things with every book I read. At night, after Grandma heard our prayers and tucked us in bed, and after I heard her footsteps reach the bottom of the wooden stairs, down from the second floor where our bedroom was, I pulled out a book and the flashlight I had sneaked from the dining room buffet where Grandpa kept it, and read some more. I was addicted to books.

I moved on from picture books as all children do. I have early memories of reading and loving Louisa Mae Alcott's book, *Little Women*, and feeling like Meg, Jo, Beth, and Amy were my friends. I knew them well. I especially identified with Jo, the sister who was the leader, the adventurer. I read every Nancy Drew mystery book and the entire *Anne of Green Gables* series.

There was a period of time in my life when I did not read so much. I worked full-time, and had young children who required considerable attention, a house to keep clean, clothes to wash and iron, and friendships to keep track of. I read magazines, things that were easy to pick up and put down when some responsibility overshadowed the pleasure of reading. But during my second marriage, when I was still working full-time and the house was filled with eight children from ages three to fourteen, reading became an escape, a refuge. My children still talk about how they called to me when I was reading and I ignored them. *"Mom, Mom, Mom, M-ah-ah-ah-om!"* I heard them but I knew when their calls meant something truly was urgent, and when they simply wanted me to referee some disagreement they were having. They didn't like it much that I ignored them, but reading saved my sanity by carving out that precious private space I needed. It was my time. With eight children, there was no private space, not the bathroom, not even a door on my bedroom, so I read amidst the tumult and to forget it was there. It would wait for me, I thought, and it did.

When I enrolled in college at age thirty-five, I took my first college-level literature class. I had literature in high school and we read the stuff we had to read, Shakespeare, I remember, and *Beowulf*. I was not so much enamored of those, nor of required reading, books chosen for me by others, but I learned a whole new way to read in college. I discovered that books go beyond the words on the page, that there are undercurrents, themes, and meanings that I could discover; there was depth and mystery and wonder. We read Alexandri Solzhenitsyn's *Cancer Ward*, *Things Fall Apart* by Chinua Achete, Joseph Heller's *Catch 22*, Henrik Ibsen's *A Doll's House*, and *The Bell Jar* by Sylvia Plath. I was hooked in a new kind of way.

I didn't give up escape reading, I never will. There will always be a need to separate myself from whatever is going on around me, but I have broadened the range of what I read and enjoy. I escape with women detective stories: Marcia Muller and her Sharon McCone series, Sara Paretsky and her brainy V.I. Warshawski, Sue Grafton and heroine Kinsey Millhone, Linda Barnes and the lovely Carlotta Carlyle. I like some male detective books too. I devoured John D. MacDonald and his Travis McGee series. I love Robert B. Parker's Spenser and Ed McBain's 87th precinct series. I read current authors, best sellers, books recommended by other avid readers, and the classics, some of which I read long ago and some I missed along the way. I like historical fiction and I read nonfiction usually in spurts when some activity piques my interest. In the 1970s, I read many books related to the women's movement. I like autobiographies, mostly those written by women. I read books that speak to spirituality and faith. I've read the Bible twice from beginning to end. I've read business books to expand my skills and to help me think more broadly about organizational development issues encountered in my consulting work. Eclectic is how I describe my reading tastes.

Sadly, I know now that I will not read every book in the library as I thought I would when I was seven years old. Happily, authors, who must also be readers, just keep writing books and filling shelves. For a long while, I too filled shelves in bookcases. I carted my books from one place to another, increasing numbers of heavy boxes. When Jose and I moved into an RV, there was no room for bookshelves. I stored my books at my daughter's house. After a couple of moves, and several years of being responsible for my heavy book boxes, she told me she had moved my books for the last time and I needed to do something with them. Who could blame her? It was hard for a moment, but I gave them all away, and took comfort that someone else would enjoy them as I had.

I've found that almost every RV park has a library and until the advent of computers and buying books on line, I shopped at bookstores across the country. I love bookstores like I loved the library. I salivate over my choices just as I do when I read the dessert menu at a top-notch restaurant. Who am I kidding--any restaurant. I especially love the small, independent bookstores where there is always a person who loves books as much as I do, and who is happy to recommend her or his latest favorite. Those little bookstores are disappearing, crowded out by the chain bookstores, Borders and Barnes and Noble. Now some of those are closing too, outsold by the giant online company Amazon.com.

Amazon began advertising its Kindle reader and Barnes and Noble its Nook, both electronic library devices. In 2011, I purchased a Kindle, and now at the push of a button, any book I want to read is instantly available. I love the convenience, but I will always miss the feeling of a book in my hands, avidly turning the pages to see what's next, dog-earing a page (yes I do dog-ear when it's my very own book) to find my place when I next pick up my book. Kindle dog-ears in its own fashion; every time I move the cursor to the title of the book I'm currently reading and push the enter button, I am taken back to the last page I read. It is the miracle of electronics.

I still go to bookstores, and sometimes I buy a real book, finish reading it, and then donate it to the library or give it to someone who can't afford an electronic device. I've kept up with the times in my reading methods just as I try to keep up with the times in other ways. I'll know I'm really, really old when I spend all my time reminiscing over the way things used to be.

Books have opened my mind, made me think more deeply, and taught me more about myself, others, and the world I live in. I owe as much to books about how to live a full and complete life as I do to experience. Oh, thank you, to whoever got that seven-year-old me to the library so many years ago. My life, particularly these young-old years, has been incredibly enriched by books. I'm hoping there is a library in heaven.

Technology: Is it too much of a good thing?

When I was young we had telephones that stayed in one place and four people shared the line. Washing machines had wringers and clothes were dried on clotheslines. We had an electric clothes iron, heavy, no steam. Our house was heated with a coal furnace. Electric refrigerators were fairly new and many people still had iceboxes. Most people had gas cooking stoves, not electric. No one cooked on a barbeque. Coffee was made on top of the stove. There were no blenders, food processors, or mixers, and beating food ingredients was done with an egg beater or a spoon. None of the small electric appliances, frying pans or griddles or popcorn poppers, were on the market. I believe there were waffle irons. We kids were the automatic dishwashers. Bed springs were exactly that and not covered with cloth. Sleep-number mattresses had not been invented. Few women worked outside the home but you can bet it took them all week to do the household chores. By the time I had a house to keep in the early 1960s, I had a private phone line, an electric washing machine and a gas dryer, a gas furnace, an electric stove, an automatic coffee pot, a mixer, and a steam iron.

At the time I was born, there were stationary radios, not portables, and no televisions. I got a portable radio for Christmas in 1950, and it weighed about eight pounds. My dad bought our first television set in 1950. Record players played records at seventy-eight rpms, and later, at forty-five rpms. Eight tracks became available in the late 1960s and the '70s, cassette players in the 1970s, and computer discs (CDs) in the 1980s. DVDs were available in the mid-1990s; before that movies were seen in a movie theater. Today, in the early twenty-first century, people record television programs on DVR and TiVo. Jose and I have neither.

I got my first bicycle when I was eight; there were no gears, and no one I knew had a bicycle shift. Sidewalk skates did not have shoes; they were four metal wheels mounted under a shoe-shaped metal base, which you fastened on your shoes with clamps and straps tightening the clamps with a key. I did not have a car until 1958, and that was the family car. I bought the first car that belonged exclusively to me in 1963, an old clunker for one hundred dollars. I was forty-two when my dad bought me my first new car, a 1978 Oldsmobile.

Believe it or not, the first fully programmable computer was invented in 1936, the year I was born; however, it would be thirty-eight years, 1974, before we had the first consumer computer. Office computers took up an entire room, and the hottest new office job was keypunching. The Microsoft operating system came on line in 1981, and the Apple Macintosh in 1984. By the late 1980s and early 1990s, nearly every office and many homes had computers. The first laptop came into the market in 1984, but they were not commonly used until the early 1990s. I took my first computer class in 1990, and bought my first desk computer shortly after. I bought a laptop in the mid-1990s.

The first cordless phone was invented in the 1970s, and the Federal Communications Commission authorized cellular receivers in 1982. In 1987, more than a million people had cell phones and the system was on overload. Electronic readers became widely available after the turn of the twenty-first century. I bought my first cordless phone from Verizon in 1990, and an electronic reader in 2011. Today, I have an iPhone, which is like a mini-computer, and I can receive mail, play games, post and get messages on Facebook, and more. I am never unconnected, even if I'm not talking online or checking to see if someone sent me something.

I can't imagine life today without my portable phone, e-reader, laptop, and television. Since I am retired, it isn't particularly important for me to save time, but I would say that having all of these things allows me to use time, maybe productively, maybe not. Computers certainly are an improvement from the days when I used a typewriter and had to literally erase typing errors. There was no spell-check, and I can't imagine how long it would take to write this book, edit it, and edit it again, without a computer.

As a reader, I love being able to download in less than a minute any book I want. I can find information in which I might have an interest with a few keystrokes on my computer. I subscribe to Ancestry.com, which has made searching family history less work than it would have been, and preserves what I've learned forever.

On the other hand, I may have acquired another addiction. I sometimes spend hours on my computer checking and responding to mail, checking and responding to Facebook posts, playing Scrabble with online friends, and looking up things I have a momentary interest in. I have friends on Facebook that I've never met in real life. I'm not sure how firm and fast the friendships are; I've never heard the sound of their voices.

During the last presidential election between our president, Barack Obama, and Mitt Romney, I checked an election forecasting website every day to reassure me that my guy was winning. I do my banking and make political and charitable contributions on line, check to see which movies are on at the theater, and look for a driving route even though my husband has two global positioning systems. Jose used to complain that we didn't talk anymore, that is, until he too acquired an iPhone and an electronic reader. We do have a rule that electronic devices don't belong at the supper table, but honestly, how much do people who have been married for a long while actually talk to each other anyway?

People today lose their lives because they are addicted to their portable communication devices and can't leave them alone even when they're driving. These are not all young people. New cars can now be equipped with a phone so you can talk hands off; one of my friends has one, but I still think they distract from the ability to focus on driving.

Here's what I wonder…will the number of hours people spend on computers and watching television, or playing electronic games, increase or decrease as time goes on? People today are in constant touch with others, talking electronically stream of consciousness or sending jokes. Are we losing something by not having face-to-face conversations about things that allow us to know each other better? In some ways it feels satisfying to call these brief online conversations talking to friends, but it also feels like the conversations have little depth.

In my lifetime I have experienced unimaginable technological change. Technology has made it possible for women to work outside the home and still manage their household. I wonder if, in the future, men will take on more responsibility for housework so that technology truly means more free time for women. I wonder if people who come after me will seek deep friendship, or if they will be satisfied with having casual conversation with lots of people they don't know well.

I do know conversations on line are convenient. Close women friends have recently been using email to communicate. We all live in different places, and we do share exactly what we are feeling or dealing with at the moment. We can respond when we have time to think about how we want to respond. Of course, we can and we do pick up the phone to hear their voice if what they are saying on line requires something more.

I know for sure technology is not going away. I have bought into it, and I am more computer savvy than many in their mid to late seventies. It does feel like I waste a lot of time looking at my computer screen, and I do feel like I'm addicted to staying in touch. Maybe I need a twelve-step program for technology addicts.

Celebrating a special year

In 2011, I turned seventy-five. I love being old. I say
that often and I mean it. It's easy for me to say. I am in good
health and I have enough of everything I need, and some of
what I don't need but am delighted to have. Not everyone is
in that position, so I am not only old, I'm grateful. Seventy-
five is three-quarters of a century...a milestone to celebrate.

I decided I would do something out of the ordinary
every month. I've never had a bucket list. I wanted the
monthly celebration events to be playful, have meaning for
me, and include the people I love the very most. I knew that
some would be once-in-a-lifetime experiences. I wanted a
variety of experiences, physical, emotional, spiritual, practical
and impractical, but not risky. I did not want to jump out of
an airplane.

In January, I got a tattoo. Yes, I did! It's a women's
equality symbol and on my left shoulder. The tattoo artist at
the Wicked Ways Tattoo Parlor in Apache Junction, Arizona,
was all I hoped he would be. I took pictures of all of my
seventy-fifth year activities, so I loved that he looked like a
tattoo artist in the movies might look. His head was shaved
and he had a long, gray, Fu Manchu beard. He wore a leather
vest and ragged jeans, and his arms and chest were covered
with colorful tattoos. It didn't hurt and my kids were a little
shocked. Perfect.

In February, my daughter, Julie, and I went to the all-
inclusive Miraval Spa Resort in Tucson, Arizona. This is
Oprah's favorite spa and if it's good enough for Oprah, well,
why not. Oprah could probably afford a lifetime at Miraval; I
could only afford two days and nights. We slept in cloudlike
feather beds; had pedicures, manicures, and massages; ate
tasty, healthy food; walked the beautiful grounds; and sat
around the pool taking in the mountain views.

In March, Jose and I and twelve friends hiked to the
bottom of Grand Canyon. We stayed at Phantom Ranch two

nights, and, thankfully, hiked back out. I trained for six months so I could do it. We hiked down the Kaibab trail and up on Bright Angel. Both had long stretches of ice, so we wore straps on our shoes with metal grips that dug into the ice. The hike is gradual going down, but the hike up is steep, and mostly switchbacks. It was not easy. When I reached the top Jose asked, "What do you think?" My response, "I'm glad that I did it, and I'll never do it again."

In April, Jose and I traveled to Paris, France. I never imagined I would go to Paris, but when I was making my list of monthly events I said to Jose, "I don't know what I want to

 do in April," and he broke into song. "April in Paris," he crooned. "That's it!" I yelled. Okay, this is the number one highlight of the entire year. We spent ten days, stayed in a wonderful little hotel, and saw all of the must-see sights. We were at the top of the Eiffel Tower, attended Easter mass at Notre Dame Cathedral,

wandered through Monet's gardens in Giverney, visited the Louvre and Musee de Orsay, walked on the Champs de Elysee to the Arc de Triomphe, climbed up a steep hill to Sacre Coeur Basilica where we could see most of Paris, and went underground to see piles of bones at the Catacombs. There is no such thing as bad food in Paris, and you can't buy French bread in this country, at least in Michigan, that tastes like French bread in France. We walked the streets and got lost more than once.

May was take-care-of-business month. I arranged for my cremation and wrote my obituary as a favor to my kids. We reviewed our trusts, wills, and investments. I had a thorough physical and included some extras just to make sure I am healthy. I am.

In June, Jose and I took kayak lessons. People keep asking me why we took lessons assuming we could just jump in a kayak and start paddling. Probably we could, but I wanted to do it right. Besides, as it turned out, our instructor at Power Outdoors in Newaygo was a very cute twenty-something young man who was incredibly patient and treated us like we were his equals, not doddering old fools who might not be in our right minds. It turns out there's a lot involved in managing a kayak.

In July, I went on a spiritual retreat at the Julian of Norwich Episcopal Monastery in Waukesha, Wisconsin. I've been an Episcopalian for a long time, but I didn't know they had nuns. This experience ranked right up there with Paris. I woke at five in the morning for my first of five daily prayer and meditation times with the sisters and brother who live there. They practice vows of obedience, chastity, poverty, and silence. I practice none of those, but the practice of silence for most of the five days opened my mind and my heart. I'm even kind now when friends who know me ask in amazement, "You were silent for five days?" Well, actually, I arrived on a Sunday and you don't have to be silent on Sundays or feast days. Monday was a feast day. It was a wonderful opportunity to get to know these exceptional people who commit their lives to their vows.

August was girlfriend time. I have been blessed with the best women friends ever. Together we have laughed until we couldn't breathe, cried when our hearts were breaking, raved at the injustices in this world, marched to bring attention to our causes, and sat for hours listening to each other's stories. This was my month to say thank you. My life would have been so much less without them. I gathered with some and sent notes to others. I wanted them to know how grateful I am that we have been on this Earth at the same time. By the way, my actual birthday is in August, and given the

excitement of the entire year, the day itself was somewhat anticlimactic.

Like lots of people, I have been unlucky and I've been lucky in love. Jose and I have known each other for fifty-six years, and been married for the last fourteen. Jose is an adventurer and for most of our marriage we have lived full-time in our motor home and traveled the United States, Canada, and Mexico. I was a bona-fide couch potato when I wasn't working. My idea of recreation was reading. He pulled me off the couch, dragged me out the door, and it's been an exciting fourteen years. In September, we renewed our marriage vows. We know most people who do this have been married much longer, but when you marry your true love at ages sixty-one and sixty-five, you can't wait until your silver anniversary. I bought a wedding gown for $5.99 at Goodwill, Jose rented a tuxedo, and we said "*I do*" all over again.

In October, we traveled to the International Balloon Festival in Albuquerque, New Mexico, and as the song says, we went "Up, Up and Away in A Beautiful Balloon." We shared the basket with another couple and the balloon operator, sailed over power lines, and landed in somebody's back yard. The mass ascensions were an amazing sight: More than six hundred colorful balloons filled the sky, and at night the balloons glow in the dark. If the balloons don't provide enough color to fill your senses, there are fireworks that light up the desert sky.

Next, I spent time with my kids, Brad, Brian, and Julie, in a house I rented near Phoenix. They are hardly kids anymore but you know how it is with moms, they are always our kids. We sunned by the pool, played board games, and ate too much of the favorites they always want me to cook.

My sons and daughter-in-law played a little golf, and we spent a night at a casino in Laughlin, Nevada. The kids politely listened to my stories about my joy in them as babies, the nerve-wracking teen years, and the pride I feel that they are the wonderful, responsible, caring adults I hoped they would be. I politely listened to their stories of teen-age escapades that I'd really rather not know about.

In December, I wrote the story of my seventy-fifth year, and it was published in the February, 2012, issue of *North Shore Woman's Lifestyle* magazine. It is my hope that those who read it will feel the joy I have felt in this celebration of old age, and that when the time comes, they will embrace their own old age. I'm thinking about what I might do to celebrate my eightieth birthday, and my ninetieth, and, hey, what should I do to celebrate one hundred?

What does it mean to have faith in God?

My friend Janeane Morrissey asked me in her last
months of life, "Do you believe in God?" Her question was the
beginning of a long discussion and a lot of thinking. My
maternal grandmother, Lulu Hershey Hier, loved hymns, and
we gathered around her at the piano and sang as she played.
Since the age of seven, I have known the words of her
favorites, but she never went to church. No one in my family
went to church, and the word God was never mentioned
except occasionally in vain. However, it was while living with
Grandma that I found my first faith mentor, Mrs. Lane. I
don't know her first name or anything about her except that
she lived on our street in Grandma's neighborhood in the
early 1940s, and she invited the neighborhood kids to her
house once a week for Bible lessons.

We sat quietly on the floor around her, and she began
her story while placing flannel cutouts on a flannel board. The
story of Christ's birth started with a cutout of Mary and the
angel Gabriel. Then she removed Mary and placed cutouts of
Joseph and the angel who told Joseph that Mary would bear
the child of God. She put up several people traveling to
Bethlehem, including Mary and Joseph. We watched as she
formed the manger scene, and the three wise men following a
star and bearing gifts for the Christ child. We learned about
Joseph and his coat of many colors, Noah and the ark and the
animals two-by-two, and the multitudes and the loaves and
the fishes. We saw Jesus baptized by John, asking his disciples
to follow him and He would make them fishers of men. He
walked on water and asked Peter to do the same. At the Last
Supper he told his disciples to take bread and wine that
represented his body and blood and to do it in remembrance
of him. Jesus asked the children to come unto him. We
learned that Jesus was someone who lived on this Earth and
showed us how God expected us to live; someone who died,
bleeding, on a cross, so that we would be free of sin. We were

captivated. I wasn't sure what sin was, and I sort of thought of Jesus as a superhero.

Mrs. Lane invited me to her church, a place where people publicly accepted the Lord Jesus Christ as their personal savior by marching up the aisle for a blessing when the preacher asked who wanted to be saved. One Sunday, overwhelmed with emotion, not understanding entirely what it meant to be saved but feeling compelled to respond to the preacher's plea and wanting to be part of the excitement, I walked the aisle. Mrs. Lane was pleased. I expected to feel different, but what I felt was pleased with myself.

I moved from my grandparents' neighborhood at age ten. That was the last contact I had with church until I was seventeen and attended the Methodist Church in Pentwater on Easter Sunday at the invitation of my best friend, Shirley Coon. I liked dressing up, and it was the only occasion where I had ever worn a hat. After graduation I moved to Muskegon and did not attend church. It never occurred to me to do so.

In 1957, I was engaged to marry. His mother was a committed Catholic and attended church every Sunday. She expected us to be married in the Catholic Church and I wanted to please her. My future husband did not attend church, but he too wanted to please his mother. I did the necessary work to become a Catholic. We both attended the required premarital counseling and I had instructions with, or was it from, the parish priest. He explained my responsibility to be respectful to my husband as the head of household and as a mother raising Catholic children. It was required that my children be baptized in the Catholic faith. When I did have children, they were baptized and given middle names that are saints' names: Brad Stephen, Brian Thomas, and Julie Ann. My mother-in-law was my guide on all things Catholic and told me this was the appropriate tradition.

In the beginning of my marriage I attended church regularly with my mother-in-law. My husband did not. As time went on, I slacked off and became an intermittent

345

churchgoer. It was becoming more difficult to respect my husband and given the conditions at home, survival was my top priority. My next contact with the priest would be for counseling, at my mother-in-law's request, because I was thinking of divorce. At that time the Catholic Church was very specific about not recognizing divorce. The parish priest told me that he understood why I had to leave the marriage, but I was required to raise my children as Catholics. He said that I should not expect to remarry, and if I did, I must explain to my children that I was living in sin. I was only twenty-six years old. It was unlikely I would stay single my entire life, and even more unlikely that I would tell my children I was living in sin if I did remarry. I never returned to the Catholic Church.

When I married the second time, it was in the Methodist Church. I decided that my marriage might be more successful if the entire family attended church, my husband and I and eight children. Because I was working full-time outside the home, Saturdays were spent cleaning and organizing. Sunday morning church preparation, over time, and with little help, was overwhelming. By the time I got to church I was frazzled, and spent much of my time trying to keep the kids who were wiggling still and the ones who were dozing awake. It was difficult to get into the spirit, and after a while our attendance dropped off and we eventually stopped going.

You will notice that my religious experiences had little to do with faith. I thought I believed in God, but I didn't engage in any spiritual practices other than to call out, *Oh God, please help me*, when I was in some kind of misery. I basically had little faith in the church as an institution, and not much of a concept of what it meant to have faith in God. I either was going to church because it seemed like the right thing to do or because I wanted to please someone else.

That is, until I met Judy Fleener and her husband, Father Bill Fleener, an Episcopal priest. We worked together as community activists. I saw that in their marriage they greatly valued and respected each other, their similarities and their differences. They personify Christ's love in their actions toward everyone with whom they come in contact. They do not proselytize, but they talk matter-of-factly about their faith. Judy has a great sense of humor and Bill is humble and self-effacing.

Although the way the Fleeners lived their faith impressed me, I did not immediately translate it into something that might be important in my own life. But, in mid-life, I was driven to my knees. I was in emotional pain. My children, whom I had raised mostly alone, were now in college or on their own. My nest was empty and so was I. I was working day and night as director of Every Woman's Place helping survivors of domestic violence and sexual assault. I was exhausted. I had not been re-elected to the City Commission, and Jose, the man I loved, was ending our ten-year relationship. I didn't know who I was, or what I wanted, or how to fix the pain.

One Sunday morning after a too-long sleepless night, I literally found myself at St. Gregory's, the Episcopal Church where Bill Fleener was the priest and Judy Fleener and two of my support group friends, Pam and Jane, attended. I don't remember making the decision to go. I sat with my friends, tears running down my cheeks throughout the service. One moved to each side of me and they quietly held my hands. After church, when everyone left the pews, I stayed and knelt and prayed the universal prayer of broken people...*Oh God, help me, help me, help me*. The next day I called and made an appointment to counsel with Father Fleener, and every Sunday after that I returned to church.

I began to *do* church and *pursue* faith like it was a job I was getting paid for. I committed my whole self to it. My baptismal vows were renewed and I became a member. I began to study the Bible. I learned to pray. I became an acolyte and served at Wednesday morning mass. I was elected to the vestry. I served on a search committee for a new bishop for our diocese. Unlike other things to which I had committed my whole self, this did not deplete my energy, it added to it.

And then a friend invited me to participate in a De Colores retreat weekend, a Cursillo. The Catholic and Episcopal Churches have their own Cursillo tradition, but the Cursillo I attended was ecumenical and participants, all women, came from many faith backgrounds. It's hard to describe a Cursillo weekend except that love is poured on everyone who attends by the Cursillistas serving for the weekend, people who have made a Cursillo themselves. There is music and teaching, and each time I returned to my sleeping space, there were small gifts on my cot. Cursillistas prayed for us and prepared our meals. We shared hugs and laughter. I was surrounded by love. Something opened up in me, my pain eased and I was filled with gratitude for these people and for my life.

Over the next seven years my faith deepened as I continued to learn and grow in the Episcopal faith. I prayed, kept a faith journal, and read from spiritual and inspirational books every morning. And I listened. Church was my renewal day. Sundays were to hear someone else's ideas about faith and how to live a faith-filled life.

In 1988, I moved to Greenville, Michigan, and again attended the Episcopal Church. At that time the church was without a priest. Sunday services were led by a deacon. The church had an opportunity to hire a woman priest and chose not to because the majority of the congregation did not support the ordination of women. I did not feel fed, and I felt alienated from those who could not believe in the possibility of a woman priest. But I continued going to church and carrying out my daily faith practices.

And then one Sunday I picked up the *Grand Rapids Press* and saw a story about a woman pastor and her two sisters who had started a nondenominational church about five miles from Greenville, in a little town called Harvard. I decided to visit, and on my first Sunday there I was in shock. The Episcopal Church is an old faith, rich in tradition. I love the tradition and the predictability. Not so at Harvard Christian Freedom Church. There were people from all walks of life. The music was noisy and so was the prayer. "Amen," the people shouted out as the pastor spoke, but the congregation was welcoming and there was something undeniably special about the church leader, Pastor Lynne. It was clear she had a very personal relationship with God and that she was at peace. You knew when she looked at you she loved you. I wanted what she had.

I kept going back. Pastor Lynne and I became close. She has a gift for seeing others' gifts, sometimes gifts you didn't even know you had. I attended Bible studies and I learned the most important thing I was ever to learn: that God created each of us to be exactly who we are. He created us in his image and we are more than good enough. There is no one exactly like us. He created us for a purpose, and he gave us all that we need to live a life fulfilling that purpose.

It may not sound like a revelation to you, but it was to someone like me who as a child was shifted from foster home to institutions and back to foster homes, who had been violently abused by the father of her children, and who had never dealt with her pain but simply papered it over with accomplishments, with doing. I never understood that it wasn't accomplishments and doing that counted. I did not know that we count just because we exist. It was a revelation and the beginning of a bona-fide healing, a real relationship with God.

I moved from Greenville to Chicago in 1990, and attended Fourth Presbyterian Church on Michigan Avenue where more than two thousand people worshipped every Sunday. It was the church closest to my condo and I could walk to it. The choir, professional singers, sounded like angels must sound. There were small groups you could join to do good works or simply to connect with others. The minister was an accomplished speaker and I left every Sunday with something to think about. I continued my personal spiritual practice of reading, writing, and prayer.

When I moved back to Muskegon two years later, I married Jose, the same man who left me twelve years earlier. I believe that he is back in my life because I have learned that I am worthy of love, and that people who believe they are worthy of love will attract others who have the capacity to love. Pastor Lynne performed the ceremony. We attend church together, back in the Episcopal tradition where both of

us are comfortable with the liturgy and traditions.

Only once since committing myself to faith in God have I questioned. That was when my dear friend Janeane (left) asked if I believed in God. She was living with and dying from cancer. Janeane was an atheist, but also one of the most caring and committed people I knew. She devoted her life to trying to raise up those who lived in poverty. If anyone deserved to be raised up and to live her afterlife in a place called Heaven, she did. But I had been taught that because she did not believe, she would not go to Heaven. She believed her purpose was fulfilled on this Earth, and when it's over, it's over. She was okay with that.

I asked myself many times during her illness whether I believe in God because I cannot face my inevitable end on this Earth. I acknowledge there is no tangible proof. It was a struggle. Thanks to Janeane, I read more and thought more deeply. The struggle was an important part of my faith journey, and I am left with these thoughts:

Faith is what it is, believing without seeing, knowing with no tangible evidence. It's a choice. If it was invented by human beings to soften the inevitable end, it doesn't matter. Creation is a mystery, and we were each created to be exactly who we are. I believe that God's greatest gift to us is free will, the ability to choose and decide for ourselves, and that it is in making those choices and decisions that we become fully human. That is His divine plan. I believe there are miracles and that those miracles are delivered through people who care. I believe that a man named Jesus lived on this Earth, and that he taught lessons about how we are to treat ourselves and others, how we are to live our life, and that if we do our best to follow his teachings we will leave this world a little better than it was when we came into it. I try to live that way. I fall short. I try again. I pray. I read. I write. I forgive myself. I am forgiven. That's good enough. It works for me. That's what it means to have faith in God.

My state of the union address

The span of my life has been a time of major social change. Before I turned ten, we fought World War II, which lasted four years and ended with a clear and decisive victory for our country. This is the last war that people clearly understood, and the last decisive victory we would claim. We have engaged in nine more wars since. The Vietnam War that began in 1963 was a turning point in our attitude about war. Many young people did not want to fight a war they did not believe in, and some fled to Canada to avoid the draft. Protests were held; draft cards and sometimes our flag were burned. Eventually those who opposed the war applied enough pressure on our government to end the draft, but troops still are sent to fight unpopular wars.

The Iraq and Afghanistan Wars have divided our country. We initiated both in reaction to the loss of around three thousand American lives on American soil. Not all of the bodies were recovered. On September 11, 2001, Al Qaida, a terrorist group masterminded by Osama Bin Laden, an Arab of Syrian and Yemini descent, hijacked planes and slammed them into the twin towers of the World Trade Center in New York, and the Pentagon in Washington, D.C. Terrorists in a third plane, believed to be headed for the White House, crashed in Pennsylvania when passengers overtook them. President George W. Bush, and later President Barack Obama, pledged to find Bin Laden and gain justice for those who died on 9-11.

Al Qaida had its roots in both Afghanistan and Iraq. President Bush ordered troops to invade Iraq claiming that country had weapons of mass destruction. After we were well into the war, the American people learned there were no such weapons. Fighting two wars simultaneously has taken too many young lives and greatly weakened our economy. In 2011, our intelligence forces located Bin Laden in Pakistan, and President Obama and his advisors formed a plan, made in secret, to send U.S. Navy Seals to bring him in, hopefully alive. The Seals determined they could not bring him in alive, and the president made the tough decision that Bin Laden be killed. President Obama ended the Iraq War, and the Afghanistan War will end in 2014 while he is still in office. We could not clearly claim a victory in either of these wars, and the Middle East remains in chaos.

There have been other major social movements in my lifetime and I've talked about the two in which I was active. The first was to bring people of color, particularly blacks, into full equality. Although slavery was abolished at the end of the Civil War, segregation, particularly in the south, was strictly enforced. Blacks were prohibited from full participation in voting and in many other aspects of American life. Discrimination in the south was overt. Blacks were required to sit in the back of the bus, there were separate drinking fountains for blacks and whites, and blacks could not eat at the same public eating establishments or sit anywhere they wished in movie theaters. They were prohibited from living in white neighborhoods even if they could afford to live there, and laws prohibited interracial marriage. Black and white children went to separate schools. Black men could be and were killed for looking at a white woman. The military was segregated. Discrimination in the north was more covert; segregation was *de facto*, unwritten. Discriminatory practices in employment and housing were the norm.

Vietnam war protests awakened young people and gave them a sense that they could bring about change, end oppression, and organize for justice and equality. Dr. Martin Luther King and Jesse Jackson, both ministers of southern churches, and many other activists, organized young people, black and white, from the north and south, and slowly change occurred. It was a long fight and many lost their lives. Dr. King was assassinated. This shocked America and led to more change. It has been a long fight. At the beginning of the twenty first century, legal segregation no longer exists, but full equality has not been reached. Black people continue to live with the effects of segregation and discrimination. They are still more apt to be in poverty and in prison, undereducated, and not as healthy. The election of President Obama in 2008, and his reelection in 2012, raised hope and brought the largest number of black voters to the polls ever in the history of the country.

The black civil rights movement reawakened women to the differences in opportunity between women and men. Women won the right to vote in the early twentieth century, but ten year later the Great Depression hit and focus on women's rights waned. I've written about how my life was affected by gender discrimination and the effect that the women's movement had on me. Generally speaking, White women have progressed further than people of color in many ways, primarily because we are the wives and daughters of white men, who have always held most of the power in this country. The fight for equality is not over. Violence against women in and outside the home continues. The battle is still being waged over whether women have a right to decide if they wish to bear a child or not. Inequality and sexual harassment continue in the workplace. While more women work outside the home, they still carry most of the burden of work inside the home. We have not yet had a woman president, and women are a considerable minority in congress. Only three of the nine Supreme Court justices are women, two appointed by our current president.

The environment has also been the focus of an important social movement. Scientists have told us that our planet is warming, and that our wasteful and thoughtless practices will destroy the Earth if we don't change. Automobile emissions, mining methods, misuse of land including abandoning buildings we no longer wish to use, mishandling industrial waste, and more are problems. Regulations have been established, but when there is a contest between the environment and profit, too often profit wins.

We have been talking about alternative energy sources for many years, but progress is slow. Windmills, nuclear power, and solar energy are all available, but not yet widely accepted. Recently, auto manufacturers were required to increase the miles per gallon of fuel that can be achieved. Efficient public transportation is absent in all but the largest cities, so most people own at least one car and many own two.

The most recent social movement is being fought to gain acceptance and full legal rights for those who are gay, lesbian, transgender, or bisexual. Sometime in the twentieth century, gays began to stand up and speak out, clearly articulating that homosexuality is not a choice; it has always existed and always would exist. As more and more people become open about their sexual orientation, most of us have recognized that we have family members and friends who are gay. The stigma created by differentness is lessening.

This year, 2013, the Supreme Court determined that married same sex couples are entitled to federal benefits and by declining to hear a case from California, effectively allowed same sex marriage there. The rulings leave in place laws in some states banning same sex marriage and the court declined to say whether there was a constitutional right to same sex unions. Currently there are thirteen states that allow same sex marriage. There is still much work to be done to overturn existing laws and constitutional amendments prohibiting these marriages in the states where they are banned. All social movements take time and there is considerable momentum to ensure this will happen.

Presidential politics have always interested me and I definitely can be described as liberal, progressive, and a Democrat. My mother was apolitical and my father a Republican. There have been thirteen presidents in my lifetime, seven Democrats and six Republicans. I registered to vote when I turned twenty-one, and in 1956 voted in my first presidential election for Adlai Stevenson, who lost to Dwight Eisenhower. John F. Kennedy's election in 1960 was a day of joy. He was a charismatic leader, young and handsome, with a beautiful wife and two beautiful young children. It was he who initiated space exploration that resulted in the United States being the first nation to land humans on the moon. His assassination on November 22, 1963, in Dallas, Texas, was a time of national shock and grieving, and nearly everyone alive at that time can tell you where they were when they heard news of his death. We won't forget the heartache when his brother Robert Kennedy was murdered while running for president five years later on June 5, 1968. Only the election of Barack Obama lifted me to the same level of joy as that of President Kennedy.

One other president has been shot in my lifetime, Ronald Reagan. Fortunately, he lived and continued in office. Another troubled time in presidential history was the Watergate scandal. In June, 1972, police discovered a break-in by five men at Democratic National Headquarters in the Watergate building in Washington, D.C. Forty-three people were indicted, tried, and convicted, and several were Richard Nixon's presidential appointees. It became apparent that Nixon knew and probably supported the break-in, and he resigned before he could be impeached

The other presidential scandal in my lifetime was President William Clinton's inappropriate relationship with a young White House intern. He is not the first president to engage in an extra-marital affair. Presidents Franklin Roosevelt and Dwight Eisenhower both had a mistress. What was different with Clinton was that in the past people ignored presidential peccadilloes, but in this case, a Republican Congress was determined to impeach Clinton. He and his wife, Hilary, were investigated the entire time he was in office, and the affair was the only accusation that stuck. We now consider fidelity in marriage an admirable trait in our presidents.

Politics have changed in my lifetime. Today, civil discussion is rare and differences between liberals and conservatives precipitate major dissension. In the past, we could depend on accurate, unbiased news reporting. News people reported what was going on in the world, our country, and communities. Most were objective and did not tell us how to think about what was happening, but instead gave us information so we could decide what we think. Now we have opinion programs and individuals, more often personalities rather than news people, who try to tell us what we should think and denigrate people who think differently. Many people have difficulty telling the difference between what is factual, entertainment, or opinion. This worries me.

Violence is on the rise. Young men, mostly black or Hispanic who live in poor neighborhoods, see too little in their future and are killing each other. Drug use has increased among the young in black, white, and Hispanic communities. There have been several mass murders in the past few years, mostly perpetrated by young white men. The most recent is the murder of twenty-six people in a Connecticut elementary school, twenty of them first graders. The country is engaged in a heated debate about the proliferation of military-like weapons and magazines that allow fifty to a hundred shots in a very short time. Many want these weapons banned and others believe this is an infringement on the second constitutional amendment that provides for the right to bear arms. People on either side of the issue are firm in their positions.

The Hispanic population is growing in the United States. In a few years Hispanics will outnumber whites. Many have crossed the border from Mexico to improve their economic status and are here without documentation or have overstayed the time permitted by their documents. The country is divided on this issue, too. Some think that undocumented workers are taking jobs that belong to young citizens, and others believe they are hard workers doing jobs that young citizens don't wish to do. Many undocumented workers have been in the country for a long time and have raised their children here. It becomes a problem for the children when they want to go to college or work after their education is completed and they have no papers.

Children are growing up faster these days. They are exposed to so much more on television, in video games, and movies. Drugs are available to most teenagers if they choose to use. Parents worry about their children's safety. When I was a child we could roam the neighborhood, but most children do not have that kind of freedom today. Play is organized. They are driven almost everywhere, and few walk to school, for example. When I was a child we could play freely with hours to daydream, no schedule. My children rode throughout the neighborhood on their bikes, and walked three-quarters of a mile or so to school without an adult present. I didn't worry about their safety until they were teens and wanted to push their limits. The amount of information available is much greater and children are expected to learn more. School is tougher today. I never had the amount of homework children have today.

There has been amazing positive change too. Affordable air travel allows many to explore the world, or at least our own country. Improved farming methods and worldwide food distribution gives us access to a wide variety of food options, although we still have people who are hungry. In my lifetime, access to education has been available to those who sought it. My grandparents' generation rarely finished high school, and working-class people in my father's generation rarely went to college. There is still a problem in the way in which education prior to college is funded, through property taxes, and this affects quality, particularly in poorer neighborhoods. Our health systems have improved, and we now can cure many diseases or conditions that took the lives of our ancestors. Again, there are problems that need to be solved, particularly access and affordability for those at the lower end of the income scale.

During my entire lifetime, the United States has been viewed by the world as the richest, strongest and most generous nation on Earth. We have been the leaders. As I write this many are worried that we no longer hold that position. I don't believe it matters whether we are the richest and strongest; I do believe it matters whether we are the most generous and caring. I do want us to continue to be a place of opportunity, a country where we work together to solve our problems. I want us to understand that even if we have different priorities and points of view, we can compromise to achieve as good a life for future generations as I have enjoyed. That is what I ask for in my daily prayers, what I hope for those who come after.

Who am I and what have I learned?

My young life was not easy. I was moved from here to there, and my parents came and went, all of it without an explanation. They were not aware of how their choices affected me. They had difficult childhoods, too. I was not the first child with a broken heart, nor will I be the last. Scars are formed, and fears begin, fears of abandonment and rejection, fears that you're not good enough, you're not lovable enough. Those fears led me into unhealthy marriages, more pain, and some drama creation of my own.

And then, by grace, I was given the experiences I needed to become who I was meant to be. Some were difficult and confusing and unwelcome, but I learned from them. Others were gifts, miracles delivered by the people who came into my life: the foster mother who loved me and told me I was beautiful, my parents and grandmother who told me I was smart and strong, and the teachers who reinforced it. In a time when women were kept in traditional roles, I had a boss who fought for and promoted me. The children in my life gave me the gift of acceptance; my own children and my granddaughter provided an opportunity to love unconditionally. A group of women recognized the value of passion over a college degree and hired me to found an organization that changes lives for women who were abused as I was. When I have faltered, women friends have encouraged me with affection and wise words. A married couple modeled a faith I could believe in and a woman pastor taught me what God intended when I was born. Someone took me to a library, which began my love of books, and books helped me imagine a better life and taught me to accept what I couldn't change and to change what I couldn't accept.

I think it's nearly impossible for anyone to fully know who he or she is. We have built-in protective devices that help us to think that we don't have characteristics we dislike in others. On the other hand, we sometimes think we are less than we are and we are hesitant to ascribe qualities to ourselves that we like in others. I believe that in the way I live my life, and in the things I say out loud and in writing, people will draw their own conclusions about who I am. They will undoubtedly be as right as I am in the following attempt.

I am a mixed bag. I have failed to do some things that I wanted to do because I thought they were impossible, but I also have stepped out of my comfort zone and done things that I thought I could not do. I can be confident and not care whether I am liked when I am driven to speak out about something I believe is unjust. At the same time, abandonment by those I love is a fear I've carried my entire life. I can and have spoken on a stage to hundreds and been at ease, but I dislike walking into a party of ten strangers and I wonder what I could possibly have to say that would interest them. I love spending time with friends and family, but I am the most content when I'm alone reading a book or sitting in a dark movie theater losing myself in a film.

Here's what I like best about me. I value loyalty and go to great lengths to stay in touch with the people I love. I believe that close friends are forever. I can keep a secret. I would take a bullet for my children and my grandchild. I care deeply about social justice issues. I strongly believe that when people say things that are racist, sexist, homophobic, or against any religion, or when anyone is abused by someone stronger or with more power, I have a responsibility to speak up, and that if I don't they can assume I think like they do. I love learning new things. My faith is the basis for my values and my politics come from what I believe that my faith says is required of me. I have a sense of humor and I like to make people laugh. I love to dance. I am good at noticing and commenting on someone's good qualities, and it is always genuine. I like feeling competent.

Here's what I like least about myself. I have never been able to feel completely content with how I look. I care less now that I am old, but I still care. Being right is way more important to me than it should be. I am not always patient with needy people. I waste too much time playing games on my computer and keeping up with Facebook posts. It's somewhat addictive and I don't have that many years left on Earth. There are lots of things that are much more worth doing. I'm not one for instant love. It takes time for me to fully let people in. I sometimes talk more than I listen. I'm getting better at that but it needs more work. I am defensive when I'm told how to do something that I've been doing adequately for years.

I believe everyone who came before me is part of who I am. I inherited from my dad my gift for words and the ability to see my cup as half full. Compassion for others and the ability to forgive came from my mother. I see these qualities in my children and I am happy about that.

I have written a story of the people and events that most shaped my life. It is the story of things that happened over which I had no control, things I might have done better and didn't, and things that I did as well as I could. All of them count. All of them contributed to who I am. I gained strength and confidence from the gifts of those miracle bearers. I gained the courage to get an education and increase opportunities. I became healthy enough to recognize and attract a healthy person. We married and he has taken me into one adventure after another. We have grown old together. My children have become good people. I continue to expect grace and miracles and I wish grace and miracles for everyone who reads my story.

EPILOGUE

THE REST OF MY LIFE

Where has the time gone?
I was so busy, hustling here, bustling there,
never a moment to myself, and now,
the children all off on their own adventures,
scarcely a look back.
Youth and its unnoticed privilege, gone
Leaving wrinkles, age spots, questions without answers.
Youthful dreams fulfilled or not,
dreamed by someone else, the girl I used to be,
and remembered by the old woman I am.

Nearing the End
Beverly Geyer, 2013

Most of us think old age is at least ten years older than we are, maybe twenty. It is easy enough to label someone else as old and harder to label ourselves as old. People are living longer, delaying the thought that they are old. We used to think that sixty was the beginning of old. Perhaps sixty-five, the age we are eligible for Medicare, is the magic number that labels us as old. Most of us would probably believe that when we are in our eighties, we are old.

In my young- old years, free of full-time work, I was able to choose how I wished to spend my time. I worked at being healthy and fit, and although doing that is no guarantee, I am healthy and fit. The celebration of my seventy-fifth year reflects what kind of young-old I have been. Those years were filled with travel, learning, connecting with others, lots of doing. I continued to work as an organizational consultant in the summer months in Michigan. I have had time for reflection, reading, writing, and doing nothing, but mostly I was doing something.

I am just entering my old years. Nothing has magically changed since my seventy-fifth birthday, but I do notice a slowing down, a lessening of energy compared to the beginning of my young-old years. My mind is sharp, but the memory files are recovered less quickly. I exercise regularly, but I have more body aches than I had ten years ago. I know that one major health incident can change my active life and that I can't control that. I know that I will lose people I love. That has already started, each death saddens me, and I know each death hereafter will sadden me.

I still have goals. I want to get better and better at truly living one day at a time. I want to perfect the ability to be content with whatever is going on in my life. I want to continue to exercise, even though it's harder, because I feel better when I do. I want to continue to travel, but stay longer in the places to which I travel. I would love to spend six months in Europe. It would be fun to visit every continent if I could afford it, but I won't be regretful if that doesn't happen.

I want to pay as much attention to my children and grandchild as they are comfortable with. I want my marriage to continue to be a comfort and a joy. We get closer every year and I expect that to go on. I want to learn something new on a regular basis. I don't have a bucket list, but I look for opportunities to try new things. I want to keep doing that.

I will continue to read and would be happy to have my obituary say I died with a book in my hands. I will go to the movies as long as I can take myself, and after that, as long as I can get someone to take me. I will connect with my friends, in person when I can, and by email and phone when I cannot. We will laugh together, maybe mostly about our failings, but sometimes about the foolish things we did when we were young. I want to be present to them, to listen to the stories in their life.

I will always be interested in how we as a people are treating each other, who gets elected president, who is my representative in Congress, who is mayor of my hometown. I will always want us to move as a people to a place where we care more about the Earth we live on, and more about each other and those who have less than we do, especially children. I will always hope for no more war, for equality of opportunity for all people, for less greed, for acceptance of others' rights to think differently, for civility in public discourse, for less judging of others. I may not have voted for the person who is president of our country, nor be aligned with the direction he or she is taking, but I will always respect that he or she was the choice of the majority and, therefore, has the right to set his or her own agenda. If I don't like the direction, and enough people think as I do, we are blessed to live in a land where there are rules to follow to make change.

Should I live to be old-old, it is my hope that I will accept the changes that are sure to come. I believe it will be more likely if I practice acceptance regularly along the way, and I can only hope the biggest changes hold off until I am old-old. I want to see what happens next with my children and my grandchild, but even more than that, I want to leave this Earth before they do. I want love to be my strongest motivator and fear to be my weakest until the day I take my last breath. What I want most is to live with a sense of wonder, without fear that keeps me from being all that I am capable of and loving myself and others as deeply as possible. And I want to keep writing.

THANK YOU

This writing adventure began in winter, 2010, when I read a posting of activities at Canyon Vistas RV Resort in Gold Canyon, Arizona, where my husband and I spend part of the winter. Another resident, a former teacher, scheduled a class entitled, *"Write Your Life"* every Tuesday afternoon. I talked with friends and learned that two of the men in our circle, Gary Borton and Jim Hagadorn, had attended the first class and they urged me to try it. Thank you Gary and Jim. It was one of the best recommendations I've ever gotten.

The next Tuesday I showed up for the class and the teacher, Coleen Ehresmann welcomed me and provided a book that would be our guide. We were to divide our life into time periods, carry a notebook at all times, and jot down anything we remembered. Our weekly assignment was to write one story, one episode, about anything in our life we wished to write. Each week we read aloud whatever we had written. She made suggestions about ways in which we could make our writing more interesting. Those who attended became close as they shared their personal history, some of it sad, some of it funny, some of it matter-of-fact. I am deeply indebted to Coleen for giving her time and expertise and for her unfailing support, and to my classmates who listened to my stories and encouraged me to keep writing.

It took a little over two years to write this story and nearly a year to get it to where it is now. I read it over and over but knew from listening to others that there were things I would miss. I asked three friends to read my almost finished product, all avid readers, skilled grammarians, and straight shooters who would not worry about whether they were hurting my feelings if they said something didn't work. Colleen Burns, Peggy Jensen and Gail Trill waded through more than three hundred fifty pages, pencils in hand, commenting and questioning. It was a tedious job and they dug in. Their work made all the difference in ensuring that periods and commas were in the right place, duplications noted and clarifying questions asked. I can't thank them enough for their help.

I met Ann Weller at, of all places, the funeral of the mother of a friend. We chatted over coffee after the service, asking what do you do questions. Ann said she was an editor, a professional editor. I asked her if she would do the final edit on this book and she readily agreed. She is a pro and luck was with me when we met. Thank you Ann for your commitment to making sure my work was as good as I was capable of producing.

Finally, thank you to my husband, Jose Olivieri, whose patience never failed as I spent hours and hours on this work, sometimes at the expense of carrying my share of the household responsibilities. He pitched in, left me to my work, never complained and was my best cheerleader. You are a treasure my love.

32967614R00208

Made in the USA
Charleston, SC
30 August 2014